Four Contemporary
Russian Writers

To the memory of
Kostya Bogatyryov

ROBERT PORTER

Four Contemporary Russian Writers

BERG

Oxford / New York / Munich

Distributed exclusively in the US and Canada by
St. Martin's Press, New York

First published in 1989 by
Berg Publishers Limited
Editorial Offices:
77 Morrell Avenue, Oxford OX4 INQ, UK
165 Taber Avenue, Providence R.I. 02906, USA
Westermühlstraße 26, 8000 München 5, FRG

© Robert Porter 1989

British Library Cataloguing in Publication Data

Porter, Robert, *1946–*
    Four contemporary Russian writers.
    1. Russian literature, 1945–. Critical studies
                I.   Title
                891.7′09′0044

ISBN 0–85496–246–8

Library of Congress Cataloging-in-Publication Data

Porter, R. C. (Robert C.)
    Four contemporary Russian writers / Robert Porter.
                p.   cm.
            Bibliography: p.
            Includes index.
    ISBN 0–85496–246–8 : $30.00 (U.S. : est.)
    1. Russian literature — 20th century — History and criticism.
    2. Rasputin, Valentin Grigor'evich — Criticism and interpretation.
3. Aĭtmatov, Chingiz — Criticism and interpretation.   4. Voĭnovich, Vladimir,
1932–   — Criticism and interpretation.   5. Vladimov, Georgiĭ, 1931–   —
Criticism and interpretation.   I. Title. II.   Title: 4 contemporary Russian
                writers.
            PG3022.P67 1989
            891.7′09′0044—dc19

1000440732

Printed in Great Britain by Bookcraft, Midsomer Norton, Avon

Contents

Preface

Broadly speaking, this book has two purposes. Firstly, it seeks to examine the literary strengths of four leading contemporary Russian writers. Each of these authors now figures regularly on university syllabuses and many of the works discussed here have been translated into English. It is, therefore, hoped that the book will appeal to the serious student as well as to the more general reader.

The current popularity of all four writers has no doubt been engendered in part by the several excellent critical works in English that have alluded to them. However, there has been little discussion in English of their most recent works, and anyway, somewhat lengthier treatment of these authors would now seem to be appropriate in view of their wider reputation.

Taken together, Rasputin, Aitmatov, Voynovich and Vladimov represent some of the very best of contemporary Russian writing, but also some of its weaknesses. These four authors demonstrate the diversity of Russian writing today, and the diversity of its practitioners and their circumstances.

This leads on to the second purpose of this book, which is to illuminate through four 'case studies' some of the developments in Soviet and Russian literature from the 1960s to the 1980s. Thus this book should serve as an introduction to the vast topic of Russian literature from Khrushchev to Gorbachev. In the following pages there will be some discussion of Socialist Realism, literary dissidence, *samizdat*, human rights, the third emigration and the new departures now attempted by Gorbachev. A book like this cannot by its very nature be in any way 'definitive', but it may better equip the student of twentieth-century Russian literature to begin to grapple with a subject which, as it develops, never ceases to surprise even its most astute observers.

Many people have helped me, either consciously or inadvertently, with this book. I should like to thank all my friends and colleagues in the British Universities Association of Slavists Twentieth Century Studies Group, who at their annual meeting in Oxford each autumn have, over the years, educated me. Though it is invidious to single out individuals, I must mention Michael Nicholson, Geoffrey Hosking and Rosalind Marsh. Not just their erudition, but their common sense and unfailing sense of humour leave me much in their debt. Thanks are due also to Tony Briggs for his careful reading of the first draft of the work.

I should like to thank the editors of *Forum for Modern Language Studies, Canadian Slavonic Papers* and *Scottish Slavonic Review* for permission to re-use material previously published by them.

I must, lastly, thank my wife, Lissy. She did not type out sections of the book, nor did she offer constructive criticism of it. Hers was the much more onerous task of putting up with me while I wrote it.

Robert Porter
Bristol, 1988

Note on Transliteration

In transliterating Cyrillic I have tried to be reasonably consistent without being pedantic. On the whole the soft sign at the end of a word is denoted by an apostrophe, but not in words that have become well known in English, notably *glasnost.* Soft signs occurring within a word or with well known proper nouns are generally not denoted unless it has been felt that a very precise transliteration is appropriate, for instance in quotation of whole phrases. Moreover, I have adopted the established spelling of certain proper nouns even though this may lead to some inconsistencies, e.g. Aitmatov but Voynovich.

Translations are my own unless otherwise indicated.

Introduction

It has become commonplace to state that since the 'thaw' which followed Stalin's death in 1953 Soviet literature has developed in all sorts of intriguing ways, and has gone far beyond the generally recognised boundaries of Socialist Realism. In the area of Soviet literary criticism there has been a marked tendency over the last twenty years or so to broaden the definition of Socialist Realism so as to accommodate the renaissance in Soviet letters, to discuss meaningfully the diverse and exhilarating literature in the Soviet Union, while attempting to pay lip service to the parameters established in the 1930s. The Soviet literary press still frequently refers to 'Socialist Realism', 'the positive hero', the ideological content of works, and so on. However, just as frequently, discussion can be conducted without recourse to the received terminology; and any serious reader of Russian twentieth-century literature will in any event be fully aware of the enormous differences between, on the one hand, the stereotyped published literature of the 1930s, with its resolute heroes and its easily identified sympathies, and on the other hand, the questioning, doubts and moral ambiguities thrown up by more recent Russian literature.

This is not to say that Soviet literary criticism has abandoned its traditional role of censorious moralising. Like its Western counterpart, it is more often than not concerned with ethics and degrees of social responsibility. The Soviet critic, like many of his colleagues elsewhere, refuses to countenance the writer as egoistic rebel. In his novel *Flaubert's Parrot*, Julian Barnes makes great play with this fixation that the critic and the public have with creative writers as guardians of moral values. Barnes imagines a defence counsel in some trial over a real work of literature, basing his case on 'simple defiance':

Is this book sexy? M'Lud, we bloody well hope so. Does it encourage adultery and attack marriage? Spot on, M'Lud, that's *exactly* what my client is trying to do. Is this book blasphemous? For Christ's sake, M'Lud, the matter's as clear as the loincloth on the Crucifixion. Put it this way, M'Lud: my client thinks that most of the values of the society in which he lives stink, and he hopes with this book to promote fornication, masturbation, adultery, the stoning of priests and, since we've temporarily got your attention, M'Lud, the suspension of corrupt judges by their earlobes. The defence rests its case.[1]

The Western commentator on Soviet literature can often find sympathy for those Soviet writers, and more especially their heroes, who kick over the traces, by denouncing Soviet society as corrupt and unjust — the critic provides the rebel with a cause.

Of course, Socialist Realism, whether regarded as a theory or a genre, is arguably more vulnerable than are ill-defined notions of civic-mindedness and propriety which one finds in other countries — for Socialist Realism has been formally adopted by the establishment. First propounded in 1932, much expatiated upon at the First Writers' Congress in 1934, it has lists of prescriptive injunctions and tenets; its textbook definitions have been adjusted over the years, but on the whole the formula must remain the same: the work of art must be didactic, must set an example, must be optimistic. It must be loyal (i.e. 'socialist') and unequivocally comprehensible (i.e. 'realist'). A work with an unacceptable political message may be dubbed, at best, 'atypical' or 'subjective'; a work with no message may be open to charges of 'formalism'.

The death of Leonid Brezhnev in 1982 did not see the demise of Socialist Realism as an injunction to be invoked when the necessity arose. The short-lived President Konstantin Chernenko, addressing the Union of Soviet Writers on its fiftieth anniversary in 1984, repeated 'words well known to you. . . Socialist Realism'.[2] Even as Mikhail Gorbachev's policies got well under way there was still scope for a senior Kremlin official Yegor Ligachev to voice misgivings and insist on traditional values: 'No matter what novelties are offered to us by home-grown innovators or foreign advisors, we shall not deviate from our class principles, from the principles of socialist realism in the arts, from a Communist direction in culture, in the moral sphere, and in Soviet education.'[3]

Literaturnaya gazeta ('The Literary Gazette') carried an article in July 1987 which neatly set out the current problem of Socialist Realism, and referred specifically — conveniently from our point of view — to Rasputin's works *Posledniy srok* (*The Final Stage*, or *Bor-*

1. J. Barnes, *Flaubert's Parrot*. First pub. by Jonathan Cape, London, 1984. Quoted here: Pan (Picador), London, 1985, p.133.
2. *Literaturnaya gazeta*, 26 September 1984, No. 39, p.2.
3. M. Walker, 'Glasnost puts strain on Politburo', *The Guardian*, 14 July 1987, p.8.

rowed Time as it has been translated) and *Pozhar* (*The Fire*). The article began: 'What extremes in the interpretation of socialist realism we have encountered recently! From assertions of its obsolescence, exhaustion, outdatedness to recurrences of the normative understanding of it as a set of clichés and stereotypes.'[4]

Arguing along the lines that it would be wrong to try and detect literally 'the spirit of socialism' and 'the depiction of reality in its revolutionary development' in every line and every image of a work, the author maintains that 'revolution' and 'socialism' are to be found rather in the 'ideological orientation' of the work. Thus in Rasputin's novel *The Final Stage* Anna is the bearer of 'the best characteristics of the people's morality, which enriches socialist morality'. The novel, we are told, was published two years before the first decree against alcohol was issued in 1972 and paints a horrific picture of drunkenness. 'In this way can one possibly consider that Rasputin's works do not serve to carry out one of the basic tasks of the art of socialist realism — "the ideological remaking and education of the working people in the spirit of socialism"?' Alluding to *The Fire* the author argues that he 'cannot agree with those critics who in analysing the story reach conclusions about "the harsh changes in the social-ethical structure of the people as a whole". If "as a whole", then who began and is continuing to realise restructuring [*perestroika*]?'

The article concludes that:

> Present day Soviet writers have comprehended the new tendencies in social life, and in their best works have subjected to harsh criticism stagnant phenomena, have analysed the most acute ethical, philosophical problems of being of our contemporary man. And all this has been done *in the name of the revolutionary development of reality*. (I emphasise these words specially, which define one of the qualitative categories of the method of socialist realism, so as to show that this formulation is not so outdated as N. Khudaiberganov [a critic cited earlier in the article: R. P.] thinks.)

This article is an excellent example of how the conventional Soviet critic, clinging to Socialist Realism, can think only in terms of civic-mindedness. Here, Rasputin is seen as implementing specific Party policies on alcohol abuse and 'restructuring' even before they have been announced. Somewhat impudently, given the Party's view of its own leading position, the author implies that real artists may well be a step or two ahead of the politicians, but that essentially the

---

4. B. Goncharov, 'Sotsialisticheskiy realizm: problemy razvitiya: korotkoye slovo "Lish"', *Literaturnaya gazeta*, 29 July 1987, No. 31, p.3.

interests of both groups coincide.

These comments on Socialist Realism should be set against the stirring developments in the media and the arts unleashed by Gorbachev's policies of *glasnost* ('openness' or perhaps more accurately 'vocalness') and *perestroika* ('restructuring'). Newspapers and journals regularly carried exposures of corrupt practices, economic inefficiency and widespread criminality. Specifically, in the literary world a number of key new appointments were made and the literary journals embarked on a programme of rehabilitation for several erstwhile *literati non grati*. The weekly middle-brow glossy magazine *Ogonyok* ('Flare'), under the new editorship of V. A. Korotich, gave prominence to a number of hitherto risqué poets of the past. Nikolai Gumilyov, shot by the Bolsheviks in 1921, Marina Tsvetayeva, an émigrée who returned to Russia only to commit suicide in 1941, and Osip Mandelshtam, who died in a camp in 1938, were among those introduced by the poet Yevgeniy Yevtushenko.

One of the more purely political rehabilitations that the magazine undertook was that of Fyodor Raskolnikov. This case illustrates how Gorbachev's *glasnost* was meant to go further than the thaw instigated by Khrushchev, yet it also demonstrates that Gorbachev's policy has no foregone conclusions and like other reforming rulers of Russia, Gorbachev, like Khrushchev, could be swept off course.

Fyodor Raskolnikov (1892–1939) was a fully committed revolutionary who was imprisoned and exiled by the Tsarist government. He was personally acquainted with Lenin, and became a hero of the Civil War. Captured by the English in 1918, he spent some five months in jail in Brixton, before being swapped for nineteen English officers held by the Russians. In the 1920s he edited the journals *Molodaya gvardiya* ('Young Guard') and *Krasnaya nov'* ('Red Virgin Soil'). From 1930 to 1938 he was ambassador to Estonia, Denmark and finally Bulgaria. Raskolnikov watched with increasing alarm as Stalin's purges gathered pace, and realised that he too, as a member of the Bolshevik Old Guard and a diplomat, was in jeopardy. Attempts were made to bring him back to the Soviet Union but, suspecting a trap, he defected. In France in July 1939 he learnt he had been declared an 'enemy of the people'. Before his death from meningitis in the September of that year, he wrote an open letter to Stalin, justifying himself, refuting the accusations against him, and concluding:

> Your mad bacchanalia cannot continue long. The list of your crimes is
> endless. The list of your victims is endless, it is impossible to enumerate

them. Sooner or later the Soviet people will put you in the dock as a traitor to socialism and to the revolution, as the main saboteur, as the original enemy of the people, as the organiser of famine and judicial fabrication.[5]

Raskolnikov was posthumously rehabilitated by a decision of the Supreme Court on 10 June 1963. His remains, it was decided, were to be brought back to the Soviet Union and reburied in Kronstadt. His widow and daughter were made welcome in Moscow. However, by September 1965, with Leonid Brezhnev firmly in control, the tide turned; he was again publicly accused of Trotskyism, desertion and with working for 'White Guard and fascist scum'. For some twenty years afterwards Raskolnikov was under a cloud, but now once again, because of *glasnost*, he is a true communist and revolutionary hero.

This episode shows that Gorbachev's policy aims to complete what was unfinished by the Khrushchev era or to continue what was reversed under Brezhnev; more particularly this episode shows there is now a renewed effort to divorce the new regime entirely from Stalin and his legacy. Khrushchev and his contemporaries were compromised and weakened by their complicity in Stalin's crimes. This also applied very much to the writers of the Khrushchev era. Possibly only Boris Pasternak had retained his integrity throughout the Stalin years and it was no wonder that it was to him alone that the younger generation would turn for sound spiritual guidance.

As 1987 wore on *Ogonyok* became involved in more highly significant partial rehabilitations, political, literary and scientific, to take them in descending order of political importance, rather than chronologically. Gorbachev had somewhat disappointed many observers when in his address on 2 November 1987, heralding the 70th anniversary of the October Revolution, he recalled Nikolai Bukharin as 'the darling of the Party', but fell a long way short of rehabilitating him. At the end of the month *Ogonyok* carried a six-page feature on the Old Bolshevik who had been executed in 1938 after a notorious show trial.[6] His widow and son had been quietly rehabilitated by Khrushchev in the early 1960s, but there the matter had rested. Now the popular weekly recounted how on taking leave of his wife, knowing he would not return, he had pleaded with her to memorise his testimony and transmit it to 'the future generation of the Party'. Bukharin, a right-wing Bolshevik whose practical ideas on economics, as much as anything else, put him at odds with both

5. V. Polikarpov, 'Fyodor Raskolnikov', *Ogonyok*, June 1987, No. 26, pp. 4–7, p. 6.
6. *Ogonyok*, November 1987, No. 48, pp. 26–31.

Trotsky and Stalin in the late 1920s and the 1930s, could well have something of interest to say to Soviet economic reformers of the late 1980s. His case was one of those to be reviewed by a special judicial commission established under Gorbachev to deal with the victims of Stalin's purges. Only time will tell if full rehabilitation will indeed come about.

The main literary rehabilitation undertaken by *Ogonyok* was that of Vasiliy Grossman, or more particularly, of his major work *Zhizn' i sudba* (*Life and Fate*).[7] In publishing an extract from his enormous epic novel about the Second World War, and especially the battle of Stalingrad, *Ogonyok* was in effect overturning the assertion which, allegedly, the Party's leading ideologist Mikhail Suslov had made to Grossman in 1960, that his ideologically harmful novel 'would not be published for two hundred years'.[8] Now *Ogonyok* was beginning to tell the full story of Grossman.

The sympathetic treatment that *Ogonyok* accorded to the geneticist N. I. Vavilov (1887–1943) was more routine when compared with the piece on Bukharin which it preceded by one week, or to the Grossman feature which had appeared in October.[9] Vavilov had fallen victim to Stalinism mainly as a result of his opposition to T. D. Lysenko (1898–1976), the bogus scientist who denied the very existence of genes and whom Voynovich mocks so effectively in his major novel *Private Ivan Chonkin* (see Chapter 4, especially pp. 108–12). Vavilov had been largely rehabilitated in 1965 when Lysenko was finally discredited and full recognition was given to the science of genetics. *Ogonyok*, perhaps more sure of its ground over Vavilov than it was over Grossman and Bukharin, carried a portrait on its front cover and included reminiscences of Vavilov's fellow prisoners.

Ogonyok's final coup of 1987 came in December with the publication of an extract from *Doctor Zhivago*, presaging the full publication in *Novyy mir* ('New World').

The transformation that *Ogonyok* underwent was echoed throughout the media, and interestingly there seems to have been no real pattern as to which journal carried what. In the late 1950s and the 1960s it was clear that there was a fair degree of polarisation between the liberal *Novyy mir* edited by Aleksandr Tvardovsky and the conservative *Oktyabr'* ('October') under Vsevolod Kochetov.

7. *Ogonyok*, October 1987, No. 40, pp. 19–23.
8. V. Voynovich, *Antisovetskiy Sovetskiy Soyuz*, Ardis, Ann Arbor, Mich., 1985, pp. 201–4.
9. *Ogonyok*, November 1987, No. 47, pp. 10–15 and front cover. A. Takhtadzhyan, 'Kontinenty Vavilova', *Literaturnaya gazeta*, 25 November 1987, No. 48, p. 12.

During the 1970s this picture became blurred and such journals as *Nash Sovremennik* ('Our Contemporary') and *Druzhba narodov* ('Friendship of Nations') often carried the most 'liberal' literary works. Under Gorbachev there has been no clear evidence of simple polarisation.

The literary renaissance engendered by *glasnost* can be seen in various ways. Firstly, there was fuller rehabilitation for Soviet writers hitherto published only selectively. The most obvious examples here are Boris Pasternak and Anna Akhmatova. In the wake of the Eighth Writers' Congress in 1986, Andrei Voznesensky was appointed to head a commission to investigate Pasternak's work. In any event the bulk of his *oeuvre* had already appeared in print (a handsome two-volume edition had come out in 1985), yet the prose part of *Doctor Zhivago* was still officially unknown (indeed unmentioned in all the elaborate editorial apparatus in the 1985 edition); but it was quickly announced that the novel was at last to appear in the first four numbers of *Novyy mir* in 1988. It was of course appropriate that *Novyy mir* should publish the work, as it was this journal which had rejected it in 1956, stating: 'The burden of the author's views . . . is that the October Revolution was a mistake, that the participation in it of sympathisers from among the intelligentsia was an irreparable disaster, and that everything which happened afterwards was evil.'[10] Introducing some of Pasternak's poems in July 1987, *Ogonyok* mentioned *Doctor Zhivago* and said: 'The novel was written without any hint of malice or disparagement of the October Revolution'.[11]

It might be argued, though provocatively, that the full publication of *Doctor Zhivago* was small beer, since the most successful part of the book, the poems, had already been published, and anyway much of Pasternak's 'message' seems at times obscure and 'difficult' to the general reader. However, this could hardly be said of Anna Akhmatova's poetic masterpiece *Requiem*, which, written at the height of Stalin's purges, finally found its way into print in the Soviet Union in 1987 in the pages of *Oktyabr'*, a journal once regarded as extremely conservative. Arrest, imprisonment, exile and execution are the key themes in the work, while the simplicity with which the outrage is expressed makes the work all that more challenging:

> And if they gag my tormented mouth
> with which one hundred million people cry,

10. See: R. Conquest, *Courage of Genius: The Pasternak Affair*, Collins (Harvill), London and New York, 1961, p. 138.
11. *Ogonyok*, July 1987, No. 29, p. 10.

then let them also remember me
on the eve of my remembrance day

[. . .]

. . . even in blessed death I am terrified
that I will forget the thundering of the Black Marias[12]

As already noted, Gumilyov (incidentally, Akhmatova's first husband) was also partially rehabilitated. Of course a good number of
other ex-Soviet writers have yet to be treated as they deserve. In
pointed contrast to the silence in the Soviet press the émigré newspaper *Russkaya mysl'* ('Russian Thought') ran a series of articles in
1987 commemorating Yevgeniy Zamyatin, the author of the banned
anti-Utopian novel *We*, who died in emigration. The last issue
dealing with Zamyatin also gave great prominence to the news that
a new unofficial publication, impudently entitled *Glasnost*, had been
launched in Moscow.[13] However, plans to publish *We* in the Soviet
Union in 1988 were eventually announced.

A second way in which *glasnost* had an immediate effect on
literature was to be seen in the number of works that had been ready
for publication from the early 1960s but which had not seen the light
of day. These included Aleksandr Bek's novel *The New Appointment*,
Andrei Bitov's *Pushkin House* and, most sensationally, Anatoly Rybakov's *Children of the Arbat*. There had been émigré editions of the first
two works, but Rybakov's novel, completed in 1966 and revised in
1983, was relatively unknown hitherto. It was again *Ogonyok* that
carried a batch of letters by prominent writers and others, including
Yevtushenko and Okudzhava, to Rybakov praising his work.[14]

A third way in which *glasnost* operated on the literary scene was in
the partial rehabilitation of Vladimir Nabokov. Hitherto unmen-
tionable except in derogatory terms, a number of works now appeared: *The Defence*, essays on Gogol and Pushkin, a sample of his
verse, and in *Ogonyok* the short story *The Circle*.[15] However, all this
was naturally only a token gesture towards proper rehabilitation.
The editor of the journal *Moskva* ('Moscow') which published *The
Defence* replied in answer to a query about the possible publication of
Lolita: 'We do have certain moral standards'.[16]

12. A. Akhmatova, 'Rekviyem'. *Oktyabr'*, 1987, No. 3, pp.130–5.
13. See *Russkaya mysl'*, 26 June 1987, pp. 8–9; 3 July 1987, pp.8–9; 10 July 1987, p.
9; and p. 1 and p. 6 for the report on the journal *Glasnost*. The subsequent issue of
Russkaya mysl' reprinted the first issue of *Glasnost* as a supplement.
14. *Ogonyok*, July 1987, No. 27.
15. *Ogonyok*, July 1987, No. 28, pp.10–11.
16. S. Laird, 'Soviet literature — what has changed?', *Index on Censorship*, July–

No one would deny that all these events marked something of a new era in Soviet cultural life. Taken in conjunction with the extraordinary developments in Soviet film-making and, on a more mundane level, the routine exposure of malpractices in everyday life, it was small wonder that a healthier climate pertained. There were even suggestions, ill-founded as it turned out, that Solzhenitsyn was to be published.[17]

Which brings us to the very real limits of *glasnost* in the literary world. For the fact is that, with the exception of a tentative offer to Yuriy Lyubimov, the theatre director, to return to the Soviet Union, and the token publication of Josef Brodsky,[18] there has been no rehabilitation of any living Russian representative of the arts. In some ways, while it should be apparent from the following discussion of Voynovich and Vladimov that in theory they could easily be accommodated under the new dispensation, in fact there have been renewed Soviet attacks on them. It should also be obvious that in some ways they are now more 'acceptable' in Soviet terms than might be certain aspects of Aitmatov or Rasputin. This paradox justifies the — hardly original — contention behind this book, that one should seek out the individual literary merits of a work of literature, rather than assess it in terms of its alleged Soviet or anti-Soviet qualities. Recent developments in the Soviet Union have, moreover, lent weight to the notion that there is little point in trying to label Russian writers according to their given circumstances, and that there is in fact only one Russian literature, no matter where or how it is produced.

The literary renaissance under Gorbachev, for all its shortcomings, has surely demonstrated for one thing how irrelevant and indeed inapplicable is the term 'Socialist Realism', no matter how one wishes to define, redefine or stretch it. What could be a better illustration of this than an excellent work devoted to Soviet literary criticism which appeared in 1986? Galina Belaya's *Literature in the mirror of criticism* surveys Soviet literary criticism as it has developed from the 1950s to the 1980s and focuses within her wide-angle view on a number of specific authors, including Rasputin, Aitmatov and Trifonov. In some 350 pages the term 'socialist realism' occurs only once, and 'positive hero' crops up just twice, undergoing an intriguing transformation: the first time it appears as *'polozhitel'nyy*

August 1987, Vol. 16, No. 7, pp.8–13, p. 10.

17. *The Independent*, 4 March 1987, p. 8. *The Guardian*, 6 March 1987, p. 8.
18. *The Guardian*, 7 January 1987, p.6; and Josef Brodsky, 'Niotkuda s Lyubovyyu' *Novyy mir*, 1987, No. 12, pp.160–8.

geroi', the second as *'pozitivnyy geroi'*.[19] This latter variant is very much the innovatory form, used as if the author is straining every muscle to escape a form of words that has become so compromised over the last few decades.

Rasputin, Aitmatov, Voynovich and Vladimov all have their differences as well as certain affinities, but one thing uniting them is that in their best works they cannot be compromised — as at times their critics, including the present one, may well be.

---

19. G. Belaya, *Literatura v zerkale kritiki*, Sovetskiy pisatel', Moscow, 1986, p.25, pp. 26–8, p. 348.

–1–

Valentin Rasputin
The Sombre Siberian

In the early 1980s two Russian critics, once leading figures in the world of letters in the Soviet Union and now living in emigration, crossed swords over the state of Russian literature today. They were Yuriy Maltsev and Andrei Sinyavsky, and the topic of their disagreement was, to use Maltsev's term, 'intermediate literature' (*promezhutochnaya literatura*), works published officially in the Soviet Union which were light-years away from hack writing, yet whose authors enjoyed the status, privileges and indeed acclaim accorded many a conformist.[1] Maltsev cited Trifonov, Abramov, Belov, Astafyev, Mozhayev, Shukshin, Rasputin and Tendryakov as good examples. In his article Maltsev was in effect continuing arguments found in his book *Volnaya russkaya literatura* ('Free Russian Literature'),[2] namely that only underground — and hence dissident, émigré — literature was genuine literature, and that Western observers, not knowing the Soviet Union at first hand, were not in a position to appreciate what was true and what was false in Russian literature. Intermediate writers, he argued in his article, are ostensibly continuers of the Russian realist tradition, but somehow fail to live up to it. 'The essence of the tradition of Russian realism is not in verisimilitude [*pokhozhest'*] "just like life" but in the catharsis of truth, in the spirit of truth [*katarsis pravdy, pafos istiny*]'.[3] Maltsev found all his chosen examples wanting in some way, arguing that their works added nothing to our understanding of life and Soviet society, and that far from liberating the reader, as Turgenev had said great books did, they only made the writers and the Russian people feel more acutely their enslavement.

Andrei Sinyavsky responded to this article with a speech at a conference in Los Angeles. He reaffirmed his belief in one Russian literature and said he used the concept of 'two literatures' only for

1. Yu. Maltsev, 'Promezhutochnaya literatura i kriterii podlinnosti', *Kontinent*, 1980, No. 25, pp. 285–331. A. Sinyavsky, 'O kritike', *Sintaksis*, 1982, No. 10, pp. 146–55, and No. 11, pp. 212–15. Also O. Matich (ed.), *The Third Wave*, Ardis, Ann Arbor, Mich., 1984, pp. 23–30.
2. Yu. Maltsev, *Volnaya russkaya literatura*, Possev, Frankfurt, 1976.
3. Idem, 'Promezhutochnaya literatura', p. 292.

terminological convenience. He rejected Maltsev's dismissal of 'intermediate writers' and pointed to the way in which some of the greatest Soviet writers of the 1920s had been unaccepted at the time by the first Russian emigration: Pasternak, Mayakovsky, Khlebnikov, Babel, Zoshchenko, Mandelshtam, Platonov, Tynyanov. Characteristically, Sinyavsky dubbed his article 'an invitation to a dance' rather than a 'fundamental lecture', but he argued cogently that *samizdat* (self-publication) and *tamizdat* (publication in the West) have their effect on official literature, and that works such as Solzhenitsyn's *Cancer Ward* are banned because of government ineptitude rather than for being overtly harmful. Maltsev's attacks on Rasputin, Trifonov et al. for their apolitical nature, he went on, smacked of the official attacks on Akhmatova and Pasternak of the not too distant past. Today, he concluded, the third emigration (the second having taken place after 1945: R. P.) was dealing with a Russia that was neither alien nor closed. Part of the task of the third emigration was to build bridges and strengthen existing ones, and here, criticism — not in the form of condemnations and evaluations, but in more serious, developed and concrete examination of literary phenomena — could help.

The outside observer might enjoy the irony in this dispute: Sinyavsky, an authority on Russian literature and a virtual monoglot despite the pressures of emigration adopting a position of urbane liberalism, while his adversary, a former professor of Italian literature mobilised Proust, Joyce and (in a subsequent letter to *Sintaksis*) Milosz, to defend what appears to the benighted Western observer a rather insular, but not unassailable, position.

In any event, Maltsev himself recognised the superiority of the 'intermediates' over the conformists and singled out Rasputin for particular praise, perhaps the better to damn him:

Valentin Rasputin strikes one with the originality of his talent, the clearly expressed individuality of the writer, so rare today not only in Soviet but also in intermediate literature, where bare description [*opisatelstvo*] predominates and all authors, writing on a similar subject, resemble each other, like newspaper reporters. His poetic world is full of profound tragedy [*tragizm*], and were it not for the frequent compositional oversights [*proschoty*], detracting from the tension, weakening this tragic atmosphere, and the unevennesses, one might make so bold as to call him the foremost talent in the whole of contemporary censored Russian literature.[4]

Maltsev argues that the intermediate writers indulge in half-

4. Ibid, p. 288.

truths and vague hints, whereas they should spell things out in full. Thus, if these books are read in years to come they will need lengthy annotations, perhaps longer than the works themselves, to be comprehensible. Maltsev's view hardly explains non-Russians' satisfaction with these (unannotated) works, nor does it explain some Western critics' dissatisfaction with works overloaded with explanations (Solzhenitsyn's *Gulag Archipelago*, for example). Maltsev actually appears to be accusing Rasputin and others of not being 'just like life' when he has already argued that the real essence of the Russian realist tradition resides elsewhere, to wit in the 'catharsis of truth, the spirit of truth'. It may well be that for Rasputin and his ilk the way to the spirit of truth is through hints, associations, implication. The annotating of a symbol that strikes a chord, however vague, in any breast can safely be left to the critic. The creative writer needs no annotations for it, just as at the other extreme (*pace* Tyutchev's famous line to the contrary) a well-uttered thought may not necessarily be a lie.

Maltsev's view is decidedly provocative, given the virtual universal praise that Rasputin (and some other intermediates) have attracted. While a few doubts have been expressed about the ethos of village prose,[5] the fact remains that Rasputin as a creative writer has hitherto risen above the barriers of politics. One sympathetic Soviet critic writes of *Proshchaniye s Matyoroy* (*Farewell to Matyora*) 'never has Rasputin been so tendentious',[6] while a sympathetic article in the émigré journal *Kontinent* argues that there is not the slightest trace of tendentiousness in Rasputin.[7] Clearly the strength of Rasputin has inspired critics of various political persuasions to write warmly of him without abandoning their own allegiances. The appreciation of his novels that follows will attempt to define more closely Rasputin's artistic strength.

Writing in *Novyy mir* on the appearance of the four novels in one volume, Yekaterina Starikova noted that their publication in reverse chronological order enhanced the 'completeness' or 'perfection' of Rasputin's work.[8] Bearing this in mind, and recognising the close affinities in subject matter, philosophy, style and structure of all four works, this discussion will take two aspects of Rasputin's work and

5. K. Clark, 'Zhdanovist Fiction and Village Prose', in E. Bristol (ed.), *Russian Literature and Criticism*, Berkeley Slavic Specialities, Berkeley, Calif., 1982, pp. 36–48.
6. Ye. Sidorov, 'Preodolevaya zabveniye', *Literaturnaya gazeta*, 1977, No. 4, p.5.
7. V. Iverni, 'Smertyyu — o zhizni', *Kontinent*, 1978, No. 15, pp. 291–312, p. 306.
8. Ye. Starikova, 'Zametki o proze V. Rasputina', *Novyy mir*, 1977, No. 11, pp. 236–44, p. 236.

trace them through all four major works, and will, I hope, go some way to demonstrate that Rasputin deals admirably with the catharsis and spirit of truth.

The Mother Theme

There is a well-known legend among the people of Irkutsk that the Angara river is really the disobedient daughter of the witch Baikal. Angara runs out of the lake to join her lover Yenisei, whereas the other 335 rivers and streams connecting the lake represent the dutiful daughters of Baikal, who bring the waters to her.[9] Maternity and duty, the prominent themes in this legend, are echoed throughout Rasputin's work and it is fitting that his geographical settings should underscore his chief characters, for in the main these characters are perceived first and foremost as mothers. The arrangement of the four novels in the collected edition, with *Farewell to Matyora* coming first, reinforces the point. 'Matyora' recalls the Russian for 'mother'. *Zhivi i pomni (Live and Remember)* is about a heroine mother-to-be; *The Final Stage* has at its centre a mother now abandoned by her children, and *Den'gi dlya Marii (Money for Maria)* provides the grace notes to the theme, for though Maria is passive she is held responsible, and the reader can never escape the notion of her being the linch-pin in this family under threat. The Soviet critic Starikova has noted that her name is the biblical version rather than the more secular *Marya*.[10]

In an interview in 1976 Rasputin was strangely reticent about his family: 'My father was a peasant, he worked in forestry, served and saw action . . . In a word he was like everyone. My mother worked, was a housewife, barely coped with things and the family — as far as I recall she always had her fair share of worries.'[11] Yet one of the most salient aspects of Rasputin's mature work is his fixation with elderly women and the extraordinary insights into their psychology he displays. Barely forty years old when writing *Farewell to Matyora*, the author chooses Darya — a woman of about eighty — for his heroine. Even more intriguing is his close identification with her; at least one reviewer has called her 'Rasputin's *porte-parole* in this essentially monophonic novel'.[12] Darya is in fact the *prima inter pares*

9. V. Dioszegi, *Tracing Shamans in Siberia*, trans. from the Hungarian by Anita Rojkay Babó, Anthropological Publications, Oosterhout, 1968, pp. 23–4.

10. Starikova, p. 236.

11. V. Rasputin, Interview, *Voprosy Literatury*, 1976, No. 9, p. 142.

12. J. Dunlop, 'Valentin Rasputin's *Proshchaniye s Matyoroy*', in E. Bristol (ed.),

in what is above all a feminine and matriarchal society. With one glaring exception, the men in *Farewell to Matyora* are generally hostile, destructive, alien and peripheral. By contrast, most of the women are mutually supportive, custodial and possessed of a sense of history and continuity. By and large, the author's narrative shares these latter qualities. The book's opening paragraph uses the words 'and' and 'again' to draw out this sense of continuity. Significantly, we are introduced to *three* women (Darya, Sima and Nastasya) at the outset. The novel's main characters span *three* generations of the Pinigin family (Darya, Pavel, Andrei); the author tells us that the island was first inhabited some *three* hundred years ago. Darya's three children are all dead. Three families have already gone, then another three move. The indivisibility of the number (echoed elsewhere) contrasts subtly with the notion of *couples* that one would expect in a society less ravaged by war and other hardships: for the most part, the men once close to the heroines of Matyora are now dead or gone.

The sense of unity existing between the women is also to be found between them and their natural environment. 'Mother-river' (*Mat'-reka*) is something of a commonplace in Russian folklore and the island of Matyora is to some extent under the motherly protection of the Angara river. Never is the river (which is to cover the island once the dam is built) seen as a hostile force, whereas the men of progress are. The final pages of the novel have the Angara desperately keeping the men at bay as they seek to land on the island to remove the last few inhabitants. Elsewhere people happily bathe in the river and old Yegor refuses motorised transport to cross it.

If the Angara is mother to the island, Matyora is mother to those who dwell on her: 'The first peasant who some three hundred odd years ago thought of settling on the island, was sharp-eyed and discerning [*vygadlivyy*], having reckoned that he'd find no better land than this. The island stretched for over five versts and not in a narrow ribbon, but like a flat-iron, — there was room for grazing, forest, frog-infested swamps . . . '[13]

The simile of the flat-iron is particularly appropriate, summoning up notions of domesticity and order. It anticipates Darya's last day in her hut when she whitewashes, cleans and tidies, knowing full well her home is to be burnt down the next day. Those appointed to clear the island conclude she is off her head, yet the narrative, as much through hints such as the one cited above as in more explicit ways,

---

Russian Literature and Criticism', p. 64.
13. V. Rasputin, *Povesti*, Molodaya gvardiya, Moscow, 1980, p. 16.

testifies to her sanity and sense of propriety. The muted tone of domesticity here also contrasts with scenes of dislocation and upheaval later on. When Yegor and Nastasya move out, we are given an impressive catalogue of their domestic accoutrements, but no one knows where they should be put. The Matyora that had a place for grazing, forest and whatever has changed:

> Nastasya was clutching at everything, piling everything up in a heap — old man Yegor was shouting:
> 'Where? Where? You bloody woman' [*mat'-peremat'*].[14]

Yegor's untranslatable term of address (*mat'* can be a common form of address to women, but Yegor uses the term as one of abuse here) is mildly ironic, given the circumstances of home-breaking and dispossession. Now nothing seems to have a place.

The reader is constantly made aware of the strong links (almost of ownership) that have existed between the Angara, Matyora and the inhabitants — in particular, Darya:

> The right, wide sleeve of the river . . . hugged the low bank opposite . . .; the left sleeve, more tranquil and close by, as if belonging to Matyora, hanging down from her steep bank, seemed at this hour in the quiet sunshine, motionless. That's what the people on Matyora called this sleeve: our Angara . . . But from end to end, from bank to bank, there was enough room [*razdolye* is the word here implying both 'space' and 'freedom'], wealth, beauty and wilderness [*dikost'*] and all sorts of creatures in pairs [*po pare*] — all this, separated from the mainland, she had a sufficiency of — was not this why she bore the resonant name of Matyora?[15]

This passage might be construed as one of Darya's inner monologues, as she contemplates the scene. Significantly, the wild life is mentioned in pairs (unlike the human life which history has shown to be more self-destructive). Matyora then has a history, an identity and is self-sufficient. In all these qualities she parallels Darya herself.

Both heroine and island have a timeless quality, Matyora having been settled over three hundred years ago, and Darya's age, over eighty, only approximately reported, since the church records have disappeared and the women's recollections do not exactly coincide over such details. She is the oldest and the others turn to her in the

14. Ibid, p.62.
15. Ibid, p.43.

face of catastrophe, Bogodul being a welcome guest and Katerina actually moving in with her.

More important is the question of identity. Apart from the closing paragraphs of the novel, Darya is utterly certain of herself, she is self-possessed and self-sufficient, just like her island. Unlike 'Darya' several of the other proper nouns in the story have variants. No one is certain if Matyora's sister island is called Pogmoga or Podnoga. Petrukha, the good-for-nothing, drunken son of Katerina, is really called Nikita, but he has been renamed in a manner more befitting his character[16] (Petrushka is the Russian equivalent of Punch). Sixty-year-old Afanasiy Koshkin is pressured by his relatives into changing his name to the more prestigious-sounding Kotkin, for they feel that it suits better their new situation in the more re-munerative *sovkhoz*.[17] 'Sold your surname for a half-litre [of vodka]?' is one gibe he earns. These seemingly trivial acts of betrayal could never be perpetrated by Darya and her closest allies. Her strength of character never falters.

Most strikingly, Darya is a religious figure. Her nearest relative in modern Soviet fiction would be, of course, Solzhenitsyn's Matryona and there is no need to dwell on the connotations of this name. Like Matryona, Darya is simple-hearted, stoical in extreme hardship, observant of ritual to a degree that possibly leaves her open to charges of superstition rather than Christian devotion. Naturally, Soviet ideologues would recognise no distinction between the two. None the less, in neither heroine could the strength of conviction be denied and it is, or was particularly in the early 1960s when Solzhenitsyn's story appeared, surprising that such figures could find a place in Soviet fiction. However, village prose has now established itself to such a degree, and done so much to restore the religious aspect of rural life, that attempts in fiction to abolish or denigrate religion seem rather thin. Tendryakov's early anti-Christian story *The Miraculous Icon* (1958) is embarrassingly crude, while his novellas *On Apostolic Business* (1969) and *The Eclipse* (1977) might suggest that far from defeating religious convictions he came to find them inconveniently alluring. Rasputin delves more deeply into his heroine's psychology than does Solzhenitsyn.

Would it be too fanciful to see the community of Matyora as a latter-day Old Believer commune? Its best adherents strive for chastity and reject material riches. It is cut off from the world at large and resents changes imposed from above. On a more meta-

---

16. Ibid, p.52.
17. Ibid, p.106.

physical level, it could be recalled that the first Old Believers, many of whom came to populate Siberia just at the time when that first inhabitant set foot on Matyora in the late seventeenth century, were convinced of the imminent destruction of the world. True, the inhabitants of Matyora cannot pinpoint the anti-Christ quite as readily as the Old Believers could, but the reader might well verbalise him for them: technological progress.

Darya's enactment of her religion is in clear defiance of the social norms established from without. Nothing illustrates this better than the scene where the old women, egged on by Bogodul, prevent the cemetery from being cleared. The result is a temporary victory for ritual and tradition over the new anti-Christ. The unseemly brawl in the cemetery contrasts sharply with Darya's return there and her last day in her own home. In these passages everything she says and does is governed by a sense of propriety and ritual. Addressing her deceased parents, she adopts a praying posture, rocking backwards and forwards (almost trance-like), makes a form of confession and then hears an instruction to tidy her hut. Her consequent actions take on all the airs of liturgy. She decks the hut's interior with grass and fir twigs: 'The firs immediately exuded the forlornness of a last farewell, reminded one of burning candles, sweet doleful singing. And the whole hut immediately assumed a mournful and rejected visage [*lik*]'.[18]

Darya's hut has been transformed into a church, the images are entirely ecclesiastical now. Darya spends all night composing a prayer and it seems as if her words catch something and carry it off into the distance. She removes her funeral belongings and allows the men to burn her home, her only injunction being that they should not set foot inside. What draws Darya on throughout at this stage is unknown. Searching for the firs she senses that someone is 'following her', 'guiding her'.[19] The ritual she performs is only half-remembered. Instinct predominates over reason. Yet elsewhere, Darya is eloquent in stating her convictions, and her religion is surprisingly down-to-earth.

Perhaps rather schematically, but none the less quite understandably, her grandson, Andrei, is furthest from her in his views, her son Pavel being in every sense a half-way house. The author denies none of these characters a high degree of morality and sincerity. This makes the clash of values all the more poignant. Andrei's promethean view is summed up in a phrase, which, taken in the

18. Ibid, p.171.
19. Ibid, p.171.

context of the whole novel, is notorious: 'Man is the tsar of nature'.[20] This attitude, not uncommon in any young man, is of course ideologically very convenient. Andrei's convictions coincide more with the slogans of the first five-year-plan. Darya counters with notions at once more personal, more pithy and ultimately more transcendent:

'Gran, you said that you felt sorry for man. For all men. Do you remember you said that?'
'Yes; how could I forget?'
'Why are you sorry for him?'

The key word here in Russian is *zhalko*, and it carries a number of connotations which are lost in translation: 'sympathising with', 'pitying', 'sparing', 'having mercy on'. More specifically in regional dialect *zhalko* is used (as is the verb *zhalet'*) to mean 'love'. Thus it is quite proper that it takes Darya some time to answer fully her grandson's seemingly straightforward question. A little before this exchange, the author describes the days of enforced idleness during the harvest, when the inhabitants of Matyora have time to ponder on the purpose of life, and Rasputin concludes for them:

The truth was not in what you felt in your work and in the songs and joyous tears, when the sun was setting and the world cooling, yet when in one's soul a sense of disquiet and love was welling up, and a yearning for even greater love, of the kind which only rarely occurs, the truth was in that the hayricks should be there. That's what they were here for. But then came doubts too: that's how it was, but it wasn't quite right either. After all they would stack up the hayricks and cart them off, the cows would polish off everything to the last blade of grass by spring, all their work, and those songs after work when it was as if it was not them, the people, singing but their souls, all joined together — so sacredly and primordially did they trust the artless words being sung and with such zeal and unity were the voices raised; this sweet and alarming dying in the evenings before the beauty and fear of the approaching night, when you don't even understand where you are and what you are, when it seems gradually that you're silently and smoothly gliding above the earth, scarcely moving your wings and taking the blessed path opened to you, noticing in detail all that is passing by beneath; this quiet, deep pain which has arisen from you know not where, that you did not even know your own self until this minute, you did not know, not only what you carry within yourself but also what is not always noticed, what is around you, and to lose it once is more terrible than losing an arm or leg — that is what will be remembered for a long time and will remain in the soul like an unfailing light and a joy. Perhaps only this one thing and eternally

20. Ibid, p.109.

only this, transmitted like a holy spirit from man to man, from fathers to children, and from children to grandchildren, disquieting them and guarding them, guiding and cleansing, would one day bring them to what generations of people had lived for.[21]

The ineffable element in man described here is made up of apparent incompatibles: 'disquiet' and 'love', 'sweet' and 'alarming', 'beauty' and 'fear', 'pain' and 'joy', 'disquieting' and 'guarding'. Transmitted through generations, it provides the meaning of life and defeats death. Despite the overtly ecclesiastical touches (ascension, wings, 'blessed', 'holy'), the notions are not tied to any formal religion and when taken up elsewhere in the novel, might be seen as advocating a vague, pagan spirituality. Certainly in pre-Christian Russia, there were no gods as such but rather a belief that God was to be found everywhere in nature. It is against this background that Darya answers Andrei's question. At the core of Darya's spiritual dimension is the same spontaneity and harmony of mixed emotions which characterises the harvest singing and the transcendentalism it brings. She replies:

> He does what he doesn't want to ... Look [at him, man], take a good look. He just doesn't want to laugh, maybe he ought to cry, but he laughs, laughs ... And when he talks ... he's crafty at every turn, not saying what he means. And if you ask him to say what he means, he won't, he'll keep quiet. If you have to go one way, he'll go the other [. . . .] You ask me why I feel sorry for him? How could I not be? Get him off his high horse and you see he was born a little kid and all his life long he stays a kid [. . .] And as for death ... How he, a Christian man, fears it! You've got to feel sorry for him just for that. No one in the world is so afraid of death as him .....[22]

Darya's credo, much abbreviated here, illustrates that there is as much content as form in her religion. By contrast, Andrei's shibboleths about machines and the modern age seem remarkably hollow. It would be difficult to classify Darya's religion. She talks of 'Christian man', using a corruption (*khristovenkiy*) of the standard word, recognises the soul; her actions at the cemetery when it is being desecrated and her transformation of her hut into a sort of church display an awareness of Christian ritual. When she decks her hut out in firs, it reminds one of Pentecost or Palm Sunday, when the peasants bring greenery to church. Yet she says God is within man not in heaven, she prays to her parents, and for a Christian her

21. Ibid, p.105.
22. Ibid, pp.119–21.

thoughts are singularly unteleological, for she is unconcerned about ultimate ends. She seems to have little interest in the after-life and it is left to the author to hint at one in the closing passage of the novel. Here the characters are reduced to disembodied voices. Darya's teleology is limited to the self-evident business of procreation. She recognises forebears, descendents, and family, with all their imperfections. Thus Darya's religion, both in form and content, is very much a personal, private affair, but it is precisely this which endows it with strength and authenticity. In spelling out her religion's content she is a dutiful mother and grandmother; in enacting it she is a daughter so dutiful as to put Angara to shame, if the legend of that river be true.

If *Farewell to Matyora* enjoins us not to forget, *Live and Remember* shows us Rasputin taking his own advice in a most positive manner. All his major works take place at approximately the time they were written, with this one exception. *Live and Remember* takes the reader back to 1945 and in this instance Rasputin can be compared to some degree with a number of other Soviet writers who have sought to reappraise the war years. It would appear that the time for celebrating the undeniable valour of the Soviet people is over, and the boldest writers have turned their attention to the psychology of individual soldiers and have focused, sometimes sympathetically, on those whose actions in war have hitherto attracted only opprobrium. The anti-war theme can be discerned in Bulat Okudzhava's early story *Good Luck, Schoolboy!* (1961). An understanding of the deserter is to be seen in Vasil Bykov's *Sotnikov* (1970). For a thorough-going debunking of the Soviet war effort one has to go to Vladimir Voynovich's *Private Ivan Chonkin* (published 1975 and 1979) for a satirical view, or to Vasiliy Grossman's *Life and Fate* (first published 1981) for a coldly realistic exposure of the unseemly factors involved in Stalin's victory.

Not that the main theme of *Live and Remember* is the war, but Rasputin has recorded that the idea for his story was sparked off by the recollection that as a young boy he had seen a deserter brought through his village.[23] From this point he would seem to have turned to the mother theme again, for the *prima facie* hero is Nastyona. However, the 'mother theme' manifests itself in a variety of ways in the novel, not all of them directly connected with her.

Nastyona is fated to be a mother not so much by her sex as by her

23. V. Rasputin, Interview (see note 11), p. 142.

circumstances. In the famine years of collectivisation she has to take charge of her younger sister. Immediately one is aware of an interdependency: 'Without her [little sister] Nastyona would probably have been lost . . . Only Katka, for whom Nastyona was left in place of a mother, forced her to bestir herself, ask for work, beg for a crust'.[24] The mother's role is quickly exchanged for that of Cinderella when she is attached to the Guskov family until her marriage to Andrei. Then follows four years of relatively happy conjugality, marred only by her inability to conceive. When Andrei comes back from the war — when the story opens — the relationship has to be re-made, and significantly Nastyona frequently assumes a maternal role vis-à-vis her husband. Firstly, she must protect and feed him, on one occasion as she would a child.[25] Nastyona's actions and attitudes are marked by a comprehensive vision based on empirical knowledge as well as intuition. She alone knows the full situation regarding her husband, but cannot tell. She immediately intuits his presence when household items go missing at the start of the story.[26] Ironically, her knowledge forces her to lie and deceive at every turn. By contrast, Andrei is persistently wrong about his wife and when confronted with an unpleasant circumstance resorts to violence to assert himself. The only violence Nastyona perpetrates is on her own conscience and eventually her own person. The occasional violence, both threatened and actual, which he shows her is never reciprocated, but is rather greeted with reproach, explanation or consoling gesture, in fact with the responses of a patient mother to a wayward child. As a child might, Andrei takes certain sayings at face value, teaching himself to howl like a wolf ('if you live with wolves howl like one' being the equivalent of 'when in Rome . . .') and trying to bite his own elbow ('your elbow is near but you can't bite it'; 'so near and yet so far' being a possible English equivalent). His alternating suspicion and naivety are frequently misplaced. He thinks Nastyona will betray him. His act of desertion is committed on impulse with no thought for the consequences and later he is keen to persuade himself that fate is entirely responsible. On hearing of his wife's pregnancy he says: 'I know . . . now I know, Nastyona: it's not for nothing I came here, not for nothing. It's fate . . . that's what pushed me, that's what brought it about'.[27]

Moreover, as Nastyona's omniscience goes hand-in-hand with tolerance and forbearance, Andrei's egoism becomes all the more

24. *Povesti*, p.204.
25. Ibid, p.233.
26. Ibid, p.200.
27. Ibid, p.272.

pointed. The story as we have it leaves Nastyona dead and Andrei still at large, though throughout he is the one most convinced of his own imminent death and the one most determined to survive in the form of his offspring, no matter what burden that might place on mother and child : 'You're to have the baby — that's what's got to be done. Even if you die, have it, that's our whole life [*v etom vsya nasha zhizn'*]'.[28] Andrei's metaphysics are bought at the expense of another's life and only his ego, though trapped in time and circumstance, is the victor. His morality is highly dubious.

Andrei is in constant need of a surrogate mother, studiously avoiding contact with his real one. It is not promiscuity but this which draws him to Tanya, the dumb girl who shelters him after he deserts. She manages to teach him some deaf and dumb language 'with the same love and patience as a child is taught to speak'.[29] However, his innate suspiciousness manifests itself with her too: 'He could not escape the unpleasant feeling that Tanya was not the person she pretended to be',[30] and decides home is the only place he can go. Arguing with Nastyona, he suggests his mother would prefer not to know his circumstances, that mothers do not believe notifications of sons' deaths, and that he and she will meet in the next world. There is a rough-hewn logic to a lot of what Andrei says, but on the whole he acts on impulse and his ego is of paramount importance. For all his reasoning about the need to avoid his parents, the reader has a feeling that in fact the naughty boy is simply afraid to go home.

Andrei's egoism, his abandoning of Tanya, dominance and suspicion with regard to Nastyona, his coolness to his parents, all this comes clearly to the fore when he finds a calf and kills it. As is often the case in Rasputin this utterly realistic episode contains a strong element of the irrational and acquires a profoundly symbolic quality.

On his hunting forays Andrei stays overnight in a cave, which becomes more than just a physical shelter:

The island stuck out now particularly bare and nondescript [*nekazisto*], but Guskov wanted to go there right away, without hesitation, he wanted to because of the cave in which he spent the night when hunting and which brought him success. If he didn't stay in that cave, he wouldn't know if he'd be lucky or not. It tempted him with a sort of special, secret, forbidden power akin to him, and tempted him also for the secret which had been able to reveal itself or which could be concealed there. Till now Guskov believed that he'd spotted the cave not by accident, but it was nothing other than the will of fate which was at work in his stumbling on it.[31]

Given the dominant 'mother' theme of the work the cave would appear to hold Freudian affinities with the womb. From this 'womb' Andrei emerges to take a calf from its mother and, failing to shake off the cow, to kill its offspring before its eyes. On seeing the calf Andrei feels that his loss of dealings with domestic livestock, though not as important as other losses, is 'painful and incomprehensible' and contains something 'with which he does not want to be reconciled'.[32] After butchering the calf, he is neither 'surprised nor overjoyed': the meat in the bag apparently has strained and drained all his feelings. 'Even now he did not know if he had killed the calf only for the meat or for the sake of something else which had since firmly and powerfully started to reside in him'.[33]

Andrei's violence and impulsiveness are utterly in keeping with what one knows of him throughout the novel, yet in this instance he seems divided against himself even more than elsewhere. The resemblance here to Dostoyevsky's Raskolnikov, noted again by Starikova, is well founded. Like Dostoyevsky's hero, Andrei is set apart from the rest of society and also suffers from a split personality. Moreover, his act of near gratuitous violence against the calf can be construed as an expression of free-will and defiance. Ensnared by the ironies of reality the individual still insists on his own autonomy. In Andrei's case his autonomy is bought at the expense of an offspring's life, and given his insistence on his own procreation, one can only conclude that he is in effect going some way to destroying himself in destroying the calf. Once again the connection with Raskolnikov will not be lost on the reader.

Another area where the 'mother theme' is prominent is in the case of Nadya, a 27-year-old war widow with three children to support. While the facts of her situation speak for themselves, the corollary of those facts is that motherhood is perceived as an enslavement, not to say a death sentence — in a word, as the very antithesis of the way Andrei sees procreation. Significantly, it is to Nadya that Nastyona is drawn and to whom she flees for shelter when her pregnancy is discovered. Nadya is at her wits' end to provide the children with their daily crust and it is left to Nastyona to offer them maternal affection. Nadya's situation provides Nastyona with insights into motherhood of which Andrei could never even dream. Moreover,

31. Ibid, p.333.
32. Ibid, p.335.
33. Ibid, p.339.

Nadya completes our awareness of Nastyona's entrapment, because Nadya can at least shout and scream her protests, beat her children or sing and drink at a celebration. Her situation is forever on display. Nastyona's is locked within her. She is a prisoner without a voice:

> Remaining unobtrusive, Nastyona kept silent. She could neither speak, nor weep, nor drink with all the others — as never before, Nastyona realised that here nothing was possible: she had no right. Whatever she might do, it would all be deceit, pretence — all that was left to her was to listen to and watch cautiously what the others did and said, not giving herself away and not paying attention to herself.[34]

Given that Nastyona's probity is of the highest order, her suicide is inevitable. It cannot altogether be viewed as an existential act of free-will nor as a gesture of defeat. Her continuing to live would lead to her husband's discovery. Her death would mean the death of their child and in her husband's words the end of 'their life'. (In his child-like fashion Andrei remains unaware of the possible illogicality of his injunction that she should give birth even if it kills her.) If one seeks a list of moral priorities in *Live and Remember* Nastyona's honesty would have to come at the top. Though trapped and silenced throughout the story, except for those brief moments with Andrei, though separated from her own community by a situation not of her making, she is finally laid to rest in ground among her own people. 'He [Mishka-the-farmhand] wisely intended to bury her in the cemetery for drowned people. The women would not let him, though. And they gave Nastyona to ground among her own people, only just a little bit to the edge by a rickety fence'.[35]

Writing about Rasputin's second novella *The Final Stage* Vladimir Shaposhnikov says: 'The "coefficient of respect" both for the land and for one's elders in the present-day village has diminished noticeably, because young people in the village have acquired certainty in the future, have acquired the widest opportunities for arranging their lives in accordance with their own demands and inclinations'.[36] This statement does not cater for the significant numbers of disrespectful youngsters to be found in Soviet 'town prose' and anyway it is questionable whether greater individual freedom *ipso facto* makes for greater disrespect. However, Shaposhni-

34. Ibid, p.261.
35. Ibid, p.393.
36. V. Shaposhnikov, *Valentin Rasputin*, Zapadno–Sibirskoye knizhnoye izdatelstvo, Novosibirsk, 1978, p. 35.

kov's words do touch on a central theme in *The Final Stage*, namely the gulf between the octogenarian Anna and her five surviving children. In this story the mother is virtually rejected, virtually isolated. The only support and understanding for her comes from outside the family. Rasputin would appear to be far less sanguine about Soviet life than his critic Vladimir Shaposhnikov is.

In *Farewell to Matyora* and *Live and Remember* motherhood is an active and vital phenomenon. But in *The Final Stage* it is in the past. Anna has borne many children, yet only five have survived, and only one of these, Mikhail, still lives with her. Mikhail's wife addresses Anna as 'Mummy', but this merely emphasises the fact that Anna's offspring have deserted her. The family reunion at her deathbed brings out the differences between them all. None of them understands the mother, and the favourite daughter, Tanchora, does not even respond to the call to come. The two brothers get blind drunk on the vodka intended for the wake. Tired of waiting for mother to die, the family disperses again and Anna dies that very night. Echoes of family life elsewhere are similarly discouraging. Varvara has had many children just like her mother, but they have brought her little joy. She rows with them and one of them is in prison. The five-year-old Nina, Mikhail's daughter, is simply bribed with sweets and employed to smuggle food to her father and uncle as they get drunk in the bathhouse.

Such is the picture we have of family life, and against this background it is worth examining the ways in which the concept 'mother' occurs in this story. Anna's own thoughts on motherhood record the inevitable combination of joy and sorrow which makes up the stuff of life. Her 'kids' (*rebyatishki*), whom she must feed and provide for, form an essential part of the eternal cycle (*vechnaya krugovert'*) of life.[37] Anna would not appear to place great store by any immortality for herself acquired through the agency of her children (as Andrei in *Live and Remember* does). Rather the fullness of her own life which children have given her allow her to face death with complete equanimity, even self-possession.

> The old woman had thought about death many times and knew her as well as she knew herself. In recent years they had become friends, the old woman frequently conversed with her and death, having stationed herself somewhere to one side, listened to her reasoning whispers and sighed understandingly. They agreed that the old woman would depart during the night.[38]

37. *Povesti*, p.530.
38. Ibid, p.525.

As long as there is breath in Anna's body she will have her sorrows and anxieties, but these are nothing in comparison with the anguish which her children apparently suffer. The children persistently try to persuade their mother and themselves that she will not die, and their deceptions and self-deception stand in clear contrast to Anna's certainty. Anna's death mocks not her, but her children.

In Anna's sentiments death has become a familiar friend; in her utterances it becomes a mother. '*Mat*" and its diminutives (especially *matushka*) are widespread in popular speech as nouns in apposition (*mat'-reka* has already been noted). Anna coins the phrase 'mother-death' (*matushka-smertyn'ka*),[39] quite in keeping with her view of death as a familiar friend. Yet in coupling the concepts of 'mother' and 'death' in this fashion Anna establishes her ascendency over her wayward children. Her authority triumphs.

The other instance where the term 'mother' is broadened is in the lament that Anna teaches her daughter Varvara to repeat in anticipation of her performing folk death rites. Twice we have 'mother of the church of God' and finally the more prosaic and 'folksy' 'mother damp earth':

> A iz matushki bozhzhei tserkve
> V matushku syruyu zemlyu
> Ko svoyemu rodu-plemenyu[40]

The final line revitalises what would otherwise be a dead metaphor and points up the notion of 'family'. Though of little direct comfort to her now, Anna recognises that the concept of family is the *sine qua non* of a full existence.

In *The Final Stage* 'mother' has religious and folk connotations; it stands on a par with the two great mysteries of life and death. More immediately it stands for the supremacy of the family over all else. Social and geographical mobility, economics and ideology may all threaten Soviet family unity, but in Rasputin's work the family is always central and in this he is hardly alone among his contemporaries — one thinks immediately of Fyodor Abramov and the émigré Vladimir Maksimov. It would be easy to attribute a didactic element to Rasputin (and indeed some of his Soviet critics have), but in fact his method and his philosophy are more subtle. Ultimately his characters speak for themselves.

39. Ibid, p.544.
40. Ibid, p.550.

Money for Maria differs from Rasputin's other major works in that we have a hero rather than a heroine at the centre of the story. Despite the novella's title, Maria is entirely passive throughout, and her husband Kuzma holds the stage. Unusually in Rasputin this male character is a more traditional hero, but not in any Socialist Realist sense. A highly moral human being, he finds himself a victim of his society; his psychology is played off against that of all those around him to reveal an enormous rift between town and country, resulting in deeply ingrained social stratification. Few would deny that this is the main interest of Rasputin's story; so how then does the 'mother' theme manifest itself?

Kuzma's prime concern is his family and how to keep it together. Maria is paralysed with fear at the thought of imprisonment, pleading with Kuzma to 'save her', yet unable to do anything for herself. She is noticeably less resilient than Rasputin's other heroines. In his attempts to borrow the thousand roubles necessary to make up the deficit which Maria has incurred, Kuzma receives varying degrees of help from all quarters, the most coming from the collective farm chairman. But our chief concern here is with the women Kuzma encounters. There appears to be an ever-growing degree of comfort from women as the story progresses. Maria creates the problem and is useless in its solution. She calls in Komarikha the local fortune-teller, for whom the down-to-earth Kuzma has no time. The complex structure of the story — his train journey to town interspersed with flashbacks — serves to draw out the increasing comfort offered by the womenfolk. At the station the ticket girl and conductress are boorish and off-hand. When Kuzma recalls his visit to Stepanida to borrow money, we witness a nasty scene of domestic strife between her and her niece Galya. Stepanida could be of some financial assistance but for Galya's loud-mouthed lack of diplomacy.

The train journey under way, Kuzma encounters the old couple who provide a rather idealised picture of marriage. Significantly, the old woman does most of the talking in this account of marital fidelity and compatibility. Then a flashback takes us to Natalya's sickbed. She willingly hands over to Kuzma the money saved for her own funeral. This is the last act of generosity in the story as we have it. We shall never know if Kuzma's brother will give him the money outstanding or if, as Maria expects, he will refuse. Thus the men in this story are ultimately less dependable and comforting than the women.

We have little direct information about Maria and what we see of her first-hand tells us nothing. Yet before this crisis she was clearly a good, caring mother and the mainstay of the family. The way in which she tries to prevent the menfolk from squandering their money on vodka, the fact that the shop can be opened for anyone's convenience at all times, the shop as a social focal point, all these factors testify to Maria's maternal qualities. By contrast Kuzma is reduced to a child-like state by the financial crisis. Frequently tongue-tied, embarrassed and inept, he is at the mercy of the schoolmaster's patronage, the collective farm chairman's toughness and experience (which admittedly pays off), the brashness of the young well-paid wastrel he meets on the train, the condescension of the members of the Soviet upper class over their cognac and cards in the first class carriage, and even his own brother, now urbanised and remote in every sense. Komarikha's superstition, Stepanida's tight-fistedness and even Galya's coarseness represent on balance less of a threat than that posed by the men.

Though the mother theme is undoubtedly muted in *Money for Maria*, it does recapitulate on the out-and-out veneration for women that is so clearly present in *Farewell to Matyora* and which occurs in the other works discussed. Each of the stories shows us families faced with imminent destruction. In each, with the exception of *Money for Maria*, the women bear the brunt. Hence the title of this story is mildly ironic, and doubly so. The story is not primarily about Maria and the money is something alien to the family's way of life. Kuzma never feels they have lived badly and there has always been something to eat. This high regard for subsistence living and lack of concern for money are, of course, in keeping with the values of a primitive agricultural community. The anthropologists tell us that in agricultural societies, unlike among hunters and nomads, women generally enjoy a somewhat higher status, for they are viewed by men as helpmates, providers of food and as symbols of fertility. In Rasputin they are additionally preservers of tradition and moral values under threat from the twentieth-century hunters and nomads created by urbanisation and industrialisation.

The Theme of the Irrational

While Rasputin is clearly the village prose writer *par excellence*, it would be wrong to see him purely in such terms. He introduces into his text a universal element which liberates the finished work from the confines of its immediate subject matter. The early village prose writers of the late 1950s and early 1960s were concerned primarily with the *a priori* truths of life in rural Russia. Deming Brown writes of Yefim Dorosh for example:

Efim Dorosh is the writer of sketches who seemed best able to see things through the eyes of a peasant and at the same time to convey a sense of the complex historical, social, geographical, and psychological factors that conditioned the countryside. An acute observer of the details of village life, with a strong practical understanding of how Russian agriculture operates and should operate, Dorosh also showed a poetic appreciation of the beauties of the countryside and a deep concern for the preservation of the Russian national character. Obviously a democrat with strong liberal convictions and a deeply respectful solicitude for the Russian peasant and his culture, Dorosh combined critical realism with a tone of pragmatism and reasoned persuasiveness.[41]

These remarks might equally apply to Rasputin but more would need to be added. The Soviet critic N. Tenditnik puts her finger on the nature of Rasputin's works: 'The multisignificance [*mnogoznach-nost'*] of the subtext in V. Rasputin's prose, his symbols are always strengthened by a firm realistic graphic quality [*obraznost'*], they grow out of the real world of human relations.'[42]

Obraznost' might also be rendered as 'figurativeness'. In other words there is a strong poetic quality in Rasputin's prose and the resonances that are struck rely to an extent on an irrational element.

The novel of the irrational has, of course, a long pedigree in Russian literature, from Gogol's *Dead Souls* through to Bulgakov's *The Master and Margarita*, and more recently Vladimir Orlov's *Danilov the Violist* (1980). Rasputin's works are primarily realistic in a traditional sense, involving flesh and blood characters, real-life situations and a very real sense of temporal and geographical location. However, one of the chief elements contributing to the poetics of his work is the irrational, the introduction into the text of phenomena that cannot be comprehended, or accommodated by logic. Mysticism, religion, magic, conjecture, the ineffable all have a part to play in Rasputin, and together with the other elements in his work provide the very drama, tension and adventure of the novel.

The irrational in *Farewell to Matyora* permeates the work in many ways, but primarily in the figure of Bogodul, in the Master (Khozyain), the religious motifs and the larch tree.

Bogodul is a mystery in every way. His name has uncertain status and origin. It is not clear whether it is his Christian name or surname, or more likely a nickname (*prozvishche*) as stated in the text.[43] It is pronounced in the Ukrainian manner with a 'kh' after the

---

41. D. Brown, *Soviet Russian Literature since Stalin*, Cambridge University Press, Cambridge, 1978, pp. 226–7.
42. N. Tenditnik, *Otvetstvennost talanta*, Vostochno–sibirskoye izdatelstvo, 1978, p.69.
43. *Povesti*, p.16.

'g' and literate people feel the name is closer to '*bogokhul*' implying 'blasphemy' or 'blasphemer'. He says he is Polish by origin but he uses only Russian, and little more than Russian obscenities at that. He is only rarely capable of coherent conversation and then only with the old women. The reader has no direct evidence of this. His speech consists primarily of the obscenity '*kurva*', nearly always stammered, but it serves him better than others' verbosity does.

Similarly, Bogodul's age and history are indeterminate. There are several suggestions that he was exiled to Siberia for murder, but this strikes one as a more pre-Revolutionary than Soviet course of events. In appearance he has not changed over the years 'as if God had allowed him to live through several generations'.[44] Someone quips that he perhaps served under Peter the Great or Ivan the Terrible.[45]

Moreover, Bogodul's domestic arrangements are highly eccentric. He boards with various old women in the village in winter and in summer occupies a hut that, we are reminded repeatedly, was used by Admiral Kolchak's White troops when they seized the island in the Civil War. The connotations here are highly anti-Soviet. Kolchak was notorious for his atrocities against any who wavered in support of him. The Czech Legion withdrew its allegiance to him because of his behaviour. He was blatantly backed by Britain in his endeavours.[46] Thus Bogodul is outside Soviet power as much as outside history.

Of course, his appearance and his life style are strongly reminiscent of the traditional 'God's fool' (*yurodivyy*) of the Russian village. Significantly, tradition had it that 'God's fools' frequently attached themselves to the most established and respected figures in the community. (Here, one might recall the career of Rasputin's notorious namesake.) Often foul-mouthed and eccentric, they were still much respected. Bogodul in many ways fits the pattern of the 'God's fool'. However, as is frequently the case in Rasputin, there are affinities with other elements of traditional Russian life or folklore which prevent the character becoming a stereotype. The representatives of authority in the office think he is a 'wood demon more than a person'[47] and this, of course, links him to the 'Master of the island', and when the workmen try to destroy the larch tree they liken it to Bogodul, referring to him as 'our master [*nash khozyain*]' and thus completing the circle of references. If one wanted a further link

44. Ibid, p.33.
45. Ibid, p.138.
46. E. H. Carr, *The Bolshevik Revolution 1917–1923*, Vol. I, Penguin, Harmondsworth, 1973, pp. 356–9.
47. *Povesti*, p.132.

between the larch and Bogodul one can recall that Kolchak's men hanged two traitors on it[48] and later threw the bodies in the Angara (incidentally, Kolchak's body was thrown in the Angara after he was executed by firing squad in 1920).

Thus Bogodul, outside the law, outside history, his name and abode associated with blasphemy and treason, his human status frequently in question — Andrei says he's 'a beast not a person'[49] — is an unlikely candidate for the reader's sympathy. Yet he gains it. Firstly, he is the only male character in the work to represent something other than a threat to the women's way of life. He, like them, shuns alcohol — in stark contrast to several of Rasputin's other male characters, and in this story to Petrukha particularly. He is the one to warn them of the 'alien devils', as he puts it, who are clearing the cemetery and to tell Katerina that Petrukha's hut is on fire. Like the Master, his strength is in his perception rather than in his powers of expression. The closing paragraph of the story has the Master making an utterance for the first time, and Bogodul unable to see anything because of the fog. Outwardly violent and intimidating, Bogodul is rendered powerless at the end, closer to the old women than ever before.

Barely capable of speech, Bogodul can hardly be seen to act rationally. He operates on the level of instinct and his likes and dislikes are instantaneous and uncompromising. He rejects the town as he rejects alcohol. In essence then, Bogodul epitomises an irrational yet integrated element in man. Close to the everyday women-folk in the story, yet at one with the wild, natural elements (he goes without shoes and can let a snake bite his bare foot), having clear affinities with other motifs in the work, he cannot fairly be dismissed as 'colourful but superfluous' (*koloriten, no, v obshchem-to, izlishen Bogodul*) as the critic Ovcharenko puts it.[50]

The other irrational elements in the story seem to merit at least a little more consideration from Soviet critics. Starikova writes:

As I was reading *Farewell to Matyora*, when I first reached the part where suddenly amongst all the worries about the hay and the potatoes, the Master appears — he is either the house-spirit of the peasant huts doomed to be burnt, or a wood demon who has preserved the unity of the island dwellers and their flooded land, I trembled with delight, with aesthetic satisfaction.[51]

48. Ibid, pp.159–60.
49. Ibid, p.127.
50. A. Ovcharenko, et al. 'Proza Valentina Rasputina', *Voprosy literatury*, 1977, No.2, pp. 3–81, p.69.
51. Ibid, p.76.

This appearance she calls a 'bold sortie from humdrum routine into the fantastic, which immediately raises the poetic level of the narrative'. However, his appearance, or rather his call, at the end of the story she feels is 'a superfluous finishing touch'. While one can readily concur with Starikova that the irrational element in the work contributes to the story's poetics, it is less easy to see why she finds fault at the end of the work.

When the Master makes his first, dramatic entry, it is as much a shock to the reader as the arrival of the cemetery clearers is to Matyora's earthly inhabitants. Yet it is soon made clear that the Master has been part and parcel of the island for ages, knowing and seeing everything, unlike the 'alien devils' from the Sanitary and Epidemic Station. The Master is alive to the minutest sound, a bubble bursting or a twig creaking. His most intriguing quality is his contemplation of the here and now. The infinity of the sky 'disquietens him': 'let people look up to the sky for comfort'.[52] There is an essential ambiguity in the Master's attitude. On the one hand, he is a spirit, and one can speculate about all the spiritual qualities of man he might represent. On the other hand he, seemingly, rejects the 'dreams' and 'aspirations' of man. The Master's spiritual comfort is to be found in the sights and sounds all around him, to use a cliché, in the miracle of nature. He makes no attempt to rationalise this or to build a philosophical or religious system out of it. In this sense he is close to the heroine, Darya, whose obviously religious outlook is never specified or systematised. Indeed, the implication of the Master's outlook might well be that it is *man*-inspired religious systems which are to be avoided.

Like Bogodul, the Master has a lair, but is essentially a wanderer. His movements are random but he often gravitates towards Matyora village. On his visits there he always starts his round from Bogodul's hut. He has a remarkable foreknowledge, and the notion here must be that only unearthly spirits can know the future. The prognostication of human beings is thus presented as highly dubious. Andrei insists that 'man is the tsar of nature' but he has no inkling of the Master, and he has no reliable knowledge as to what the future holds, either for himself or his society.

The Master makes two other appearances: when Katerina's hut is burnt, and obliquely, when 'a small animal' follows Darya the day her hut is burnt down. The wood demon can assume many guises in Russian folklore, sometimes man, sometimes beast. But the common factor in the wood demons would seem to be the notion of encounter

52. *Povesti*, pp. 54–5.

between human and demon. It is interesting to note in *Farewell to Matyora* that no one meets the Master, or is aware of him. In Darya's case he tries to 'look her in the eye', but apparently without success. Moreover, the wood demon can sometimes be threatening or unruly.

It is also the case that folk tales often have a human character making some kind of pact with a wood demon.[53] Rasputin's Master, though, is content to watch, listen and remain unobtrusive. In *Farewell to Matyora* then, the humans on the whole seem to be out of touch with this element of spiritual life. Lastly on the subject of the Master, it must be borne in mind that he is not wholly supernatural. When the humans depart so will he. Their end is his end. So ultimately the Master can be seen to embody well-founded human aspirations and intuitions, rather than a divinity that rules over mankind.

While the religious dimension in the work is to be found primarily in the figure of Darya, it is difficult to escape some kind of analogy with the Old Testament story of the Flood. However, in *Farewell to Matyora* we have a version of the biblical story shorn of its original comforting features. The ark, in the form of the new settlement across the water, is spurned by the old folk of Matyora. There is to be a flood not because of retribution, divine or otherwise, for sins committed, but for utilitarian considerations which Darya and her friends cannot understand. There is no righteous character equivalent to Noah — Vorontsov, the bureaucrat responsible for resettling the islanders, is painted in very dark colours. More especially, in stark contrast to the biblical story, there are no symbols of peace and restitution at the end. There is no dove bearing an olive branch, and the rainbow, an emblem of agreement between heaven and earth, is nowhere to be seen. This is a society dispossessed and abandoned, a society at odds with the powers that rule over it. No wonder Soviet reviewers were uncomfortable about the story's tenor, while at the same time admiring the artist's skill.

Darya's religion has already been discussed to some extent. Her blend of Christianity and possibly Buddhism — her mother was Buryat — shades into a kind of paganism, especially when she is pursued by the Master, for wood demons are traditionally associated with pagan mythology. One recalls that the wood demon fears fire and iron (Siberian shamans often wore iron trinkets to ward off evil spirits), the very things that threaten Darya and her kind. By extension one might say that the overt Christian imagery in

53. Much of this incidental information on wood demons is taken from E. Pomerantseva's *Mifologicheskiye personazhi v russkom folklore*, Nauka, Institut etnografiyi, Moscow, 1975.

the work is more than amply counterbalanced by pagan elements, by the persistent presence of the ancient elements: earth, fire, air and water.

Another image associated with the irrational is the *Tsar-listven'*, the larch tree.[54] As elsewhere in the novel this seemingly inanimate object is personified and is also highly symbolic. It is referred to by the locals as 'Tsar' and 'he' (despite the feminine gender of the Russian word for 'larch'). It appears terrifying (*groznyy*) and unconquerable. It would also appear to have god-like qualities, since in the old days the villagers gave it gifts at Easter and Whitsun. Here one notes a perfect blending of Christian and pagan belief. As we have already seen it is associated with death (the two men hanged from it by Kolchak's men); there is also the legend of the boy who jumped in the nearby pit, never to return, but instead became the husband of a water nymph (*rusalochnyy muzh*). A young girl, disappointed in love, hanged herself from it and a boy fell from it and was killed. The bed of discarded foliage beneath it is called a *kurgan* — burial mound. The larch has then been an instrument of death, indomitable — once lightning beheaded it, but failed to destroy it. There is also a belief among the islanders that its roots fix Matyora to the river bed and thus join it to the whole earth. Matyora will last as long as the larch does. Poignantly, the one thing to be spared by the larch is the birch tree some twenty metres away. The larch has had mercy on it, and perhaps even the roots of the two trees are entwined. It is only natural that Darya should be found sitting by this symbol of Matyora when her home has been destroyed.

The larch is fully integrated into the system of interlocking symbols in the novel. We have seen that when the 'aliens' come to destroy it they liken it to Bogodul, but refer to him as 'master', which links the larch to the wood demon. Unable to destroy the tree with axes, petrol or power saws, the men turn their, now utterly gratuitous, violence on the nearby birch. Here then we have violence for violence's sake directed at the very poetics of the work. One could draw parallels with the powerful scene in *Live and Remember* where the deserter Andrei slays a calf.

It is well known that the birch tree occupies a special place in Russian folklore — it figures in countless songs (one of them cited by the men trying to fell the larch) and proverbs. Perhaps the most relevant proverb here might be 'The birch's tears flow when you tear the bark from it' (*U beryozki slyozki tekut, kogda s neyo korku derut*).

These four elements — Bogodul, the wood demon, the religious

---

54. *Povesti*, pp. 44–5 and pp. 158–60.

motifs and the larch tree — all contribute towards the irrational in the work. They stand mid-way between the familiar and comprehensible and the mystical and unknown. In this way they urge man to reach beyond himself. In this sense *Farewell to Matyora*'s message goes far beyond immediate ecological issues.

Any irrational element in *Live and Remember* is encompassed within human experience, or more especially, human behaviour. The overtly magic and mystical elements of *Farewell to Matyora* are gone and the reader is presented instead with a set of human actions which defy common sense yet are utterly convincing in their execution. Reactions to this story concentrated too much, for the author's liking, on the figure of the deserter, and when the critic Ovcharenko shifted the emphasis to the heroine, Rasputin responded warmly: 'I was delighted by your article not out of the usual vanity that a writer has, but because you understand me, you understand that I was writing not simply and least of all about a deserter, whom everyone for some reason is getting at, but about a woman.'[55]

None the less the figure of Andrei provides an essential counterpoint to the tragic Nastyona in that he operates on instinct rather than good sense, and represents the dark side of human personality. Andrei possesses many qualities which mark him out as the Dostoyevskian self-willed hero *in extremis*. He enters the story as a mystery, graduates to near-nightmare status and then assumes, like Svidrigailov, a harrowing reality. He engenders the enigma with which the story opens (the missing axe); when Nastyona encounters him she wonders if he is not a 'werewolf' (*oboroten'*);[56] he has the appetite of an animal and his affinities to the animal world are maintained throughout the story. He learns to howl like a wolf. On one occasion Nastyona refers to him as a 'mole'.[57]

Moreover, he is a criminal, an outsider, a rebel — and not merely by virtue of his one impulsive act of desertion but by his entire ambience. When he first meets Nastyona he takes her to 'his' village, Atamanovka, which

> received its present name from a different one, more sonorous and frightening — Razboynikovo [from *razboynik* — thief: R. P.]. Once upon a time, in the old days, the local peasants thought nothing of pursuing a

55. A. Ovcharenko, Introduction to *Valentin Rasputin: Izbrannyye proizvedeniya v 2-x tomakh*, Molodaya gvardiya, 1984, Vol. I, p.14.
56. *Povesti*, p.211.
57. Ibid, p.268.

quiet and profitable trade: they checked out the gold-diggers going from the Lena. For this purpose the village was ideally situated: the crest went almost right through to the Angara, and there was no way of skirting the village. At the narrowest spot by the river, desperate men used to watch out for the Lena gold prospectors — and so the village acquired a lasting reputation. The name Razboynikovo passed from oral tradition on to paper, but even before Soviet power was established someone in the district council felt that it seemed in bad taste and so it was changed to 'Atamanovka' — the meaning was the same but it did not offend the ear. However, the local folk did not agree with this change of name for some reason. And to this very day, many years later, old men from Karda, or Rybnaya and other villages, as if by common consent, would keep saying:

'The whole village used to be involved in robbery, and then they wanted to put the blame on some ataman. But it won't do.'[58]

The old men's probity and the village's unsavoury history echo the contrasts that one finds in Andrei. He is an outlaw, but has fought valiantly hitherto; he has been violent to his wife but has real moments of love and tenderness; more particularly, in a manner strongly reminiscent of Lermontov's Pechorin, he has a tendency to impose his own will on circumstances when it suits him, but when things go wrong to shift the blame to fate, or God, or some unseen force. Personal responsibility vies with free-will in Andrei for supremacy and the *perpetuum mobile* is still in operation when the story closes. When we last see him,[59] he talks almost in the same breath of killing himself and 'getting at' Nastyona even in death if she betrays him. The Russian here ('*Myortvyy pridu i strebuyu*') might suggest killing her as well as demanding she account for herself. Like Pechorin and many a Dostoyevskian hero, he suffers from self-deception. Having convinced himself he will be allowed home after hospitalisation, he is ordered to return to the front:

> He thought of the field-hospital authorities as some kind of unearthly, malicious will [*volya*] which could not be governed by human strength, just as, let's say, you can't avert a rainstorm or stop it hailing. God on high decided on something without rhyme or reason and others had to consent. But he [Andrei] was a living person — why couldn't he be taken account of? True, no-one had made him any promises, he had deceived himself.[60]

This half-admission of his own responsibility is never acted upon and Andrei's behaviour goes uncurbed by conscience. Moreover, it

58. Ibid, pp.203–4.
59. Ibid, pp.372–4.
60. Ibid, p.217.

infects others, notably his wife. She too is forced into estrangement from the rest of the community; she 'learns how to steal';[61] the two thousand roubles she is advanced is seen as a 'trump',[62] which suggests a reliance on gambling and fate which we would not have suspected in her earlier; she also takes on certain animal characteristics, 'brooding like a chicken in a coop', while the ravens 'chicken-like' spread their wings.[63] Or she is 'like a beast'.[64]

In addition to Andrei's animal characteristics and the manner in which they spread to his wife, one might consider the hero's own relationship to the animal world, and here one perceives his real crimes, as opposed to the ostensible misdemeanour of his desertion. He becomes almost king of the jungle, learning from the wolf rather than fearing it, killing a goat and deliberately letting it die slowly and then, as discussed above, going out of his way to slaughter a calf in a near-sadistic fashion. One should compare these actions with his father's binding affection for horses and Andrei's feelings at eating horse meat during the battle of Stalingrad and shielding himself from gunfire behind a horse carcass.[65] He concludes that if his father had been in his position he would not have been so bold as to say that he would never eat man nor horse even if he were dying. Though Andrei enjoys an easier relationship (or at least convinces himself so) with his father he succeeds in this way in rejecting his father's values and, ironically, is closer in temperament to his mother, given his shifts in mood and his unpredictability.

On occasion Andrei's irrationalism is pointed up by seemingly chance remarks, and echoes of a paranatural world are to be heard. Seeing him with a beard, Nastyona calls him a 'wood demon' (*leshiy*) and an 'evil spirit' (*nechistaya sila*).[66] When he learns of her pregnancy he calls her 'my Mother of God' (*Bogoroditsa ty moya*).[67] This religious motif is taken up towards the end of the story when Nastyona's unborn child takes on a Christ-like function in Andrei's eyes, delivering them from evil:

> The baby is our salvation. You've been dirtied quite a bit by this business of mine too. Yet you've got a conscience, you're uneasy. Give birth and you'll feel better. The baby will save you from evil. Can there really be in the whole world such guilt that couldn't be covered over by him, our

61. Ibid, p.229.
62. Ibid, p.224.
63. Ibid, p.227.
64. Ibid, p.270.
65. Ibid, p.304.
66. Ibid, p.232.
67. Ibid, p.273.

baby. There's no such guilt, Nastyona . . . I know; you're going to have to walk over hot coals . . . but bear it, Nastyona.[68]

Indeed, Andrei is frequently content to let others do the suffering for him. He blames the war for his situation, or 'fate' which 'sent him',[69] and all his actions are directed at others. He vows suicide,[70] but it is his wife who kills herself. Nevertheless, for all his illogical explanations and aggression, he cannot be totally condemned. For there is an endearing side to his irrationalism which manifests itself in his dreams and in his memories.

His earliest childhood memory is of his uncle being led away by partisans for having fought on Kolchak's side in the Civil War. Elsewhere he and Nastyona recall their courtship, the superstition that she might be able to conceive if they are away from home;[71] and there is the dream which they both have independently suggesting a common understanding and mutual affection despite the barriers thrown up by war or other circumstances.[72]

In *The Final Stage* the primary manifestation of the irrational is death itself. Anna herself faces it calmly, even positively:

> She was not alarmed: what had to be revealed to her, would be in due course and was not to be for the time being, it was not the [right] time. The old woman believed that in dying she would learn not only this but many other secrets, which were not to be known during one's life and which when all was said and done, would tell her the eternal secret — what had been happening to her and what would happen to her.[73]

However, her children take refuge from it, Ilya and Mikhail in drink, Varvara in theatrical outbursts, Lyusya in memories; and Tanya ('Tanchora'), who never comes, presumably in indifference. Rasputin is at pains to see things through the eyes of his heroine and often the author's voice is tantamount to Anna's inner monologue. There is no attempt to alleviate the solemn tone of the story. Death is accepted as an imponderable phenomenon that cannot be defeated by dubious religious prognostication about an after-life or by ideologically motivated optimism about the future of the human

68. Ibid, p.364.
69. Ibid, p.276.
70. Ibid, p.372.
71. Ibid, pp.292–4.
72. Ibid, pp.179–80.
73. Ibid, p.488.

race as a whole.

For all her incoherent musings and occasional delirium Anna actually possesses an acute eye and a good deal of insight into others. She is fully aware that the men are getting drunk in the bathhouse, despite all their subterfuges. She gets the measure of her children well; Ilya has changed radically, while Lyusya is a 'complete town girl' (*vsya gorodskaya*).[74] Her vivid memory of her own sin in once stealing milk is neatly contrasted to the tasteless joking and celebration of their own degeneracy that the drunken menfolk go in for.[75]

Running throughout the story is the juxtaposition of real scenes of country life, involving reason and logic as well as shortcomings, and the sporadic references to life in the town, which appears incongruous. Tanya now lives in Kiev and towards the end of the story Anna, in confusion, recalls her youngest daughter in terms of the Nazi occupation. Modern technology deceives rather than aids: the telegram fails to bring Tanya, and Mikhail, in a rare moment of decency, has to invent a second telegram to explain her absence. Anna's old friend Mironikha blames aeroplanes for her absence.[76] The radio has broken, so Anna relies on conversation with her friend, while the drunkards in the bathhouse criticise the songs on the radio for treating one like a fool.[77] One might compare the nonsense of Stepan the village drunk boasting of regularly reading three newspapers (which have clearly made no impression on him) or of Ilya suggesting that Anna might visit and come to the circus, with the sense and reality of the village that Anna has known and which is now changing:

> In recent years summer and autumn had, as it were, changed places: it poured with rain in June and July, and then right up to Pokrov [October 1st, Festival of the Protection of the Virgin: R. P.], there was fine weather, which was a good thing because it was fine weather, but bad because it hadn't come when it should. So just let the women try and guess when they ought to dig up the potatoes: in the old days now was the time and there was the will too, while the weather was like it was, to water the potatoes as they should be — give them the sort of drenching they'd had in the summer, when they were swimming in water like fish. Yet if you waited any longer the weather would turn nasty again, and then you just try and pick them out of the mud. No matter how hard you tried no one knew exactly where you'd find them or not. And it was the same with the

74. Ibid, p.423.
75. Ibid, pp.491–3.
76. Ibid, p.486.
77. Ibid, p.504.

harvest: one person would stack up the hay as in the old days and it would all rot in the rain, and someone else would just spend all that time getting drunk, wouldn't go out to the field as he kept meaning to, and he would hit lucky. The weather had started getting all mixed up, just like some old woman who'd lost her wits and couldn't remember what she was about. People said it was because of the seas which had been made on almost every river.[78]

Certainly one detects from this passage that the dislocation caused by the modern world is perceived as making inroads into the life of the village. In the village there has hitherto been a rhythm and a tradition which is quite absent in the town. Much of the reminiscing in *The Final Stage* may be idealised or even incongruous, but it endows the characters with more humanity. On her rural walk recalling her childhood — a frightening encounter with a threatening stranger, the farm, the horse, childhood friends — Lyusya grows in the reader's estimation. She experiences fear, doubt and curiosity. The notion of betrayal is never far away in Rasputin, and here there are echoes of it as Lyusya recalls calling the horse a deserter, and remembers some captured Vlasovites. (General Vlasov and his army defected to the Germans in 1942 and his name is synonymous with the worst kind of traitor.)

A more disturbing mystery than death and closely associated with the town is the figure of Tanya, who haunts the story. Anna perceives her as different from all her other children; she is the only one who bothers to write directly to her and Anna cherishes her letters which she has read to her by various people, being illiterate herself. The photograph she keeps of her depicts a country girl. Yet Anna apparently deceives herself over Tanya. This youngest daughter has promised to visit before but never has; she chooses a means of communication which cannot really work (letters to an illiterate!); and moreover, she never thinks of even sending a telegram back to explain her absence — her reticence exposes Anna's wishful thinking.

Thus the real pathos of *The Final Stage* resides not in the death of an old woman, but in rifts brought about within the family by the modern world. Geoffrey Hosking concludes that Anna's children will, after this episode, never meet again.[79]

The irrational, incomprehensible aspect of the town as glimpsed in *The Final Stage* comes into sharper focus in *Money for Maria*. The

78. Ibid, p.409.
79. G. Hosking, *Beyond Socialist Realism*, Collins (Granada), London, 1980, p.73.

simplest of Rasputin's stories, it depends for much of its effect on the deliberately dislocated time sequence, which is brought about by a series of dreams and flashbacks.

Money for Maria is also the least poetic of Rasputin's novellas and indeed its main theme is strikingly unromantic and prosaic — a family in debt. This subject matter is indeed low key in comparison with the chords of apocalypse, desertion and death that are struck in Rasputin's other major works. None the less *Money for Maria* established Rasputin's reputation at a stroke.

For readers outside the Soviet Union the fact of Maria's debt does require some explanation. In Rasputin's story we are never told how much Kuzma earns, and indeed his own casual attitude to money suggests that it does not matter too much: 'All his life Kuzma's attitude to money had been very simple: if it was there — fine, if not — well, okay then.'[80] The American journalist Hedrick Smith provides some anecdotal information on the status of money in the Soviet Union: 'I busily went on making computations until Russian friends tipped me off that it was not money that really mattered but access or *blat.*' In Armenia Smith met a field hand 'who told me he made less than 150 rubles a month at harvest time and less out of season, and that without his private plot he could not make ends meet'.[81] These remarks date from the early 1970s. Calculating the earnings of a *kolkhoznik* is a notoriously difficult exercise, since they depend on his private plot as well as on work done on the state farm and can take the form of cash as well as kind. Certainly the 'man–day unit' on the collective farms increased by over 200% between 1953 and 1962 and there was an increase in the proportion of this paid in money.[82] Between 1953 and 1967, one authority states, the average annual wages on collective farms almost tripled.[83] Clearly, money throughout that period began to play a more important part in the peasant's life. Still in the early to mid-1960s (when Rasputin's story takes place) the *kolkhoznik*'s total income was roughly 75% that of the *sovkhoznik* and two-thirds of that of a worker in local industry.[84] Even allowing for Kuzma's semi-skilled job as a driver he would be one of the lowest paid workers in the Soviet Union. If the 'special-

80. *Povesti*, p.604.
81. H. Smith, *The Russians*, Sphere, London, 1976, p.22 and p.255.
82. J. Karcz, *Soviet and East European Agriculture*, University of California Press, Berkeley, Calif., 1967, p.210.
83. J. Millar (ed.), *The Soviet Rural Economy*, University of Illinois Press, Champaign, Ill., 1971, p. 218.
84. Karcz, *Soviet and East European Agriculture*, p.204.

ists' on his farm (the agronomist, the vet, the zoo technician, the mechanic) together with the chairman earn between them 640 roubles a month,[85] one can assume Kuzma is lucky to get about 100 a month. He is astounded by the young forestry worker's boasted earnings of 250–400 roubles a month.[86] Thus Maria's debt is about a year's wages for them. Kuzma's forlorn hope that the auditor might have calculated in old roubles (and thus the amount would be reduced tenfold) refers to the currency reform of 1 January 1961.

It is tempting to see *Money for Maria*, as Deming Brown does,[87] as an implied indictment of the harshness of Soviet law. This may be so, but it is doubtful, on the facts, if the law will take its course. Kuzma has about 460 roubles from the specialists (the vet's wife has demanded her husband's wages back and the mechanic has asked for 20 roubles back), 100 from Yevgeniy Nikolayevich, about 150 from Natalya, and the offer of 15 from Gordey. He needs less than three hundred to clear the debt, and in addition to help from his brother, there has been no mention of his own earnings that month or to direct help from the sympathetic farm chairman. At the end of the story he tells himself he could have still raised the money in the village.[88] This is not to say that the story is optimistic; its tragedy resides in the social and psychological rifts that we encounter as Kuzma makes his journey round the village and then into town.

The religious connotations of Maria's name have already been noted but there are other faint echoes of a religious dimension to this story. Shaposhnikov, in pursuing a broadly sociological examination of the work comes uncomfortably close to notions expressed in Solzhenitsyn's early story *Matryona's Farm*:

> And so here V. Rasputin's novella presents us with a splendid opportunity of reflecting on the processes which are occurring now in the life of the village and which to a large extent are determining its fate in the future. Reading *Money for Maria*, one sees for oneself how much the fate of the village depends at times on one person, on one inhabitant . . .[89]

Solzhenitsyn concludes his story of the stoic religious peasant woman as follows:

> We all lived beside her and did not realise that she was that righteous person without whom as the saying goes, the village cannot stand.

85. *Povesti*, p.630.
86. Ibid, p.619.
87. Brown, *Soviet Russian Literature since Stalin*, p.251.
88. *Povesti*, p.653.
89. Shaposhnikov, *Valentin Rasputin*, p.23.

Nor the town.
Nor our whole land.[90]

One might detect certain atmospheric qualities which link *Money for Maria* with Chekhov's story *Student*; thus again a religious note is struck. *Money for Maria* takes place over one night and the weather is cold and windy. Indeed the wind is persistently referred to: 'wind, wind, wind — wind in the forest, wind in the field, wind in the village.'[91] Compare this with Chekhov: 'Now hunching himself up from the cold, the student thought that just this sort of wind would have been blowing in Rurik's day, and Ivan the Terrible's and Peter's and that in their day too there had been the same rampant poverty and hunger.'[92] Chekhov's story recalls Peter's denial of Christ and as the young theology student — he is twenty-two — retells the Bible story he moves from the blank pessimism as cited above to a dubious optimism. The Romantic element in him is a betrayal of reality, as unintentional as is Peter's denial of Christ.

Maria is betrayed by a faceless system. Generally speaking the village community supports her and there is a widespread acceptance of her moral superiority over the system's. Even the auditor is willing to cover up for five days and the authorities are seen as alien and hostile. 'Don't give me up to *them*'[93] (my italics: R. P.), pleads Maria, while Yevgeniy Nikolayevich, himself an intellectual and hence somewhat remote, says 'you tell them'.[94] At no time does anyone consider following the letter of the law. Returning the veterinarian surgeon's wages to his wife, Kuzma feels he is stealing them from his own wife 'as if he had stolen this money from Maria and she had caught him in the act'.[95] The moral superiority of those the system has deemed criminal is well established in the story. It is appropriate that, via Chekhov, *Money for Maria* should contain faint echoes of the Easter story.

In writing about those oppressed, those who are unable to relate to modern Soviet society, Rasputin in no way stands in opposition to the Soviet system. In numerous interviews and sketches his patriotism comes through, but it is a patriotism that can easily transform

90. A. Solzhenitsyn, *Sobraniye sochineniy*, Vol. III, YMCA, Paris, 1978, p.159.
91. *Povesti*, p. 561.
92. A. Chekhov, *Izbrannoye*, Izdatelstvo 'Khudozhestvennaya literatura', Moscow, 1974, p. 401.
93. *Povesti*, p.568.
94. Ibid, p.572.
95. Ibid, p.648.

itself into Russian, or more particularly, Siberian, nationalism. It has been suggested that Rasputin (together with Viktor Astafyev) has been allowed more freedom in his depiction of Soviet shortcomings, because his Siberian nationalism is particularly convenient, given that China has claims on Eastern Siberia.[96] Whatever the reasons Rasputin's nationalism finds frequent expression: 'I believe that the Russians will remain Russians, the Tartars Tartars and the French French, that, while being internationalists, we will preserve in ourselves our national beginnings and that in a hundred years' time we will start to go and worship the field of Kulikovo, the field of Borodino, Pushkin, Dostoyevsky, Shevchenko and Rustaveli . . .'[97] Such sentiments are perhaps more in evidence in Rasputin's shorter prose works of the late 1970s and 1980s ('Baikal, Baikal', 'Irkutsk is with us' and 'Siberia without Romance'), than in his more successful fiction.

Rasputin also insists on the tendentiousness of art, though this quality is not on display in the best of his fiction. In 1986 he said, in pointed contrast to Chekhov's often quoted remarks about art: 'It is not true that literature knows only how to put questions without answering them, although the answers, perhaps, are not necessary, because the moral posing of a question contains a moral answer, and the immoral posing of a question, an immoral answer.' [98]

Linking the cause of literature quite explicitly with the fatherland, Rasputin states that while each writer has his own patch, their common field, not in abstract but in concrete terms 'is and will be Russia. For us there is no fate and for us no word, outside Russia. A healthy international feeling is maintained in a national feeling — it is hardly necessary to decode such things.' Rasputin concludes as follows: 'In Siberia as everywhere else, the destruction of nature and the neglect of history lead to the physical and moral destruction of man'.[99]

Several factors make Rasputin a very unlikely candidate for any elevated position in Soviet letters. He writes about the victims of Soviet power rather than about fully integrated members of Soviet society. There is a strong undertow of religious interest in many of his works. His overt misgivings about the processes of urbanisation and technological progress put him at odds with Soviet policies. His

96. R. Marsh, *Soviet Fiction since Stalin: Science, Politics and Literature*, Croom Helm, London, 1986, p.186.
97. V. Rasputin, 'Prezhde vsego — vospitaniye chuvstv', *Literaturnaya gazeta*, 26 November 1980, No.13, p.5.
98. V. Rasputin, 'Zemlya sudby', *Ogonyok*, February 1986, No. 8, pp.24–5, p.24.
99. Ibid, p.25.

avowed nationalism — despite the lip service to internationalism —
may appear embarrassingly naked in a country officially committed
to Marxism. Some of the 'political' reasons for Rasputin's accommo-
dation in the Soviet Union are well established: his convincing
portrayal of loyal, stoic, brave and tolerant Russian peasants is of
more ideological use than that of educated youngsters, ostensibly
committed to 'progress', but with their sights set on the big city and
Western values. However, one should not overlook the most obvious
element — the sheer quality of Rasputin's writing. Many a Soviet
critic — not to mention foreigner — has complained about the
difficulties of Rasputin's language, the use of dialect and substan-
dard words, but in his earthy dialogues and rich descriptions of
people and places, he creates an utterly authentic world, a world far
removed from Europe and in many instances from the twentieth
century, which is as intriguing as it is revealing.

The Fire

When *Pozhar* (*The Fire*) appeared in 1985, there was good reason to
hope that Rasputin had overcome the period of comparative artistic
sterility which ensued after *Farewell to Matyora*. This short novel
contains all the drama and richness of expression that have been
customarily associated with Rasputin. It has been noted that in
some ways *The Fire* is a sequel to *Farewell to Matyora*; one minor
character, Klavka Strigunova, figures in both stories, there is reference to the hero's former village of Yegorovka being flooded and the
inhabitants moved out.[100] Most pointedly, there is the parallel
between water and fire, two of the four ancient elements and both a
threat to mankind, while at the same time vital to his existence.

It is tempting to see the fire in biblical terms (especially since the
flood in *Farewell to Matyora* has affinities with the story of Noah). The
materialism and fixation with technological progress that destroyed
Matyora are now to be punished by fire. Indeed the confusion and
disembodiment of the protagonists that are so movingly evoked at
the end of *Farewell to Matyora* are continued and developed in *The
Fire*. There is no supernatural element in this work, and all the
characters are studiously depicted in realistic terms. Yet they are
frequently at odds with one another and all at odds with their

100. D. Gillespie, 'Valentin Rasputin's *Pozhar*', *Quinquereme* (Bath University), July
1986, Vol.9, No.2, pp.201–13. Ye. Starikova, 'Ishchushchaya dusha', *Novyy mir*,
1985, No.12, pp.232–6.

environment. Rootlessness is the order of the day. Confusion is caused ostensibly by the conflagration, yet it would be there in the souls of its heroes, even without the age-old scourge of Russian village life.

The Russian saying 'My hut is on the edge (of the village), I know nothing' (*moya khata s krayu, ya nichego ne znayu*) refers of course to the fear of fire in the countryside — the edge of the village was the safest place to live; however, the phrase also raises questions of conscience, in the way it implies 'I'm all right, Jack'. Rasputin's story, no less than all his other works, raises questions of personal responsibility and involvement, of conscience.

The Fire tells the story of how one night there is a conflagration in the village settlement of Sosnovka. The hero, Ivan Petrovich, a man in his middle years, tries, along with other bold spirits, to fight the fire, while a good many of the inhabitants, particularly the younger ones, go in for looting and wanton sky-larking. One of them, with the curious feminine name of Sonya, attacks Khampo the watchman, who is trying to stop the pilfering, and both are killed. Ivan Petrovich is dismayed as much by the corruption of the establishment — for once he sees inside the threatened warehouses and discovers all the goods which never seem to reach the ordinary folk — as he is by the fecklessness and criminality of his fellow men.

The hero with no home, but with a pronounced sense of justice, is hardly new in Russian literature. In *The Fire* Ivan Petrovich fills this role, as do some of Rasputin's other heroes. Once again there is a strong sense of urgency at the back of the hero's actions and his ideas. Like *Money for Maria*, the work is constructed on a series of flashbacks and reflections, so that the end product is indeed complex, and even bewildering.

Ivan Petrovich's inner turmoil is communicated to the reader in a number of ways, not least by the liberal use, even by Rasputin's standards, of dialect words. Starikova found some of his coinages 'unnecessary' and 'not very aesthetic'. She also noted a lack of artistic 'finish' (*zakonchennost'*) and felt that the closing paragraph of the story was 'an enigma'.[101]

> Ivan Petrovich walked on and on, leaving the settlement and, so it seemed to him, leaving himself, forcing himself step by step into his new-found solitude. And he felt it as solitude not only because there was nobody else with him, but also because he felt emptiness and monotony within himself too. This state was either weariness, a brief enchantment or the first hardening of the spirit — how was he to know? — but he walked on

101. Ibid.

lightly, freely and evenly, as if he was haphazardly finding his own pace and his breathing, as if at last he had been set on the true path. There was a smell of resin; a woodpecker was hammering at a dry tree trunk, but it was not the woodpecker, but his heart making the noise, it was his heart responding to something gratefully and hastily. He saw himself from a distance: a little man walking over the spring earth, having lost his way and despairing of ever finding his home, and soon he would be on the other side of the wood and would disappear forever.

The land was silent, either greeting him, or seeing him on his way.[102]

In his courage and diligence in trying to put out the fire and save the goods, Ivan Petrovich displays all the qualities that one associates with village prose heroes and there is no difficulty in accommodating them to the canon of Socialist Realism. But such an apparently blurred ending as the one cited here does indicate an uncomfortable degree of doubt and uncertainty on the part of both hero and writer.

In fact the ending of the story is totally in keeping with all that has gone before. *The Fire* is shot through with motifs of the inexplicable. It is worth noting that while the Soviet critic quoted above seems rather at a loss to explain the work, one émigré critic Maria Shneerson has no problem in interpreting it: *The Fire* depicts the utter corruption and decay rife in the Soviet system and cannot be more explicit than it is because the work is of course subject to censorship.[103] Starikova, ironically, complains that the work is too 'publicist', while presumably Shneerson would like to see more of the graphic descriptions of the seamy side of Soviet life.

However, it would be hard to improve on Rasputin's chilling references to throat-cutting, alcoholism, theft, corrupt officialdom, and his account of the murder of one key character. *The Fire* is neither a diluted account of social decay, nor a fudged attempt to present a new positive hero. It is more exactly an endeavour to record once again the 'intuitive side' of man, especially when man is under pressure. At times man's intuition may coincide with received norms of social behaviour, sometimes not. Thus a 'partisan' critic will find what he wishes to in *The Fire*, but he may not find the whole.

The intuitive side is seen, broadly speaking, and with a good deal of overlap, in three ways in the work: through religion, through the work ethic and through certain 'blurred' passages, such as the

---

102. V. Rasputin, 'Pozhar'. *Nash sovremennik*, 1985, No.7, pp.3–38, p. 38.
103. M. Shneerson, 'Kogda vsyo vokrug zamatilos . . .' *Posev*, No. 12, 1986, pp. 46–9.

ending of the story.

As in *Farewell to Matyora* the religion is not specific. One detects elements of pantheism and even reincarnation and mysticism: 'Every stone before your birth had foreknowledge of your coming and waited for you, every blade of grass in the new spring brings you something for the preservation or support of former times, and a subtle ancestral watch is kept over you everywhere and in everything.'[104] Ivan recalls on one occasion how his wife lifted a huge box of sand to put out a fire and save her husband's life. Unable to explain how she found the strength, Alyona says: 'It wasn't me. Someone else was there to save you. He got hold of my hands and put all his strength into them.'[105]

Religion goes hand in hand with the work ethic in Ivan's psychology. At one point he demands a 'plan' for human souls to take account of all those who have been lost. The author notes his hero's relationship to work:

> Work is not done solely for His Excellency the Belly. How many people who are doing little or no work are filling their bellies none the worse. That's easy these days.
>
> Work is what remains after you. . . . In his work, a man doesn't remember that these are kilometres, cubic metres or roubles; he rises above them to a higher plane where there is no accounts department, there is only movement, rhythm and festivity . . . it would seem to be relevant to his soul, to its pristine inclination; up there he is wholly transformed into the answer to someone's urgent call, his soul tunes up and begins to reverberate openly and in freedom.[106]

Rasputin's hero may have as much commitment to hard work as, for example, Aitmatov's Boston in *The Execution Block*, but his values are not based so much on civic-mindedness and general decency as on the spiritual. He has a lot in common with Solzhenitsyn's Ivan Denisovich as far as work is concerned.

In striving to elucidate the intuitive side of man and couple it with considerations of good and evil *The Fire* comes dangerously close to incoherence at one or two points, as it comments on perfectly coherent and credible characters and situations: 'Either conscience and truth by intercommunicating are complementing one another, or they are not independent and are bowing down to something more important. But to what? The soul? Then is the soul making a

104. V. Rasputin, 'Pozhar', p.6.
105. Ibid, p.29.
106. Ibid, p.32.

fuss about reconciliation, ready to serve one side and the other side too?'[107]

At the end of this lengthy passage, a small sample of which is offered here, we read that Ivan could not fathom such questions: 'It was all utterly beyond him'. One is hardly surprised.

Rasputin, like Tolstoy, is not a successful philosopher. The inarticulate Khampo who dies in the fight with one of the louts has more coherence about him and communicates more to the reader than do some of the author's philosophical disgressions.

The Fire depicts the good side of Ivan Petrovich and his wife. Indeed she is idealised to a degree not surpassed by Rasputin's portrait of the old couple on the train in *Money for Maria* and in such a way as to be well nigh insulting to the modern woman: 'Alyona quietly occupied the place for which in girlhood she had been inadequate and which may be described as "feminine sufficiency". This means that there was exactly as much of Alyona as was needed, neither more nor less.' Or: 'Alyona was more than a wife to Ivan Petrovich. That bustling little figure, like the trinity that is one in three, was all that a woman can be.'[108] Such untainted goodness (so convenient to the more conservative male) runs parallel to the inexplicable evil-doing that marks much of the narrative. The 'thugs' or 'louts' (*akharovtsy*) are essentially drifters with no loyalties save to the bottle and their own whims. A local schoolmaster has calculated that there have been roughly as many deaths from unnatural causes (throat-cutting, beating and so on) as there were during the war. When Ivan tries to curtail the louts' drinking, his truck is vandalised. In *The Fire* we see a Russia that has lost its way, we see her strengths — at times ludicrously idealised — and her weaknesses. It is perhaps to be regretted that the author did not rely more on his poetics and less on his convoluted moralising to express the confusion that besets modern man.

* * *

It is interesting to note that 'village prose' started out in the late 1950s as a challenge to established literary norms, but that by the 1970s it had become very much part of the establishment, to such an extent that Andrei Voznesensky, veteran of Khrushchev's thaw, could gently mock rustic values in his poem of 1975 *Scientific-Technological Revolution*: 'With all due respect to water-carriers' yokes,

107. Ibid, pp.21–2.
108. Ibid, p.28.

I prefer plumbing and movement of thought'. But the village writers, with Rasputin as their best representative, had a very real
achievement to their credit. They had answered the lingering question as to what had happened — in the wake of the Revolution and
the forced pace of industrialisation — to all those peasants that
Turgenev, Tolstoy and Leskov had written about. Those peasants,
with all their quirks, vitality and resilience were still with us. David
Gillespie in his excellent study of Rasputin draws our attention to
Thomas Hardy and D. H. Lawrence who, like the Russian writer,
sought moral guidelines for the future in their regard for the past.
This is conservatism of the broadest kind, and in Rasputin's best
works it is, as in Hardy and Lawrence, more liberating than con-
stricting. Rasputin and other 'village prose' writers have in this
sense broadened the Soviet literary establishment, not simply joined
it.

–2–

Chingiz Aitmatov
The Provincial Internationalist

Kirghizia and Aitmatov's Apprenticeship

The Union Republic of Kirghizia is situated deep in the south of the Soviet Union, abuts China to the south-east and is flanked by the Uzbekistan Union Republic and the Tadzhikistan Union Republic to the west and south, and by the Kazakhstan Union Republic to the north-east. In 1979 there were 1.9 million Kirghiz in the USSR and about 90 per cent of these lived in Kirghizia, but they constitute rather less than half the population of Kirghizia. Both in terms of population and geographical size Kirghizia is one of the smaller republics, only marginally outstripping in population, for example, Jews, Latvians and Estonians. Of a total Soviet population of approximately 262 million, 138 million are Russian. Thus the Kirghiz are in a tiny minority. Frunze, the capital, stands approximately midway between Moscow and Peking.

If the location of Kirghizia is remote to most Europeans, the origins of its people and their language are even more so. The Kirghiz are closely related in race and language to the Kazakhs (a much larger ethnic group) and indeed for many years in Tsarist times the Russians referred to the Kazakhs as 'Kirghiz', possibly to avoid confusion with Cossacks (*kazaki* in Russian). The Kirghiz proper were called *kara Kirghiz* ('black Kirghiz'). This casual approach to naming these Central Asians neatly illustrates the Russians' attitude towards their colonies: 'The Russian administration of Central Asia displayed much the same mixture as other colonial administrations of altruism and cupidity, of accident and design, of indulgence and oppression, of sincerity and hypocrisy, of satiety and expansionism, of selfless devotion and tireless energy of individuals, and of neglect and obtuseness of governments.'[1]

Especially in the middle of the nineteenth century Russian Cos-

---

1. G. Wheeler, *The Modern History of Soviet Central Asia*, Weidenfeld and Nicolson, London, 1964, p. 233.

sacks were used against the Kazakhs (whom they called Kirghiz!), and despite the formidable horsemanship and martial skills of the Central Asian he was no real match for the Cossack, often equipped with two horses, a lance and a firearm.

Tsarist rule in Central Asia brought a degree of stability, especially in the latter half of the nineteenth century, but there was hardly a meeting of cultures, or an interchange of values. European Russia was producing some of the greatest literature the world had ever seen, whereas the literary traditions in Central Asia were still largely oral. Russian Orthodoxy confronted Islam. Russia, albeit belatedly by Western European standards, was industrialising; in Central Asia there was a subsistence economy.

The Kirghiz (as well as the Kazakhs and Turkmens) were mainly nomads and their literary traditions were on the whole oral until the nineteenth century. The more sedentary and urbanised Central Asians did have more of a written literary tradition going back as far as the fourteenth century. The oral tradition comprised, roughly speaking, three genres: songs and chants performed at wedding ceremonies and suchlike; then fairy tales, legends and love stories; finally, and most importantly, the epic poem.[2]

The key work here is the *Manas* cycle of epic poems. There are several versions of this enormous work and it would be an impossible task to establish a definitive text. However, as Chokan Valikhanov (1811–65), the explorer and scholar who first transcribed the work, or part of it, said: '*Manas* is an encyclopaedic collection of all the Kirghiz myths, fairy stories, legends . . . The way of life, the *mores*, the geography, the religious and medical knowledge of the Kirghiz, their international relations have all found expression in this huge epopee.'[3]

It is certainly the case with Chingiz Aitmatov that he brings alive in his works all the local colour, the history and psychology of his homeland and at the same time succeeds in his best works in divesting these of all traces of provincialism. Though for the most part his genre is the novella (*povest'*) he injects into this tight framework elements deserving the term 'epic'. Much of the critical examination of his works in the Soviet Union has been concerned, and rightly so, with the clash between a near obsolete way of life, together with an apparently obsolete literary form on the one hand, and the modern world on the other.

---

2. Ibid, p.208.
3. P. Mirza-Akhmedova, *Natsional'naya epicheskaya traditsiya v tvorchestve Chingiza Aitmatova*, Izdatelstvo 'Fan', Tashkent, 1980, p.3.

If Kirghiz literature has been slow to come of age, this is in some measure due to, and part of, the state and status of the Kirghiz language. It seems likely that some form of Turkic speech was in use all over the Steppe Region from about the sixth century, side by side with Persian. After the Muslim conquest Arabic and Persian were used in religious schools and among the intelligentsia. There was also a third literary language, Chagatay, named after one of Ghenghis Khan's sons. It was a Turkic language, but written in the Arabic alphabet. These three languages survived well into the nineteenth century, but then languages based on popular dialects appeared. Perhaps the most important of these was Kazakh, which was also used by the Kirghiz. This was the language that Valikhanov wrote in. Thus it could be said that the Kirghiz had no written language of their own until after the Russian Revolution. In the 1920s there seemed to be a real possibility of a united Islamic Central Asia which might offer serious resistance to Soviet central government. Consequently, five separate autonomous regions were created: Uzbekistan, Kazakhstan, Tadzhikistan, Karakalpak — and Kirghizia. The Kirghiz Autonomous Republic came into being on 25 August 1926, and two years later it became a Union Republic. From 1929 a Unified Latin Alphabet was introduced to replace the Perso-Arabic script and in the late 1930s this was supplanted by Cyrillic.[4] There are, of course, two ways of looking at these developments. On the one hand, they facilitated the fragmentation of the Turkic peoples and made domination and russification easier. On the other hand, it could be said that Soviet power gave these people modern literary languages, accessible to all, and these were part and parcel of the drive towards literacy, education and the triumph of modernity over antiquity. There was also, of course, a very serious attempt to make Russian the second, if not the first, language of all of the non-Russian areas of the Soviet Union.

Just as there are two ways of looking at the Sovietisation of Kirghizia, there are also two ways of regarding its greatest modern writer. Aitmatov is a magnificent example of how the Soviet system can benefit an individual of an obscure nation, how it enables talent to develop and speak to the whole world. At the same time, one can argue that Aitmatov has been obliged to abandon his own language in order to progress, and has become a literary functionary and ambassador. The retention in his vocabulary of the trappings of his culture (terms such as *aksakal, ail* or *yurt* the reader quickly assimilates, but others the author footnotes) might be construed as the

4. Wheeler, *The Modern History of Soviet Central Asia*, p.195.

embodiment of Stalin's policy towards the non-Russian Soviet cultures, that they should produce art which was 'socialist in content, nationalist in form'.

The praise that has been heaped on Aitmatov by some Soviet critics can be disconcerting:

> The humanistic spirit of Aitmatov's works really does unite good people, makes them, in some important way, close to each other.
>
> In conversations, candid talks with young and old inhabitants of Ala Too, yet another feeling was conveyed to me which possessed them: of belonging to the wide world of the Soviet peoples, to the great all-human process of liberation from inarticulate prejudices, national barriers, tribal surviving leftovers. Of course, the feeling of such belonging to the world enriches the soul extraordinarily, broadens one's awareness of life, fills the heart with the joy of participation in the cause of communist renewal of life.
>
> The short, laconic novellas and short stories of Chingiz Aitmatov do not only bring people closer together, unite the farthest corners of our earth with Kirghizia, but also, and in this resides perhaps the most important effect of art — make people, each of us, richer, more sensitive, more spiritual.[5]

There has been a strong tendency also to draw comparisons between Aitmatov and many of the major figures of world literature, notably Homer and Shakespeare. Viktor Levchenko writes (having failed in part to resist the temptation himself): 'Of course, the classics have not suffered at all because of this ... but Aitmatov would probably feel embarrassed'.[6]

Whatever the extravagant claims made for Aitmatov, he is a special cultural phenomenon. His best works are polished, realistic, lyrical, yet relevant; and he has put his nation and its culture on the map. In revealing in his fiction the shortcomings of Soviet life, he, as an outsider who has 'made good', demonstrates also the strengths of that society. Additionally, he records the richness and variety of life in the Soviet Union, not so much in the sense of the travelogue as in the psychological differences between the Asian and the European, the erstwhile nomad, now settled pastoralist, and the urbanised industrial worker. Significantly, the latter is not always seen as the superior being. It is noteworthy that the colonies that Tsarist Russia held have remained, though in changed circumstances, under the Russian thumb until the present. Conversely the British, Dutch and

---

5. V. Voronov, *Chingiz Aitmatov: Ocherk tvorchestva*, Sovetskiy pisatel, 1976, pp.6–7.
6. V. Levchenko, *Chingiz Aitmatov: Problemy poetiki, zhanra, stilya*, Sovetskiy pisatel, Moscow, 1983, p.51.

French Empires have largely vanished though no revolutions in the 'parent' countries have taken place. However, the literature produced by these erstwhile colonies might prove to be of dubious long-term value, when set against the achievement that is Chingiz Aitmatov's.

Early works such as *Materinskoye pole* (*Mother's Field*) and *Topolyok moy v krasnoy kosynke* (*My Little Poplar Wearing the Red Headscarf*) were written in Kirghiz and then translated by the author into Russian. More mature pieces were written in Russian and then translated into Kirghiz. Such a high degree of linguistic competence is in itself something to be admired, but it is also a cultural ideal which has the fullest official sponsorship. For a creative writer bilingualism sometimes carries the added advantage of making the writer all the more disciplined and solicitous. Samuel Beckett is a prime example in our own culture. In the case of Aitmatov, Soviet critics have certainly played up his linguistic prowess. Mirza-Akhmedova writes: 'One cannot overestimate the possibilities opened up by Aitmatov's literary bilingualism. The artist's rare gift allows one, without the intrusion of a translator, to comprehend totally not only the full profundity of the writer's artistic intention, but also in full measure to feel and penetrate the national element of his works.'[7]

The comment made here, in danger of sinking under the weight of its own superlatives, is another illustration of the Soviet esteem for Aitmatov. Aitmatov himself is more factual and practical in commenting on his bilingualism. At the Tashkent conference on solidarity between the writers of Asian and African countries in 1967, Aitmatov spoke on the subject of 'Man between Two Languages': 'The dying away and then the disappearance of a language that has no written form must be seen as a loss to the general culture of mankind. In our multi-national country, the Soviet Union, we proceed from these considerations and adhere to the principle of equal rights for languages within the borders of their ethnic-administrative extent.'[8]

Others have not been so sanguine about the Soviet government's linguistic policies. Nevertheless Aitmatov is aware of the problem of a young literature coming into contact with an established literature. The young literature can either 'live off' the developed literature, or take, in Aitmatov's view, the more difficult path of 'co-existence'. Kirghizia has taken this 'much harder path', but one

---

7. Mirza-Akhmedova, *Natsional'naya traditsiya*, p.7.
8. Ch. Aitmatov, *Sobraniye sochineniy v 3-x tomakh*, Vol. III, Molodaya gvardiya, Moscow, 1982–4, p.346.

that is 'much more fruitful'. Russian became the bridge-language between the greatest world writers, Cervantes, Shakespeare, Tolstoy, Balzac, and the Kirghiz people and Kirghiz culture. Aitmatov goes on:

> I belong to the representatives of Kirghiz literature. And if my works are published these days by means of Russian in many languages of the world, then it is Russian that is strengthening the position of my own native Kirghiz language, facilitates its establishment and testifies to its inner potential. I say this to share with you our experience that shows how great languages do not of necessity have to be in conflict with lesser ones, and that co-operation and co-existence between them are perfectly possible.[9]

On the specific matter of bilingualism Aitmatov argues that whether a bilingual writer opts for his own language or for his second one is not an abstract matter:

> I have to cite my own example. I write my books in Kirghiz and Russian. If a book is first written in Kirghiz, I translate it into Russian, and vice versa. In the process I gain the deepest satisfaction from this bilateral work. It is extremely interesting inner work of a writer, leading, I am convinced, to the perfection of style and to enrichment of linguistic expression.[10]

Aitmatov concludes his address with the question as to whether the freedom to write in one of two languages might not lead to the atrophy of literatures written in the minority languages. He makes no attempt to answer this point but reminds us that one's native language is a mother towards whom there are definite responsibilities.

There is nothing really new in all this. The same dilemma confronted Pushkin — namely, whether to write in French or Russian. The Czech National Revival of the nineteenth century and the Welsh revivalists have had to resolve similar issues. Many would argue that the problems of linguistic and cultural provincialism when compounded by political parochialism make the game of 'nationalism' not worth the candle. If national cultural identity means little more than quaint dress and a quaint way of mouthing Russian values then it is a nonsense. Aitmatov at his best cannot be accused of merely affecting national awareness. Yet in some works the cruder and more dated elements of Socialist Realism are discernible. That said, in

9. Ibid, p.347.
10. Ibid, p.348.

evaluating the aesthetic qualities of Aitmatov's prose it is worth bearing in mind that the first Kirghiz novel did not appear until 1937–8.[11]

Three works which were first written in Kirghiz and then translated (not by the author) deserve our attention for the parallels they form with other works discussed in this book, and for the way in which they show from what modest accomplishments Aitmatov has progressed: 'More than once people have spoken of Aitmatov's talent rising with "cosmic" speed. His rise into the orbit of mature artistry has indeed been rapid, though not at all "vertical". The Kirghiz prose writer has known a time — albeit relatively short — of literary apprenticeship.'[12]

Litsom k litsu (*Face to Face*) was first published in Kirghiz in 1957, but the Russian translation of 1958 marked Aitmatov's debut on the All-Union literary scene. Georgiy Gachev has remarked in passing that the subject of the story, desertion from the armed forces, has been taken up elsewhere in Soviet literature, especially in Rasputin's *Live and Remember*.[13] However, the reader of both works will be struck by the very strong affinities between them. We have Rasputin's own account of how he came to write his story of a deserter, but it is unlikely that he would not have known of Aitmatov's work. It seems fair to assume that Rasputin saw, possibly subconsciously, all sorts of possibilities in *Face to Face*.

Aitmatov's subject matter is explosive. In the 1930s Kirghiz writers along with all other Soviet writers had to produce their odes to Stalin and declare their country's loyalty. Yet during the Second World War there were some collaborators and deserters. One can contrast *Face to Face*, the down-to-earth story of a deserter who gets caught, with a notorious Kirghiz panegyric of 1936:

> Thou art the constant moon, Stalin,
> Thou art our shining star, Stalin,
> Thou art our lovely dawn, Stalin
> Wisdom inexhaustible, Stalin
> Courage unshakeable, Stalin
> Joy unquenchable, Stalin!
> Be immortal, great Stalin![14]

11. Mirza-Akhmedova, *Natsional'naya traditsiya*, p.20.
12. N. Potapov, 'Svet chelovechnosti' (Introduction to *Sobraniye sochineniy*, see note 8).
13. G. Gachev, *Chingiz Aitmatov i mirovaya literatura*, Izdatelstvo 'Kyrgyzstan', Frunze, 1982, p.11.
14. Quoted in E. Allworth (ed.) *Central Asia: A Century of Russian Rule*, Columbia University Press, New York, 1967, p.417.

When Stalin proved to be mortal and after Khrushchev had pronounced him less than 'joy unquenchable', it became possible to touch on, among other things, the sordid side of the Soviet war effort.

A brief account of *Face to Face* illustrates that the parallels with Rasputin's story can hardly be fortuitous or even superficial. The heroine Seide is a young mother. Her husband Ismail soon deserts after being called up. He returns by night to his wife, hides out in a cave where she has to take food to him, or he comes home at night to be fed. At one point, suffering from giddiness and nausea, she thinks she is pregnant. Seide's neighbour Totoi has three children and no news of her husband; the reader learns of his death and of the local custom of not immediately informing the bereaved. On one occasion, Myrzakul, the chairman of the village soviet, beats Seide. Elsewhere she refuses to divulge the whereabouts of her husband to Myrzakul or the NKVD. Seide longs for her cow to calve, for then she will have enough milk and butter for her insatiable husband. While all her thoughts are altruistic and loving, Ismail, like Rasputin's Andrei, becomes increasingly aggressive towards his wife, selfish and narrow. Pointedly, we read he 'becomes like a beast' (*ozverel*).[15] He has thoughts of going to his own folk in the high mountains where no one will check up on him, and this region, Chatkal, seems to the prosaic and mature-minded Seide like a fairy-tale land. Ismail steals Totoi's cow and slaughters it for the meat, telling his wife that 'if life is wolf-like, then you have to be a wolf yourself.'[16] Seide finally informs the authorities and Ismail shoots Myrzakul before surrendering. Seide brings this about by carrying their baby son towards him: 'It suddenly seemed to him that she stood high, very high, inaccessible in her sorrowful majesty, while he was weak and pitiable before her'.[17]

Face to Face is a powerful story that demonstrates, as frequently is the case in Aitmatov, that the woman, while suffering from the traditional Muslim subjugation of women, can prove strong and even independent. However, the moral issues in the work are hardly complex. Ismail has little to redeem him; he is a selfish coward from start to finish. Seide has to overcome her loyalty to him for a greater loyalty, but Aitmatov, unlike Rasputin, gives his heroine a good deal of help in the task. The deeper psychological interest in *Face to Face*, the hero's increasing animalisation and his onslaught on the life

15. Aitmatov, *Sobraniye sochineniy*, Vol. I, p.68.
16. Ibid, p.75.
17. Ibid, p.77.

process itself, are all explored more fully by Rasputin.

The self-willed female finds expression in Aitmatov's widely acclaimed story *Dzhamilya* which appeared in Russian translation in *Novyy mir* also in 1958. Louis Aragon published his own French translation of it the following year, and lavished praise on the work: 'The most splendid love story in the world'.[18] In subject matter the work stands midway between *Face to Face* and *My Little Poplar Wearing the Red Headscarf*, for it is a tale of desertion in wartime and also similar to a production novel. Dzhamilya abandons her husband who is recuperating in hospital from injury in battle, yet the reader's sympathies are with her and the new man in her life. *My Little Poplar* is another story of a marriage breaking up, but from our point of view it is particularly interesting for the affinities it has with Vladimov's *The Great Ore* and to a lesser extent Vladimir Tendryakov's *Potholes*.

My Little Poplar appeared in Russian at the start of 1961, some six months before Vladimov's novel. Like *The Great Ore* it makes a serious attempt to penetrate the psychology of the stereotyped positive hero of the production novel, though this is only one of its purposes. It was certainly the case during the first five-year plan that a lot was owed to natural enthusiasm and vigour. That vigour seems to have evaporated and there have been, especially since Brezhnev's death, repeated calls for discipline at the work place, for greater efficiency.

Aitmatov's hero Ilyas, like Vladimov's, is a truck driver who takes risks in order to succeed but ultimately fails. He is brash rather than civic-minded. Like the hero of *The Great Ore* he is too fond of strong drink. Unlike Vladimov's hero, he is rightly unsung, his decline gradual and prosaic rather than imbued with notions of death or glory. Moreover, *My Little Poplar's* debunking of the positive hero is less than half the story. Ilyas's wife eventually forms a relationship with another man, who is able to offer her more security and love than her volatile and promiscuous husband. *My Little Poplar* thus illustrates, as does *Dzhamilya*, the search for individual happiness in the face of collective dogma, whether it be of Muslim origin or otherwise. The work was also Aitmatov's first and most conscious attempt at a more sophisticated narrative structure. He writes in the first person, as a journalist participating marginally in the story, who then hands over the stage to Ilyas, who recounts events reasonably objectively but nonetheless still from his own point of view. Finally the first narrator puts a new perspective on the narrative.

18. Ibid, p.603.

Aitmatov's other three remaining early works, *Verblyuzhiy glas* (*Camel's Eye*) (1961), *Pervyy uchitel'* (*The First Teacher*) (1961) and *Mother's Field* (1962) are much more conventional. *Camel's Eye* is about production, the young hero putting up with all manner of persecution from an older workmate and finally proving his moral superiority. The ethos of Socialist Realist stories of this ilk has been unkindly called 'Boy meets tractor'. In *Camel's Eye* the boy meets girl and tractor.

> Maybe Abakir [the villain of the piece: R. P.] was already gone, bumming a ride on a freight train ... Well, on your way then, you bastard! Anarkhai will still be here and we'll manage without you ...
>
> I didn't want to think about him any more. There was work that had to be done. I had a long hard struggle before the tractor roared into life, scaring the darkness of the night. I sat in the cabin and turned the headlights on.
>
> Now I was in charge. I had a sudden wish that my darling girl with the fringe was at my side, and that she would believe me that there would be, there would be, in the wild wormwood of the steppe the splendid country of Anarkhai.[19]

One would be hard put to find a better example of a classical Socialist Realist ending than this. Young, positive hero triumphs over evil, is committed to his work; all the signs are he will get the girl of his dreams — and all this seasoned with a dash of lyrical-romantic patriotism.

In similar vein are *The First Teacher*, which deals with the triumph of Soviet education over prejudice, and *Mother's Field*, which counts the cost of the Great Patriot War. This last story is more interesting in that it is built around a conversation between an old woman and a field. The spiritual dimension of the natural world is to the forefront in this story, with emphasis on birth and renewal, as well as death. But a promethean element asserts itself at the end:

> 'Earth, mother-provider, you keep all of us in your bosom, you feed people in all corners of the earth. Dear earth, tell people, tell them [how to reach the heart of each man]!'
>
> 'No, Tolgonai, you tell them. You are a Person. You are higher than all, you're wiser than all, you're a Person! You tell them!'[20]

Aitmatov's early works earned him a great deal of attention. *Dzhamilya, The First Teacher, Camel's Eye* and *My Little Poplar Wearing a Red Headscarf* also earned him the Lenin Prize for literature in 1963.

19. Ibid, p.237.
20. Ibid, p.372.

Chingiz Aitmatov

The Hero and the Animal World

The publication of *Proshchay, Gul'sary!* (*Farewell, Gulsary!*) established Aitmatov's international reputation and set out the primary attributes of the author's mature fiction. He could readily be claimed by the ideologues as a fine example of developing Socialist Realism. By others, Aitmatov could be seen as a writer struggling against official constraints. Vladimir Voronov wrote: '*Gulsary* and *The White Steamship* capture the hearts and minds of the readers of five continents with their serious reflections on the fate of man in the contemporary world, on the humanistic nature of the new international co-operation between people which is born of the October Revolution.'[21]

In a somewhat contorted attempt to read Solzhenitsyn as signalling the rebirth of genuine Socialist Realism, Georg Lukács pointed to Aitmatov's moving story of the life and death of a horse as further evidence of the trend: 'In this novel we see the way in which the bureaucratic manipulation of the Stalin system turned against those who, for all their sectarian prejudices, worked enthusiastically to bring about the socialist evolution, undaunted by the sacrifices made of them.'[22]

Deming Brown calls the novel 'a work of ingenious socialist realism' which 'manages to suggest that the Party and the system it represents will eventually purify themselves'.[23]

As with Aitmatov's other major works *Farewell, Gulsary!* is, in political terms, all things to all men. Arguably, it fails to rise above political barriers in a way that high artistry would permit, but its worthy aesthetic qualities outweigh the shortcomings that its political checks and balances may give rise to.

It might be expected that a country whose cultural traditions were largely oral until very recently might display weaknesses when coming (late) to the written word. However, a strong oral tradition carries with it certain advantages. Firstly, as stories are handed on from one generation to the next they will be automatically adapted to the prevailing circumstances of the day to make them more comprehensible to their current audiences. Thus there is less chance of a work of art 'dating', or requiring critical and editorial apparatus, other than that which it has in-built, in the way that all written

21. Voronov, *Chingiz Aitmatov*, p.148.
22. G. Lukács, *Solzhenitsyn*, trans. from the German by William David Graf, Merlin Press, London, 1970, p.88.
23. D. Brown, *Soviet Russian Literature since Stalin*, Cambridge University Press, Cambridge, 1978, pp.283–4.

works eventually require. Oral works have immediacy, they are self-sufficient and they are timeless. Their obvious weaknesses are that they may depend too much on the individual performer for their effect; they are a fragile commodity, easily damaged in transit, and sooner or later, if they are worthy of it, they must be entrusted to paper. In this respect it is no exaggeration to say that Aitmatov has done for Kirghiz literature what Homer did for Greek literature. Moreover, a successful transcription should ensure that 'artificiality' and 'literariness', except for the practical mnemonic devices associated with the oral epic tradition, are absent. Russian literature's strength is its spontaneity, not its formalistic experimentation, and Aitmatov's work, at its best, possesses just such spontaneity. There are occasions when the author strikes a false note and these lapses can be attributed to his political balancing act.

A natural point of departure for a discussion of *Farewell, Gulsary!* has been Tolstoy's *Kholstomer*, and this story of an essentially innocent gelding with his insights into human nature, personal property and ageing, has much to recommend it as a forerunner to Aitmatov's work. When one sets *Farewell, Gulsary!* in its socio-historical context one becomes fully aware of the impact that it makes on Central Asian readers particularly. The Kirghiz precursor is the narrative work *Khodzhodzhash*, a so-called 'minor epos' which is unrelated to the more famous *Manas* cycle;[24] the song that the hero's wife Dzhaidar sings about the hunter Karagul near the end of the work possesses several affinities with the epic tradition, and these also relate to the mainstream narrative.

Dzhaidar's song is sung when Choro has died and the hero Tanabai, having been expelled from the Communist Party because of Choro, still cannot forgive him. Death and ill-feeling between people once close provide the links between the song and the main narrative. Karagul, the legendary hunter, kills all of the wildlife, but is able only to wound Grey She-Goat, who lures him up to a cliff ledge where he is trapped. He entreats his father to shoot him to ease his suffering and his father does. The story illustrates the ultimate victory of the natural world over man, and the interplay of violence and compassion. However, the idea of a person slaying a loved one out of compassion or because of ignorance of the victim's identity is a hallmark of the classic epic, as well as being an idea widespread in folk songs everywhere. In the story of Karagul there is also the

---

24. N. Chadwick and V. Zhirmunsky, *Oral Epics of Central Asia*, Cambridge University Press, Cambridge, 1969, p.280. And: Levchenko, *Chingiz Aitmatov*, p.82.

supernatural element, for the She-Goat can speak and negotiate with the hunter, and he accepts this, as does the reader, in just the same way as the ancients accepted incarnate or semi-incarnate gods in their fiction.

Kirghiz social history is also an important element in the background to Aitmatov's story. The horse was a status symbol, but also had near mystical qualities as well as being of great material value. Aitmatov's work is about Tanabai, but Gulsary is promoted to the title, and the Soviet critics have been right to talk of the hero of the work as being a centaur. The parallels between the man and his horse are manifold: they both have strength, resilience, impatience and longevity. More fundamentally, they both reflect notions of innocence as well as loss and waste. Ultimately the author tries to portray Tanabai as a victim, even though during collectivisation he was a fanatical expropriator of the peasantry, even responsible for his step-brother's fate — seven years in a Siberian camp. (The question of family relations, as elsewhere in Aitmatov, is of importance here. The step-brother Kulubai is regarded, and indeed referred to more frequently, as 'brother', rather than as 'step-brother'. The Central Asian extended family makes for blood ties and a close-knit community, which can heighten even more the familiar conflict of public and personal loyalties that one finds in literature everywhere.)

Possibly the most moving scene in this highly charged novel is the lambing season, where Tanabai struggles against impossible odds with the elements to prevent the deaths of the new-born, but fails and is punished for it. Here he more than purges his sins of supererogation. Yet in placing him persistently alongside Gulsary, Aitmatov is surely implying the inescapable imperfectibility of man. The horse becomes an ideal that a man can never fully emulate.

All the potential, both physical and moral, that life holds out to man is realised in the animal world. This is best illustrated in the scene of the *baiga*, the contests of horsemanship that have been a common feature of Central Asian life for centuries. The *djigit*'s skills are widespread throughout Central Asia, the Caucasus and among the Cossacks to this day. Aitmatov's depiction of the *baiga* neatly blends a centuries-old tradition with the modern world. The two-day event begins on May Day. There are three main events: the trick-riding, the race and the game of 'mounted football' in which a goat's torso is used instead of a ball. Aitmatov prefixes his colourful rendition of these traditional activities with a short discourse on man and horse: 'The only difference [between a famous horse and a football star: R. P.] is that a horse is envious of no-one. Horses do not know how to be envious, and people, thank God, have not yet learned to envy horses.'[25] Given the difficulties under which full-blooded Kirghiz nationalism has laboured, Aitmatov's celebration of these games is more than mere travelogue or local colour. The critic Mirza-Akhmedova recalls that there was a time (no doubt the 1930s) when people had a negative attitude to these games and saw them as relics of the past, but now no public holiday is complete without them.[26]

Aitmatov then proceeds to take a Homeric/Tolstoyan delight in the physical aspect of the contest. The horses are the real participants and they are shorn of jealousy and other human foibles, with the exception of justified pride. Being an ambler (*inokhodets*), Gulsary is more suited to the long race rather than the sprint, and his sense of pace stands him in good stead. Many aspects of *Farewell, Gulsary!* are better candidates for allegorical interpretation than the horse's style of locomotion, but it is hard to escape the analogy of an ambler being ultimately more successful, sensitive and innocent than are all the human beings in their frenzy of activity. Especially in the case of collectivisation, such frenzy proved in the long run to be counter-productive, even destructive.

In the heat of the race Gulsary is suddenly free: 'Suddenly the power of the bit and the reins disappeared, for Gulsary there was no longer any saddle or rider — in him there raged the fiery spirit of the race'. In triumph Gulsary 'knew that he was handsome, powerful and famous'.[27] Such freedom and such acclaim are never accorded to any of the humans in the story. The ideal that Aitmatov establishes near the beginning of his work eludes all its potential positive heroes. The story opens, closes and repeatedly returns to the image of an old man, Tanabai, and a dying horse, Gulsary. Moreover, man and horse are on a road whose end becomes increasingly irrelevant as the story progresses.

The system of flashbacks goes hand in hand with the judicious use of repetition to provide a structure and finish to the work. Moreover, along with other elements, such as the *baiga* scene, the legends and the struggles with the natural environment, they are suggestive of the classical epic. There is no question here of a mnemonic function, but rather of implying a generalisation, that Tanabai's fate and Gulsary's are emblematic of a whole people — for the classical epic is concerned primarily with the founding or destruction of whole nations.

25. Aitmatov, *Sobraniye sochineniy*, Vol. I, p.403.
26. Mirza-Akhmedova, *Natsional'naya traditsiya*, p.21.
27. Aitmatov, *Sobraniye sochineniy*, Vol.I, pp.406–7.

Farewell, Gulsary! can be seen very much as one of the spate of works that dealt as boldly as the 1960s allowed with the agony of collectivisation. It has been justifiably linked with Sergei Zalygin's *On the Irtysh* (1964) and Vasiliy Belov's stories.[28] The policies on agriculture initiated in 1929 led directly to a mass destruction of livestock, from which the Soviet Union would not recover for decades. The agricultural worker, either fearing he would be classed as a rich peasant, a *kulak*, or assuming in his ignorance that the new collective farm he was being forced to join would provide him with all he needed, simply slaughtered his own animals, and gorged himself and his family. Moreover, the deportation and liquidation of the *kulaks* robbed the countryside of some of its most efficient and experienced farmers. The devastation of Soviet agriculture was if anything worse in Central Asia than in European Russia. The semi-nomadic peoples depended almost entirely on the meat and milk provided by their herds. The mass slaughter of livestock resulted in the death of about a quarter of the Kazakh nation. In Kirghizia there was, according to Soviet sources, 'mass destruction of cattle', but also 'migration abroad'. Part of the frontier population moved to China taking 30,000 sheep and 15,000 head of cattle.[29]

With these facts in mind one may easily sympathise with Maltsev's view that much 'permitted' literature can only hint at real truths in Soviet life. However, the hints are certainly there in Aitmatov's work. The single most recurrent idea in *Farewell, Gulsary!* is that of loss. Gulsary himself is made into an object of vanity for the collective farm chairman, he is gelded, he grows old and dies, with no offspring and no tangible achievements. Tanabai is distanced from his son, loses his love Byubyudzhan, administers in vain to the dying lambs. A fanatical communist, he is expelled from the Party, and his reinstatement is a perfunctory duty on the author's part. Dzhaidar's recurring song (with which the work ends) about the she-camel which has lost its young, and the legend of Karagul leave a more lasting impression on the reader's consciousness. When Gulsary is shackled, Tanabai reflects on how the good skills of the past have been lost. Above all, *Farewell, Gulsary!* is a story of lost illusions.

The narrative moves between conventional realism and allegory, between the present and the past, and on occasion, rapidly between light and dark. It also moves between ideal and reality:

28. Levchenko, *Chingiz Aitmatov*, p.79.
29. V. Danilov (ed.), *Ocherki Istoriyi kollektivizatsiyi selskogo khozyaystva v soyuznykh respublikakh*, Moscow, 1963. Quoted in R. Conquest, *Harvest of Sorrow*, Hutchinson, London, 1986, p.190.

Tanabai almost fell backwards — the mountains had stepped towards
him, with the tops covered in fresh snow. How the snow suited them!
They rose into the skies in irreproachable purity clearly delineated in
light and shade, as if only just created by God. There where the snow lay
was where the deep blue infinite expanse started. And in its depths, in far,
far off blue strode the unreal distance of the universe. Tanabai shuddered
from the abundance of snow and freshness and he became sad. Again he
remembered the woman to whom he used to ride on Gulsary. If he'd had
the ambler to hand, he'd mount up and shouting with enthusiasm and joy
he would appear before her, like this white, morning snow. . .
    . . . But he knew that it was only a dream . . . Half one's life passes by
in dreams, and that's maybe why life is so sweet. Maybe that was why life
was so dear, because not all that one dreams of comes true. He looked at
the mountains and the sky, and he thought that all people could hardly
all be happy in equal measure. Each person has his own fate. And that
fate has its joys and its sorrows, like the light and shadow on one and the
same mountain at the same time. That's what life was full of . . .[30]

This passage occurs about halfway through the novel and echoes
the overall ambivalences of the work: the brightness of the *baiga* and
the darkness of the road where Gulsary dies, the ideal of the great
social experiment and its harsh enactment; and hauntingly, in
Dzhaidar's song, the black-eyed baby camel, lost, and the white
milk streaming from the mother's udder, wasted . . .

* * *

Farewell, Gulsary! illustrates an aspect of the animal world that is
similarly in evidence in *Belyy parokhod* (*The White Steamship*) — also
entitled *Posle skazki* (*After the Fairy Tale*) — namely, that animals can
be an aid to moral education.
    The educative and formative role that is assigned to all literature
in the Soviet Union means that children's literature is at least as
closely watched as adult fiction. There has been a tendency to
assume that when literary controls were at their most stringent some
writers 'took refuge' in producing works for children. In fact children's writers such as Oleynikov, Shvarts, Chukovsky and Mar-
shak turned naturally to a kind of writing that was ostensibly for
children but which, like the best children's literature anywhere, also
stimulated the adult imagination. Shvarts's plays, those 'fairy tales
for adults' as Amanda Metcalf has called them,[31] draw on the

---

30. Aitmatov, *Sobraniye sochineniy*, Vol. I, p.450.
31. A. Metcalf, *Evgeniy Shvarts and his Fairy Tales for Adults*, Birmingham Slavonic
    Monographs, 1979.

international fund of fairy stories as well as the works of Andersen and the brothers Grimm to become comedies with serious political and moral overtones — so serious that in some instances they were banned for many years. Indeed, it has always been a moot point whether Aesopian language will provide a safe conduct for a work of art when there are so many instances recorded of a *double entendre* being discovered by a censor where none exists, or the wrong *double entendre* being attributed to a given work. The Tsarist censors objected to Gogol's title 'Dead Souls' on the grounds that it was blasphemous, for the soul was by its nature immortal. It would be hard to believe that Shvarts was naive enough to think that his plays *The Naked King* or *The Dragon*, in drawing close parallels between Hitler and Stalin, would strike a chord with his audiences yet be wasted on the censors. On the contrary, such works tend to be bold, even simplistic, in transmitting messages.

Aitmatov's *The White Steamship* is one of those works that appeals equally to an adult readership and to younger readers. It has been published in illustrated editions in the format of a work primarily for children, though many would regard it as the author's most mature work of short fiction. It is, moreover, appropriate to deal with this work in conjunction with Aitmatov's other major prose of the 1970s, *Pegiy pyos begushchiy krayem morya* (*The Skewbald Dog Running along the Edge of the Sea*). Both works have small boys as their heroes and both stories seek to raise, through a skilful blend of legend and reality, fundamental questions of human conduct and morality. Both works involved motifs of travel and escape, of man extending himself beyond the confines of the routine of the perceived adult world. In each instance the growing boy is aided by his grandfather more than by his immediate parents. As on occasion in Rasputin, the young and the elderly provide through their respective naivety and near-dotage a spiritual dimension which has been lost in an adult, utilitarian world.

The main theme of *The White Steamship* might well be defined as education — in the broadest sense. The seven-year-old's grandfather Momun buys him a briefcase for starting school 'and that is probably what it all started with'.[32] The young hero is ripe for formal education, having been inspired by his grandfather's fund of stories, particularly the one regarding the Horned-Deer Mother and the origins of the Kirghiz people. He is capable of understanding and absorbing a good deal, as well as describing the world around him. He has his own names for the various rocks and boulders on

32. Aitmatov, *Sobraniye sochineniy*, Vol.II, p.6.

which he plays. Additionally, he has invented his own fairy tale, extrapolating from the white steamship he can see sometimes on Lake Issyk-Kul and the knowledge that his long since departed father was once a sailor. Indeed his two possessions, the binoculars (through which he scans scenes of domestic friction or the serenity of the lake) and his briefcase, sum up his qualities: sensibility and developing experience. The fantasy of the child contrasts with and matches his harsh circumstances of a broken home, a barren aunt whose alcoholic husband beats her and who humiliates Momun. It is this uncle who slaughters the maral deer (which the boy has assumed to be the deer in the legend, the mother-protector of the Kirghiz people), initiates a drunken orgy in which Momun along with everyone else is induced to eat the deer meat, and thus drives the boy, delirious with fever, to enact the fairy story of his own invention. The boy decides to become a fish and swim out to meet his father. The tragedy of his 'suicide' lies not merely in the death of a child, but in the destruction of all human ideals, and all sense of cultural heritage. Aitmatov made some adjustments to the end of the story when it appeared in book form (after publication in *Novyy mir*), which, according to the editors of his collected works, 'strengthened the social optimism' of the work.[33] Be that as it may, the lasting impression *The White Steamship* leaves, in both its versions, is of loss and human wickedness. The conflicts in the work are between boorishness (*khamstvo*) and culture (the Russian *kul'tura* being a much broader term than its English equivalent, implying 'decency' and 'good behaviour' as well as knowledge and good taste).

The educative process is brought into sharp focus in an exchange between the hero and a soldier he encounters. The soldier, a Kazakh from Karaganda, has never heard of the Horned-Deer Mother and cannot, as the Kirghiz can, name his seven ancestors:

'Grandad says that if people do not remember their fathers they will be ruined.'
'Who will, people?'
'Yes.'
'Why?'
'Grandad says that then no-one will be ashamed of the bad things he has done, because his children and his children's children won't remember him. And no-one will do good things because, anyway, the children won't know about them.'
'What a grandad you have!' said the soldier with genuine surprise. 'He's an interesting character. Only he's stuffing your head full of all sorts of rubbish ... Don't listen to him. We are going towards communism, we

33. Ibid, p.490.

are travelling to outer space, and what's he teaching you? We ought to have him along to our political instruction sessions, we would educate him in no time. When you grow up, you'll learn — you want to get away from your grandad. He's an ignorant, uncultured [*tyomnyy, nekul'turnyy*] man.'[34]

This soldier, admired by the young boy, and in general, depicted sympathetically, embodies the spiritual poverty of the educated Stalinist. He is by no means as evil as Orozkul, the boy's uncle, who longs for the good old days of discipline under Stalin and who is by nature a tyrant and a lout. In this passage one detects an unmistakable plea by Aitmatov for a broadening of educational values, an attempt to make official ideology respectable.

Few would deny the *The White Steamship* is a moving and successful story. It has been widely acclaimed in the Soviet Union and abroad, and epitomises the very best in Aitmatov: the ability to fuse legend and reality to the benefit of both. Given the flights of fantasy in the work, it is worth recalling the actual circumstances of its genesis, which were very much rooted in the harsh everyday world. Aitmatov recalls how he was once stranded by a snowstorm in the mountains. Subsequently he met an old man who told him that the maral deer no longer lived in the area: 'One appeared last year after a long break, but it was shot'.[35] Aitmatov conceived of the work as a short story first of all, but he had an image of a small boy in his mind's eye, and remembered that the old man indeed used to take the lad to and from a distant school each day. The critic Viktor Levchenko also records that Aitmatov and his two brothers, as boys, nearly drowned when they tried to sail on a barn door on the Imambek irrigation ditch 'out to sea'.[36] A few years later, Aitmatov's niece, the daughter of his brother Dzhaparbek, was drowned in the same ditch. The legend of the Horned-Deer Mother, Levchenko notes, is recorded by the scholar Valikhanov and exists in a number of versions.[37]

The White Steamship depicts the brutal education and death of a boy; he starts out with small chance of success given the circumstances of a broken home. Indeed, the family — or lack of it — is instrumental in his tragedy. His aunt's infertility is the *a priori* reason for his uncle's brutality. In *The Skewbald Dog Running along the Edge of the Sea*, one notes from the outset the strong family ties, which

34. Ibid, p.77.
35. Ibid, p.491.
36. Levchenko, *Chingiz Aitmatov*, p.90, note 1.
37. Ibid, pp.135–6.

eventually result in extraordinary self-sacrifice and the survival of the youngest member of the ill-starred hunting expedition.

Aitmatov was given the basis of the story from the writer Vladimir Sangi, a Nivkhi (or Gilyak) writer to whom he dedicated the work. The Gilyaks are a tiny people numbering only about 4,500 who, speaking their own language, live on the mouth of the Amur river and part of Sakhalin Island, very near Japan. Seal-culling in the Okhotsk sea is one of their most important economic activities. Sangi recounted to Aitmatov that as a seven-year-old he was taken on an expedition by some adults and they were trapped by fog at sea. They lost all sense of direction for two days until a passing bird gave them the clue as to where the shore lay.[38] Aitmatov's heroes are not so lucky and one by one throw themselves overboard to leave enough drinking water for the eleven-year-old boy Kirisk to survive.

On his visit to Britain in 1986, Aitmatov said that *Skewbald Dog* was his favourite work. To date, it is his last successful attempt to combine a Socialist Realist message with flesh-and-blood characters and fantasy. If anything, the story veers back towards his earlier, more orthodox works in its portrayal of human courage and 'correct' moral choices. Understandably, critics have drawn parallels with Hemingway's *The Old Man and The Sea*. The remote geographical setting lends the work a high degree of universality, which is greatly enhanced by the near-timelessness of the events. Apart from the occasional mention of the Winchester rifles the hunters have, the reader would scarcely know if the events were in modern times at all. As night follows day and the fog refuses to lift, the question of eternity asserts itself and history as a teleological process recedes. The family, the education and survival of the son, who will continue the family, become all-important. *Skewbald Dog* might also be compared with Rasputin's story *Live an Age — Love an Age* (1981), concerning a boy's first trip berry-picking in the *taiga*. The hero's excitement and anticipation at contact with the natural elements become soured by adult duplicity. Aitmatov's work is more intent than Rasputin's on banishing human evil from the stage for once and affirming man's basic decencies.

Aitmatov and the Novel

Strictly speaking, Aitmatov's longer works discussed so far are novellas (*povesti*), rather than full-length novels. It has been noted by

38. Aitmatov, *Sobraniye sochineniy*, Vol.II, p.492.

several commentators that in general the shorter literary forms in Soviet literature have, since the Second World War, enjoyed more success than has the novel. Some Soviet critics have argued that this is a reaction to the garrulous pomposity of the Stalin era, while the American scholar Deming Brown attributes it to the continuing constraints imposed on literary life: 'It is difficult and dangerous, in uncertain and rapidly changing times, for a democratically inclined writer to give his views the full exposure that a large novel requires'.[39]

These explanations are fair enough in themselves, but they hardly account for the strength of the shorter literary forms among some émigré writers, nor do they shed light on why some writers who have excelled in the *povest'* genre should then go on to write novels which appear artistically weaker. This is arguably true of Solzhenitsyn, the émigré and dissident *par excellence*, and it is also true of Aitmatov, the living embodiment of Soviet virtues. That the large Russian novel in the manner of the nineteenth-century novel generally is in decline, may well be the case. However, there are some very awkward and honourable exceptions to this pattern. Moreover, the disease, if that is what it is, is hardly confined to Russian literature. The explanations for the novel's decline may well be found in technological and media developments, in changing life styles and changing social patterns. At this juncture it may be safer for the critic simply to record the process and leave explanations to those with the benefit of hindsight.

When *I dol'she veka dlitsya den'* (*The Day Lasts Longer than a Hundred Years*) — also entitled *Burannyy polustanok* (*Burannyy Station*) — appeared in 1980,[40] it was widely acclaimed throughout the Soviet Union. Western readers also found much of interest in the work and were naturally apt to see veiled protests against the Soviet system in certain aspects of the work. The legend of the Mankurts, who, when captured by a foreign tribe are tortured either to death or until they lose their memory and become zombies, might readily be interpreted in terms of brain-washing and thought control. The brave Second World War partisan who is wrongfully arrested for writing his memoirs provides yet another, and rather dated, airing of Stalin's crimes. The hero Yedigei, though a Muslim and a religious man, struggles bravely against the elements and against moral degeneracy (especially drinking and sloth) in such an exemplary

---

39. Brown, *Soviet Russian Literature since Stalin*, p.145.
40. First published in *Novyy mir*. Included in Aitmatov, *Sobraniye sochineniy*, Vol.II, pp.195–489.

fashion as to be quickly hailed by Soviet critics as a positive hero; and yet he challenges the authorities in sufficient measure as to lead Western readers to view his author as a liberal and a champion of freedom.

It was the American scholar Katerina Clark who first placed a question over Aitmatov with her perceptive discussion of *The Day Lasts Longer than a Hundred Years*.[41] She identified the 'Janus-like' quality of the work by pointing out that it met the establishment's current demands for 'greater scope' (*global'nost'* and *masshtabnost'* are the key Soviet words here), while not altogether abandoning the familiar (and parochial) territory of village prose. Indeed, the work combines ancient Kazakh legend, a personal history of a few characters from the 1950s to the 1970s, and a science fiction element. All three strands are deftly pulled together in the final pages when Yedigei, on returning to the traditional burial ground of his people (which is associated with the Mankurt legend) finds it is now a space-station, from which the rockets are launched to protect the Earth from extra-terrestrials.

The blend of past, present and future, of the fantastic and the realistic, is achieved not just through the ending. There is a persistent italicised refrain running throughout the work: 'The trains in those parts ran from east to west and west to east . . . and all distances were measured from the railway line, just as from the Greenwich Meridian. . .'. The device is only superficially intriguing in its bid to endow the novel with an international, universal quality. Real universality might only come through genuine artistic autonomy, of which *The Day Lasts Longer than a Hundred Years* is ultimately bereft. The weakness of Aitmatov's longer novels becomes even more apparent in his latest work *Plakha* (*The Execution Block*). It may be as well to place this work in a broader context, the better to gauge the substance of the 'sensation' it caused when it appeared.

In contemporary Russian literature there is a growing genre of what might be termed 'the underworld' or 'the criminal', but the most explicit examples are, not surprisingly, to be found among the émigrés. Eduard Limonov in his outrageous *It's me, Eddy* (1979) painted a purple and highly amusing picture of homosexuality among drop-outs in New York. His second novel *The Youth Savenko* (1983) gave an equally graphic portrait of life among the young socially disaffected in Soviet Kharkov. Limonov seems to delight in the destruction of all received social values: rape, theft, alcoholism,

41. K. Clark, 'The Mutability of the Canon: Socialist Realism and Chingiz Aitmatov's '"I dol'she veka dlitsya den"', *Slavic Review*, 1984, Vol.43, pp.573–87.

violence, are all depicted with equal enthusiasm.

The foremost writer of this underworld genre is Yuz Aleshkovsky who, like Limonov, laces his prose with obscenities as he recounts details of muggings, debauchery and anything else that stands in opposition to accepted social behaviour. The title of his *Book of Last Words* (1984) (a literal translation) refers to the Soviet judicial practice of allowing the accused to make a final speech before sentence is passed. These speeches are, in Aleshkovsky, a hilarious mixture of legalistic and political jargon on the one hand and unbridled obscenities on the other, as the miscreant clutches at straws to save himself. In the process the author exposes the gap between social ideal and harsh reality in much the same way as Mikhail Zoshchenko had done in the 1920s in his short stories.

One of the most endemic social problems in the Soviet Union is alcohol abuse, and this has been the subject of much discussion in newspapers as well as in fiction. There is hardly anything new in the literary portrayal of drunks and wastrels and all the social problems they bring with them. The stories of Rasputin, Vladimir Soloukhin and many other 'village prose' writers contain as many alcoholic wretches as Dostoyevsky had been able to muster. In fact, the evils of drink seem to be so much on display in Soviet fiction, newspapers and real life that inevitably a certain puritanical counterweight is also to be found. As we have noted, many of Rasputin's characters positively dislike alcohol and turn to religion and reminiscing in their attempts to cope with the world in which they live.

Drug abuse is a subject which has not been widely aired in the Soviet Union, and this is one reason why *The Execution Block* is worthy of attention, though it would be wrong to see drug abuse as the only or even the main theme of the work. It is generally assumed that the drug problem in the Soviet Union is cannabis- or hemp-based, since it is in Asia and Central Asia where these drugs are produced, and there are fewer obstacles to smuggling supplies into European Russia. However, one of the earliest Soviet works which touched on drug abuse has the addicts using cocaine: Vyacheslav Shishkov's *Filka and Amelka* was first published in 1930 and it dealt with the extraordinary problem of the *besprizorniki* or 'homeless ones' of the Civil and immediate post-Civil War years. It has been estimated that in the early 1920s there were as many as 7 million minors wandering about Russia, orphaned by the ravages of war, revolution and civil war. Many of them turned to crime to survive. There were attempts to rehabilitate them after 1923, and apparently the problem was considered solved by the 1930s, with the onset of full employment and a more rigid social order. In 1931 a fuller version of Shishkov's work was published under the title *Stranniki* (*The Wanderers*), but there was, typically of the time, a subsequent enforced re-write of the text. By no means a great work of art, the novel none the less gives a frightening picture of many social ills, not least drug abuse:

Both of them lay next to each other on their backs.
'There are some here who sniff stuff. But I don't.'
'What's stuff?' asked Filka.
'Cocaine. You mean you don't know?'
'So why do they sniff it? You mean it's like "lodi-cologne" [*sic*], is that it?'
'No, it's white. They sniff it to go out of their minds, to get high!'
Filka didn't understand a thing and decided the boy was lying.
'Our riff-raff sometimes exchange what they've stolen for stuff,' Engineer explained in the tone of a connoisseur; to conceal the childish tenderness of his own voice he spoke with intentional hoarseness and looked suspiciously out of the corner of his eye at Filka, fearing the latter might mistake him for a small fry, a small boy. 'Among us a torn shirt is valued at four sniffs of stuff, and ten sniffs is enough for a pair of shoes. We use sniffs instead of money.'[42]

'Engineer' is nearly nine years old; Filka, the newcomer, is fourteen.

Another example of cocaine being fairly prevalent is to be found in M. Ageyev's work *Novel with Cocaine*.[43] The Russian title *Roman s kokainom* is of course a pun ('Love affair with cocaine' would also be a viable translation). This work covers the years 1916 to 1919; nothing is known for sure about Ageyev except that his manuscript was sent from Istanbul to Paris, where it was published in the 1930s by a Russian émigré journal. It seems fair to assume that 'Ageyev' was a Russian émigré; and he may have returned to the Soviet

42. V. Shishkov, *Filka i Amelka*. This was first published in the Soviet journal *Krasnaya nov'* in 1930. A much longer work *Stranniki* (*The Wanderers*) was published in 1931. This novel was in three parts: 'Filka i Amelka' ('Filka and Amelka'); 'Mrak drognul' ('Darkness shuddered'), and 'Trud' ('Labour'). It showed the eventual rehabilitation of the delinquents. Shishkov was obliged to rewrite the work for a new edition in 1936. A *Collected Works* was published in 1974: *Sobraniye sochineniy v desyati tomakh*, Pravda, Moscow, 1974, from which a reissue of *Stranniki* was made: *Stranniki*, povest, Sovremennik, Moscow, 1979.

There are, to my knowledge, two English translations of *Filka i Amelka*: (1) *Children of Darkness*, Victor Gollancz, London, 1931, translator unnamed, repr. by Hyperion Press, Westport, Conn., 1973. (2) *Children of the Street*, trans. by Thomas P. Whitney, Strathcona Publishing Co., Royal Oak, Mich., 1979. My details of the *besprizorniki* are taken from the translator's Afterword to this edition. The translation quoted here (pp. 3, 19–20) is faithful to the 1979 Soviet edition. 'Stuff' is *marafeta*.

43. M. Ageyev, *Novel with Cocaine*, trans. by Michael Henry Heim, Pan (Picador), London, 1985, pp. 5–6.

Union during Stalin's time and perished there. The novel has more literary merit than Shishkov's work. Indeed, N. Struve has argued intriguingly that *Novel with Cocaine* is in fact the work of Vladimir Nabokov, who published it under a pseudonym in a typical act of literary mystification.[44]

In all the works mentioned so far, whether Soviet or émigré, it is important to note that 'the underworld' is taken as a fact of life and as a subject worthy of serious literary treatment. Whether the results are comic or harrowing, successful or gauche, the writers are interested in psychology and social problems. In this sense they must be distinguished from writers of criminal thrillers, of which there are a plethora in the Soviet Union and some good examples among the émigrés. One thinks of the novels of Topol and Neznansky, for example. There is also an émigré Russian translation of Martin Cruz Smith's *Gorky Park*.[45] All these works, whether they are too frank and cynical about Soviet life to be accepted in the Soviet Union, or whether they are anodyne enough to ensure serialisation in popular Soviet magazines, treat the underworld as subject matter for entertainment. On this level, drug-smuggling also figures in plenty in Soviet fiction.

Aitmatov's *The Execution Block* purports to be a serious literary treatment of several moral and social issues, including drug abuse among the young. In a lengthy interview in *Izvestiya*, Aitmatov stated: 'Just a few days ago I submitted to *Novyy mir* my novel *The Execution Block*, the main thrust [*pafos*] of which, I hope, is precisely in this — the life of man from the point of view of the inevitable problems of ecology.'[46] On his visit to Britain in 1986 he was apparently even more coy about the work, but made a general statement on literature: 'The reader, whatever the political complications and existing contradictions, remains a human being. In literature he looks for marks of humanity and goodness.'[47]

The Execution Block is an amalgamation of two stories which are loosely connected by some shallow philosophy and a few details of plot. To this extent the novel follows the format of *The Day Lasts Longer than a Hundred Years*. However, in *The Day* the reader could give Aitmatov the benefit of the doubt and try to perceive links of an

44. N. A. Struve, 'K razgadke odnoy literaturnoy tayny — "Roman s kokainom" M. Ageyeva', *Vestnik russkogo khristianskogo dvizheniya*, Paris, 1985, No.144, pp.165–79.
45. M. K. Smit, *Park im. Gorkogo*, trans. by A. Tsvetkov, Ardis, Ann Arbor, Mich., 1985.
46. Ch. Aitmatov, 'O Neizmennom v menyayushchemsya mire', *Izvestiya*, No.117, 27 April 1986, p.3.
47. *Bulletin of the Great Britain–USSR Association*, No.73, April 1986, p.1.

arcane philosophical nature between the various stories. The work stressed an awareness of history while lighting on a theme that was remarkably topical, even ahead of its time. The science fiction part of the work involved a joint East–West space programme (shades of Brezhnev's Detente policy) which goes off course when two astronauts encounter some extra-terrestrials. The response of the earthling government is to throw up around the Earth a 'cordon sanitaire' to prevent the aliens' penetration (shades of Reagan's and Brezhnev's 'Star Wars' research — except that the novel was written before the SDI (Strategic Defense Initiative) was made public).

The Execution Block has as its hero Avdiy, a religious idealist, son of a church deacon from Pskov, a young man thrown out of a seminary before he is able to leave of his own accord. The reader's attention is drawn to the biblical connotations of his name. Avdiy is the prophet Obadiah, the author of the shortest and least significant of the Books of the Old Testament. The point seems to be that Aitmatov's hero is similarly insignificant and ineffectual.[48] Avdiy falls between two ideological stools; he is a believer and yet is too secular in his outlook for the church, so he resolves to do good by infiltrating groups that smuggle drugs from Central Asia to European Russia and to write up the true, inside story on drug abuse for his local newspaper. Aitmatov hammers away relentlessly at the religious theme. Having joined the gang of drug pushers, Avdiy helps them harvest the hemp and then he stows away on a train back to Europe, thus avoiding the vigilant authorities at the Central Asian stations. On the train he refuses to partake of the drug and is brutally beaten by the others and thrown off. While he suffers from delirium, the reader is treated to a revised version of Christ's confrontation with Pontius Pilate.

Any student of modern Russian literature will immediately see here parallels with a celebrated passage in Bulgakov's *The Master and Margarita*. Christ pleads he has been misrepresented, while Pilate is concerned more with worldly matters. At one point in Aitmatov's narrative Pilate receives a letter from his wife asking him to be lenient towards these essentially harmless cranks who actually do some good among the people. If, she says, he punishes Christ, it will have bad consequences for them both and they will never be posted back to Rome.

What is one to make of such an episode? If it is intended to restore a spiritual dimension to a militantly materialistic culture it is hopelessly out of date. Bulgakov, Rasputin and many others including Aitmatov himself have made the point far better in earlier works.

48. See also I Kings Ch. 18 verse 3ff.

Or is one to draw some inference from Pilate's wife's role in easing up on these 'dissidents'? There has been repeated speculation that Raisa Gorbachev has had a hand in the gradual rehabilitation of Pasternak and other writers.

Avdiy survives his fall from the train and is helped (by latter-day Samaritans?) to safety. His erstwhile drug-smuggling companions are all arrested and deny all knowledge of him to the police. One of the gang, Petrukha (for once in the story called Pyotr — Peter) denies him and our hero is hurt by this. In hospital he is visited by an attractive young woman whom he met briefly and has dreamed of ever since. She is a scientist working on methods of destroying the hemp which feeds the drug market. They develop a relationship, but before all the obstacles posed by her former marriage can be re-solved, Avdiy is taken on by a work team to slaughter wild antelope in the area and thus fulfil the meat quota.

Avdiy objects to the wholesale destruction of the antelope herds and his fellow workers (all 'professional alcoholics') beat him up, tie him up, later put him 'on trial' and tie him to a tree, 'crucified'. (The religious symbolism is perhaps further strengthened by the fact that the tree is a *ternovik* (blackthorn), echoing *ternovyy venets* — crown of thorns.) It is not entirely clear whether he survives the ordeal. The truck eventually returns but he is close to death.

In his encounters with the drug pushers and then the alcoholics, Avdiy has naively sought to improve, like Christ, on the human nature he finds around him. At every turn he is defeated. His plans for publishing his findings about the drug problem at first get an enthusiastic reception from his newspaper, but then the editors go cool on the idea of publication and Avdiy is shunned. The slaughter of the antelope, though aided by a bunch of alcoholics, is instigated by the authorities for purely commercial reasons, so again Avdiy has no chance of stopping what he sees as an evil action.

There is nothing new for Soviet literature in the religious symbol-ism of Aitmatov's novel (witness such titles as Aleksei Tolstoy's *The Road to Calvary* (1920–1941) and Vladimir Dudintsev's *Not by Bread Alone* (1956)); what is new in Aitmatov here, though, is that the religious symbols are so obvious that one wonders how seriously they are to be taken, or is the author indulging in some sort of joke that does not quite come off? Avdiy is denied by Peter, is 'crucified', has a pain in his side.

The third and final part of the novel is concerned with a pair of wolves, Akbara and her mate Tashchainar who have briefly encoun-tered Avdiy in the first two parts of the work. The religious element here is more satisfactory and goes hand in hand with universal humanistic values. The wolves have been driven from lair to lair by man's rapacious policies towards the environment. Their litters have died and now they are trying once more, desperately, to raise four cubs. Bazarbai, a drunk and good-for-nothing, steals the four cubs hoping to sell them to a zoological centre. Pursued by Akbara and Tashchainar he takes refuge in the camp of the wealthy, teetotal, diligent, honest and compassionate Boston, whom he envies and resents, both for his possessions and his wife. Later Boston tries to buy back the cubs from Bazarbai since their distraught parents are terrorising the camp and their howls keep Boston, his wife and two-year-old boy awake at night. Akbara and Tashchainar, personified throughout the work, pray to the wolf-goddess in their distress. One day Akbara comes into the camp and tries to take Boston's son back to her lair as a substitute for her lost cubs, throwing him across her back as she would a sheep. Boston tries to kill the wolves, but kills his son instead. He then seeks out Bazarbai, who has been blackening Boston's name and insulting him, shoots him dead and then turns himself in to the authorities.

This part of the novel is not quite as gauche as the preceding summary might suggest, and in terms of a story of the outback is engaging enough. But it is questionable to what extent it links with the other two parts. In a novel which relentlessly suggests *double entendre*, it might be that here we have a general plea for compassion and a more spiritual attitude to life, but one should take care not to be duped by formal religion, as Avdiy has been in the first two parts. The last part of the work is also concerned with the current political and economic debate in the Soviet Union; this aspect of the work will be dealt with below.

Apart from the thrill of a slightly contrived excursion into the Soviet underworld, what does the drug theme in the novel give us? The linguist will pick up some new vocabulary: *anasha* is the drug made from hemp (*konoplya*); in *The Execution Block*, *ekstra* is not a brand of vodka but an opium-style drug, as is *plastilin* (lit. 'plasticine'), a superior form of *anasha*. *Gonets* is a pusher. *Smak* is another word for *anasha*, meaning literally 'relish' (but possibly a borrowing from English here). The traditional word in modern Russian for a 'high' or a 'trip' is *kaif* and the term figures frequently in the novel along with its compounds. *Vrezat po mozgam* (lit. 'to cut into your brains') means 'to take dope'. These terms are undoubtedly only the tip of a linguistic iceberg, and for more underworld vocabulary those interested will have to go outside Soviet literature, to Aleshkovsky and others.

More searchingly, Aitmatov seems genuinely anxious to examine a contemporary scourge. Avdiy writes to his girl that drug abuse came to the Soviet Union about fifteen years before under the influence of the West (the novel takes place in 1983).[49] No one will argue that a 'drug culture' developed in the 1960s in the West which undoubtedly was felt in Eastern Europe, but, as Shishkov and Ageyev have indicated, drug abuse in Russia is much older than the permissive society.

Just as Pilate and Christ in Avdiy's delirium rehearse their respective positions of cynical materialism and spiritual truth, so too Avdiy and Grishan, the gang boss, spell out their values at their first meeting. For Grishan bliss can be obtained only from 'a high' (*Lish' kaif dayot blazhenstvo*);[50] all the promises about God, democracy, equality and so on are just words. If Avdiy can persuade Grishan's cronies away from wrong-doing, all well and good — Grishan will recognise defeat. Avdiy says that he wishes to show them 'the true path' (*istinniy put'*).[51] Oddly enough, there is little discussion and no depiction of the medical effects of drug abuse; rather we have some uncomfortable parallels between ecstatic moments brought on by music and/or religious thoughts and reported feelings of elation induced by drugs: formal religion, for the naive and inexperienced, is seen as very much an opiate. Here, Aitmatov balances his argument very finely, for he is at pains to point up Avdiy's susceptibility and naive enthusiasm. Expelled from the seminary and working as an anti-religious journalist, Avdiy finds himself up against two fortresses: 'Genuine, thousand-year-old religion and scientific thinking'.[52]

The evil effects of drugs are seen to be more or less the same as those of alcoholism — violence, sadism and death. All these evils spill over, through alcohol abuse, into the last part of the novel, in the figure of Bazarbai. His rival, Boston, is, however, an updated positive hero. He easily wins the reader's sympathy, and when he kills Bazarbai one can only approve of the action, while recognising that the law must take its course.

Boston is more interesting for his economic and political views. If we accept that the post-Brezhnev era has been characterised by a 'value-for-money' management policy which still has to cling to the traditional, but now more elastic, shibboleths concerning 'socialism'

49. Ch. Aitmatov, 'Plakha', *Novyy mir*, No.6, pp.7–69; No.8, pp.90–148; No.9, pp.6–64. *Novyy mir*, No.8, pp.120–3 — in his delirium Avdiy cannot reconcile himself to what happened between Christ and Pilate '1950 years before'.
50. Ibid, No.8, p.95.
51. Ibid, p.92.
52. *Novyy mir*, No. 6, 1986, pp.25–6.

and 'collectivism', then Boston is a good example of the *new* 'new man'. *Mutatis mutandis*, he oozes as much material success and well-being as any of the lead characters in an American TV soap opera; he has a beautiful wife, a camp with electricity laid on, two motorised vehicles, horses, herds, and several assistants — employees in all but name. At the same time he is a doting father, a teetotaller, very diligent, concerned about the environment. He is brave and enterprising. With a close friend Ernazar, he once scouted for new pastures through a snowy pass and his friend lost his life, falling into a crevasse. Boston seems fundamentally contented, with no need to get high on drugs or religion.

This hero has a persistent ideological enemy in the shape of the local Communist Party organiser (*partorg*), Kochkorbayev, who sees all that the hero does as an attack on the sacrosanct principles of socialism. Boston's policy is to try and make each family responsible for its own 'patch', and indeed his achievements have led to his name being recorded at the Exhibition of Economic Achievements in Moscow. Boston has even been selected to pay a visit to Moscow but cannot obtain permission from the *partorg* to take his wife with him. Kept awake by the wolves' howling, he reflects on the state of the world:

> He thought of various things. And most of all of how from one year to the next it was becoming more difficult to work conscientiously, and that people today, especially young people, had absolutely no shame. No one believed a word these days. And everyone sought his own advantage first and foremost. Before the war, when they were building the famous Chuyskiy canal, people came from all ends of the country and worked without pay, voluntarily. And now no one believed such things — you're telling fairy tales, they said — you're just making it all up ... Wherever you turned there weren't enough hands to help. And not because there weren't the people, but because people didn't want to work.[53]

Matters finally come to a head between Boston and Kochkorbayev, but this time a new young instructor of the district committee (*raikom*) is present. He takes Boston's side 'in principle' but the matter will be fully thrashed out in the higher echelons of the Party. Boston, a Party member and a leading worker (*peredovik*), suggests they expel him, but adds that the Party does not need men like Kochkorbayev, who only 'tie people's hands' and who need the Party more than the Party needs them. This conflict is never resolved, being suspended by Boston's killing of Bazarbai. However,

---

53. *Novyy mir*, No. 9, 1986, pp.45–6.

the readers' feelings are with the pragmatic Boston and against dogmatism and opportunism. At one point the *partorg* even suggests that young people today should be reminded of the example of Pavlik Morozov (the boy who, during collectivisation, denounced his own father and was murdered) and his Kirghiz equivalent Kychan Ozhakynov.[54]

To those who have admired the artistic merits in Aitmatov's previous works *The Execution Block* is a disappointment. Mary Seton-Watson, in one of her broadcasts for Radio 3 in November 1986, said it made her, as a Christian Western reader, 'squirm'. However, Aitmatov's national and international standing are such that full discussion of his latest work was inevitable, and was instructive, if only for the social and political content of the work.

In October 1986, on the shores of Lake Issyk-Kul, Aitmatov organised an international conference in which, among others, Arthur Miller, Peter Ustinov and Claude Simon participated. The purpose was to engender more general understanding between East and West. The previous November at a meeting in Lithuania Miller had raised the question of Irina Ratushinskaya, the imprisoned poetess, who was suddenly released just before the Gorbachev–Reagan summit in Reykjavik. He was surprised to find support — from Aitmatov.[55] Thus to some extent Aitmatov is his own man, and he is deeply concerned about serious political and moral issues. Yet the manner in which he embodies his concerns in his recent artistic works is ultimately dubious.

After the publication of the first two parts of *The Execution Block* Aitmatov gave another lengthy interview in which he spoke of the genesis of his novel.[56] He likened Avdiy to Yedigei, the hero of *The Day Lasts Longer than a Hundred Years*, in their 'thirst for justice'; he acknowledged the Bulgakov connection in the Jesus–Pilate encounter, and expressed freely his disquiet at young people today: he recalled a letter from an anguished mother to *Literaturnaya gazeta* about her two addicted sons, and he spoke of a gang of young pushers he saw under arrest. 'Yes, they had broken the law and deserved punishment, but they also needed help, and we are obliged to give it'.

The discussion of the novel in the Soviet media has generally acknowledged the importance of the social issues it has raised, but has reflected unease at the overall achievement. A television discus-

54. Ibid, p.48.
55. See R. Chernyy, 'Razum dolzhen pobedit' — mezhdunarodnaya vstrecha deyateley kultury v Kirgiziyi', *Sovetskaya kultura*, 18 October 1986, p.7. Also: M. Ratcliffe, 'Miller's Russian Tale', *The Observer*, 26 October 1986, p.23.
56. 'Tsena — zhizn', *Literaturnaya gazeta*, 13 August 1986, No.33, p.4.

sion between literary critics in October 1986 had, for instance, the following exchange:

> [Zolotusskiy] 'My impressions were most varied . . . At first it was surprise, then a let-down, then surprise again and another let-down at the end.'
> [Anninskiy] 'It was the opposite way with me. At first surprise, then incredible disappointment, then some compensation and even satisfaction.'[57]

Literaturnaya gazeta carried a round table discussion which was equally open-ended and non-committal. Chingiz Guseynov asserted:

> In his novel Aitmatov has touched on what is most pressing today, on things which, with pain and anger are spoken of in the pages of our newspapers and from the high tribunes. Are we not to worry about strengthening in the worker a feeling of being master of his own land, of responsibility for his own affairs, about freeing him from all manner of bureaucratic regulations, paper prescriptions and demagogic interdictions etc?[58]

Sergei Averintsev said, as someone who was 'not a literary critic', that he was not interested in 'shortcomings', but in 'symptoms — the symptoms of the general state of culture'. Georgiy Gachev, one of the foremost Soviet authorities on Aitmatov, countered that their role (as literary experts) was not 'creativity [*tvorchestvo*] but commentary'.

Akhiyar Khakimov stated: 'There are places in the complex and graphic structure of the images in the novel, as the participants in the discussion have noted, which engender contradictory interpretations, there are motifs, which do not always elucidate, and sometimes obscure the author's intention.'

Averintsev concluded the discussion: 'In the end books are divided not into good and bad ones — books are divided into essential ones, and those which you can manage without. Essential books are sometimes imperfect and *vice versa*.'

These responses seem to be a classic example of conventional Soviet literary discussion being unable or unwilling to get to the heart of the matter.

57. Text of discussion by Lev Anninskiy and Igor Zolotusskiy, 'Reflections on Chingiz Aytmatov's novel "Plakha" [The Block]', SU/8402/B, 1 November 1986. Broadcast 11.45 GMT, 21 October 1986.
58. E. A. Krivitskiy, et al. 'Paradoksy romana ili paradoksy vospriyatiya', *Literaturnaya gazeta*, 15 October 1986, No.42, p.4.

In *The Day Lasts Longer than a Hundred Years* the reader could construct a pattern of interpretation which would explain the affinities between the legendary past, the post-war years and a science fiction future; or between a remote railway junction in Kazakhstan and East–West relations; possibly even between the rampaging of a highly-sexed camel and the freedom of the human spirit.

However, in *The Execution Block* the only direct narrative link between the various stories is the she-wolf. The reader has to mount a considerable 'do-it-yourself' operation to give the work any real aesthetic cohesion, and the symbols have such a degree of independence one from the other that they can be made to mean anything. The best example is in the very title of the work: Mary Seton-Watson in her broadcast interpreted the title specifically and translated it somewhat idiosyncratically as 'the scaffold', having it refer directly to Avdiy's crucifixion. Aitmatov himself says:

> The block is not only a platform on which an execution is carried out, a place of execution. In the course of his life one way or another a man finds himself before an execution block. Sometimes he mounts the block, naturally, remaining alive physically, sometimes he does not mount it. In the present case the title refers to what the block costs, the cost of mounting it, to whether there is any sense in it, in this path to torture on the cross.[59]

But equally could not 'the block' be the wanton destruction of the environment by short-sighted politicians, or is it the fault of the conscienceless men 'on the shop floor'? Or is the block the curse of drug abuse, supposedly imported from the West? Or the general emptiness of youngsters' lives today? Is it alcoholism or immature religious convictions? The reader can take his pick.

There are some graphic and engaging passages in *The Execution Block*; the wolf narrative in particular can be enjoyed on the level of an adventure story while striking more serious overtones. When Akbara abducts the child, who is subsequently killed in error by his father, there are resonances of a very ancient literary tradition (Romulus and Remus) as well as echoes of folklore around the world (Kipling's Mowgli). The massacre of the antelope at the start of the story is shocking and boldly relevant to a Soviet (and an international) readership.

However, the excursions into philosophy make the work ultimately suspect. The satirist Vladimir Voynovich, now resident in the West, once expressed his own misgivings about the shallow

59. Aitmatov, 'Tsena — zhizn', note 56.

philosophy in Aitmatov.[60] Hitherto one might dismiss such comment as the sniping of one writer jealous of another's position. But Aitmatov hardly stimulates serious thought with such authorial interjections as Avdiy not knowing that 'evil opposes good just when good wants to help those embarked on evil'[61] or 'People seek out fate, but fate seeks out people'.[62] The author is at pains to highlight Avdiy's own crass and woolly philosophy ('freedom is only found in music')[63] and there are several similar instances of the hero's intellectual ineptitude. Yet these passages hardly assuage the author's own propensity for intellectual affectation: 'It is difficult to establish what human life is. In any instance, the infinite combinations of possible human relations, of possible personalities are so complex that no ultra-modern computer system is capable of integrating a general graph of common human natures.'[64]

Chekhov's famous utterance that art should ask questions without answering them is still valid. Or, one might agree with Rasputin that the moral posing of a question contains a moral answer. However, if the questions are formulated so blandly as to invite an infinite number of answers, as appears to be the case in Aitmatov's long novels, is the work that asks them a work of art? And given that *The Execution Block* aroused so much excitement in the Soviet Union — created a 'national sensation', as *The Guardian*'s Moscow correspondent reported[65] — is the new opium of the people, in fact, to be found in the contemporary Soviet novel?

In July 1987 *Ogonyok* carried an extensive interview with Aitmatov which illustrated the chief facets of the man and the writer, while revealing a little more detail.[66] He spoke of the very diverse opinions on *The Execution Block*, praised Rasputin, was pleased to see Nabokov recognised at last in the Soviet Union: 'Even what Nabokov wrote in English is still Russian literature.'[67] Regarding the state of Soviet literature today, he identified a decline but suspected exciting new developments:

60. V. Voynovich, 'O literature razreshonnoy i napisannoy bez razresheniya'; *Kontinent*, No.37, 1985, pp.439–45, p.439.
61. *Novyy mir*, No.6, 1986, p.56.
62. *Novyy mir*, No.9, 1986, p.6.
63. *Novyy mir*, No.6, 1986, p.44.
64. Ibid, p.23.
65. M. Walker, 'Pushing up the Poppies', *The Guardian*, 24 September 1986, p.23.
66. Ch. Aitmatov, Interview, 'Tsena prozreniya', *Ogonyok*, July 1987, No.28, pp.4–9.
67. Ibid, p.8.

I think that after Valentin Rasputin, who is now 50 years old, in the generations coming after him, there is a feeling of a sort of devastation in literature. Both in Russian and in the non-Russian literatures something has faltered, slowed down . . . The potential of the formula 'and the word was God' has disappeared.

Yet now, I think that a propitious time of great discoveries has arrived. And if tomorrow there appears a great novelist or poet who is going to stagger us, then it will be in the order of things. Let him oust everyone. We will accept it as a long-expected phenomenon.[68]

He went on to discuss Socialist Realism:

In principle a new attempt to evaluate literature was undertaken in our, Soviet, era. Everything that was created was endorsed by the method of what we have called socialist realism. I am not against this term, the terminology does not matter, what matters is the substance of it. One can talk about socialist realism, critical realism, magical realism, whatever you like. The important thing is that the work of art be wholly of value. But how one novel or another, or a play or a poem arises, and what its fate is in the future, all this is not subject to anyone's foresight.

I do not share the ostentatious pronouncements, the victorious rejoicings that through the method of socialist realism we have opened up a new epoch, a new era in art, that all our literature and culture are somehow unique, extraordinary.[69]

He spoke at length about social and economic shortcomings in Soviet society, complaining bitterly about Aeroflot and Soviet roads. On the international scene, he looked forward to a follow-up peace conference in Geneva after the one he had held at Issyk-Kul. He was concerned about the anti-Semitic and chauvinist elements attaching to *Pamyat'* (Memory), the Russian nationalist group founded in the early 1980s ostensibly as a conservationist group.

Aitmatov also recalled — for the first time publicly, he claimed — the repression of his father and uncles at the height of the purges in 1937.

In all, the interview is an excellent example of *glasnost*: there is distancing from Stalinism, a broadening of literary discussion that would have been unthinkable under Brezhnev and a burning concern over national and international issues. More pertinently, one might well detect in the remarks on the current state of literature that events have outpaced the established men of letters, and that Aitmatov the novelist is not of the same stature as the Aitmatov who wrote *Farewell, Gulsary!* and *The White Steamship*.

68. Ibid, p.5.
69. Ibid, p.8.

–3–

Vladimir Voynovich
The Joker

The Soviet Writer

'I must say that for me (and I think generally for every writer) the basic life supply [*osnovnoy zhiznennyy zapas*] is the stock of childhood and youth impressions.'[1] This was how Voynovich responded to a journalist's question when asked about it being easier to obtain material for his works when he lived in Soviet conditions. It is certainly the case that, Voynovich's versatility notwithstanding, the majority of his heroes are young men, frequently in the military, often at odds with authority. Unlike Rasputin and Aitmatov, Voynovich clashed with the establishment and ultimately found himself in emigration.

In addition to the five stories he published in *Novyy mir*, Voynovich had a piece in the anti-religious journal *Nauka i religiya* and a novel about the nineteenth-century revolutionary Vera Figner, *Stepen' doveriya* (*A Degree of Trust*). The publication of this in 1973 was effectively Voynovich's swansong as far as official literature was concerned. The *Novyy mir* stories represent the best of his work as an official writer. In republishing two of them — *Ya khochu byt' chestnym* ('I Want to be Honest') and *Rasstoyaniye v polkilometra* ('At a Distance of Half a Kilometre') — in emigration the author gently rebuked an émigré critic who had suggested that all that Voynovich had written apart from his novel *Zhizn' i neobychaynyye priklyucheniya soldata Ivana Chonkina* (*The Life and Extraordinary Adventures of Private Ivan Chonkin*) and the sequel *Pretendent na prestol* (*Pretender to the Throne*) could have appeared in any Soviet publication: '*Novyy mir* was the bravest and best journal for its time, but even there my prose, with the exception of my first novella 'We Live Here' only 'scraped' through, and sometimes (for example 'By Means of Mutual Correspondence') did not get through at all'.[2]

---

1. 'Vladimir Voynovich v *Russkoy Mysli*', *Russkaya mysl'*, 2 April 1981, p.10.
2. V. Voynovich, *Putyom vzaimnoy perepiski*, YMCA, Paris, 1979, p.3.

The five *Novyy mir* stories published between 1961 and 1967 display a range of subject matter and setting that makes it difficult to categorise Voynovich.[3] 'At a Distance of Half a Kilometre' and *My zdes' zhivyom* ('We Live Here') could pass for village prose. 'I Want to be Honest', *Dva tovarishcha* (*Two Comrades*) and 'V kupe' ('In the Compartment') deal with the modern urban world. However, in all of them a jocular tone is established only to be destroyed by discomfortingly serious moral and philosophical considerations. The same process is also discernible in the works that could only be published abroad.

In both the town and country stories one notes the triumph of petty detail over the grandiose scheme, the victory of reality over theory. Here one can recall Voynovich's biography. He trained and worked as a carpenter before turning to literature. A journalist who has never done a manual job is likely to be a figure of some ridicule in Voynovich, as is any intellectual, who more often than not will be utterly divorced from the real world. In his discussions of Voynovich, Geoffrey Hosking has fixed on the notion of '*zamysel*' within the human personality. Voynovich himself uses the term several times in his interviews and at one stage even planned a book with that title.[4] Hosking writes: 'Every individual should try to understand the *zamysel* which lies within him [Voynovich once said]. The primary meaning of *zamysel* is "plan, intention"; in this context it might be translated as "inner meaning, potentiality" or even "identity".'[5] Hosking goes on to trace the idea back to Voynovich's first stories. Thus one notes a high degree of consistency in his writing, although the manner of it has shifted somewhat from the realistic to the fantastic. All the *Novyy mir* stories provide rich material for the social scientist. There are numerous authentic pictures of urban and rural life in Soviet Russia, even if one leaves aside the philosophy the works offer us. But Voynovich's latest work *Moskva 2042* (*Moscow 2042*) is, by contrast, a flight of fantasy — into the future. 'I am a describer. I'm not a teacher like Tolstoy or Solzhenitsyn. I don't know how to construct life. I don't know how life must be built. My duty is to describe life as it is, not as seen

3. 'My zdes' zhivyom', *Novyy mir*, 1961, No.1, pp.21–71. Dva rasskaza: 'Khochu byt' chestnym', 'Rasstoyaniye v polkilometra', *Novyy mir*, 1963, No.2, pp.150–97. 'V kupe', *Novyy mir*, 1965, No. 2, pp.69–71. 'Dva tovarishcha', *Novyy mir*, 1967, No.1, pp.85–152.
4. See: Voynovich, *Russkaya mysl'*. Also: G. Hosking, 'Chonkin and After', in O. Matich and M. Heim (eds), *The Third Wave: Russian Literature in Emigration*, Ardis, Ann Arbor, Mich., 1984, pp.147–52.
5. Hosking 'Chonkin and After', p.151.

through a lens.'[6] The two best *Novyy mir* stories, 'I Want to be Honest' and *Two Comrades* provide good illustrations of Voynovich's powers of character analysis (*zamysel*) and his ability to describe. Respectively, they also deal with the most familiar and universal of situations: jerry-building and adolescence.

The chronic housing shortage in Russia has been exacerbated this century by the massive programme of urbanisation that the Soviet government has embarked on. Naturally, the destruction of property brought about by the Second World War only made matters worse. Under Khrushchev there was a real onslaught on the housing problem and a great many *khrushchoby* (a pun on *trushchoby*, 'slums') appeared. In the late 1950s and early 1960s many new suburbs sprang up, only to be faced with capital repairs as soon as they were occupied. Between 1959 and 1962, it has been estimated, 12 per cent of this new housing proved to be uninhabitable.[7] 'I Want to be Honest' was published in 1963.

The discussion of one of Vladimov's novels, *The Great Ore*, will show how 'classical' Socialist Realism handled the work situation. The stereotype of construction literature demanded vastness, achievement and human commitment. What strikes the reader most about 'I Want to be Honest' is the pettiness: pettiness of the technical details (a carpenter hammering in screws instead of using a screwdriver), the pettiness of human horizons (the managers want the building officially deemed finished before the public holiday — though they have trouble recalling which anniversary they are celebrating);[8] more particularly, the modesty of the hero's own aspirations, as indicated by the story's title. 'I Want to be Honest' was a title foisted on an unwilling author by a member of *Novyy mir*'s editorial board, the better to assure the work of a smooth passage through the censorship. There are several well-known examples of this exercise, notably Solzhenitsyn's *Shch–854* became *A Day in the Life of Ivan Denisovich*; *Cancer Ward*, had it been published, would have been, almost certainly, *Patients and Doctors*.[9] Voynovich's working title 'Whom I Could Become' (like 'I Want to be Honest', the phrase also figures in the text of the story) was restored by the author in the émigré edition, out of 'exclusively aesthetic considerations'.[10] 'I Want to be Honest' portrays much of everyday

6. Voynovich: interview, *Quarto*, April 1981, pp.7–8.
7. P. Sorlin, *The Soviet People and their Society*, trans. by David Weissbort, Pall Mall Press, London, 1969, p.239.
8. Voynovich: under the author's preferred title 'Kem ya mog by stat' in the volume entitled *Putyom vzaimnoy perepiski*, p.31.
9. M. Scammell, *Solzhenitsyn: A Biography*, Hutchinson, London, 1984, p.481.
10. Voynovich, *Putyom*, p.4.

Russian life, warts and all — the drinking, shoddy workmanship, deceiving the powers that be, an unwanted pregnancy, the strains on family life. All the hero, Samokhin, wants to do is be a conscientious foreman and see a job well done. Yet he is hampered at every turn by the very stuff of daily life — a shortage of materials, selfishness, laziness. Even death is reduced to matter-of-fact proportions, as when we learn that Samokhin's girl Klara may die if she has an abortion, or when the hero himself collapses and ends up in hospital. The *reductio ad trivium* lends the story a Chekhovian quality, though in Voynovich the comedy marginally outweighs the *poshlost'*, that notorious Russian quality combining mediocrity, vulgarity and banality.

The tussle over the story's title hints at Voynovich's interest in human personality. The Soviet title implies a clearly defined and universally recognised morality. The author's own title indicates not so much straightforward moral commitment, a blueprint for decency, as a longing for the realisation of human potential. Samokhin might well become a family man with a home to settle in to. While the majority of the characters are involved in an elaborate game — illicit drinking, building useless artefacts, writing specious newspaper articles — the hero struggles to maintain a sense of reality and identity. It is as if the moral question will take care of itself as long as the individual's personality can remain intact.

Two Comrades is a social comedy. That is to say, it gives us a comic picture of social attitudes and behaviour. The story is devoid of any ethical considerations for much of the time, but when the moral element breaks through, it conditions our perception of the protagonists and of the story as a whole: the comedy turns sour. Though everything in the work is rationally motivated, the notion underpinning it is that only the narrator Valeriy and his perception of things are existentially valid. Though the other characters have their viewpoints and values, the implication is that they are somehow inauthentic. Valeriy is led on for much of the time by his workmate Tolik, who gets him into scrapes with the police only to leave him in the lurch, or engineers dates with girls when the hero can manage better on his own.

The work that he and Tolik do in a factory is somehow unreal — they have no knowledge of what the enterprise is producing, but think it is something to do with space travel. Similarly, the exam that Valeriy is to take seems irrelevant and alien. Having fiddled himself a ride in an aeroplane, he reproduces an account of the experience in the exam instead of answering the questions. The teacher is so impressed that she gives him top marks. In his triumph one can detect something central to Voynovich's thinking: namely, the power of fiction over fact, the idea that fantasy (Valeriy in the exam actually makes aeroplane noises and waves his arms about, much to the amusement of his peers) is at worst harmless, but at best may actually be a surer route to reality.

Much of the first part of the story echoes the 'playing' element one sees in 'I Want to be Honest'. The lads sneak into a dance without paying, the *druzhinniki* (voluntary part-time militiamen) nab Valeriy, the regular police let him go. His mother's efforts to make him keep regular hours include hiding his trousers, but he can bully his grandmother into divulging their whereabouts by threatening to wear a skirt. The bric-à-brac of daily life is a game, and fantasy leads to reality: at the end of the story the hero does make it to flying school.

If the mundane things in life seem rather chimeric, anything more grandiose appears absurd. The story opens with the boys naked before the military draft commission ('the usual woman doctor, like a pole, black, like a gipsy, hoarse voice'). The squalid immediately gains and retains the upper hand over the mock guide-book style description of the town:

> Our town was divided into two parts — the old part, where we lived, and the new part, where we didn't live. The new part was mostly called 'Behind the Palace', because on the wasteland between the old and new parts they'd built some Palace, the biggest in the country, or so they said round our way. At first it was going to be the biggest Palace of Metallurgists in the country in the style of Corbusier. The Palace was almost built when they found out that the designer of the project was subject to the influence of Western architecture. They gave him a hard time for old Corbusier and it took him a long time to get over it. Then new times came and they allowed him to return to his interrupted work.[11]

The sneering, jocular tone, so typical of 'youth prose' of the early 1960s again connotes Voynovich's predilection for immediacy, for describing everyday trivia as against the high-falutin or abstract. Casual relationships, motorscooters, money and fun are high priorities in Valeriy's and Tolik's world. Theirs is an amoral not an immoral world.

The story turns inside out when Tolik is forced by a gang of thugs to beat Valeriy up. He subsequently tries repeatedly to justify himself to his erstwhile friend, but to no avail. The argument that if he had not done it they would have beaten them both up and worse

11. Voynovich, *Novyy mir*, 1967, No.2, p.87.

stays with Valeriy. He recalls how later on in his life and in other circumstances it is used and how dubious it is. The story ends in a muted fashion with the friendship dented and Tolik much diminished in the eyes of the reader and the narrator. However, there is no note of moral outrage or indignation — just a veiled plea for the kind of modest honesty that the builder Samokhin craves.

The Path to Dissidence

The transition from light comedy to moral searching in *Two Comrades* might serve as a paradigm for Voynovich's own career in the Soviet Union. We have Voynovich's own account of how he shifted from Soviet writer to 'dissident', a term he dislikes using. In May 1981 Voynovich attended a conference on the third emigration in the University of Southern California in Los Angeles and described in some detail what happened to him in the 1960s. The turning point for him, as for many other writers, was the arrest of Yuliy Daniel and Andrei Sinyavsky, whose crime was to publish unorthodox works abroad.

> This event shook me. Up till then I had written rather critically of Soviet life, but at the same time I was completely loyal and apolitical. I tried to write according to my conscience, but did not intrude into what did not impinge directly on my interests. I was so uninterested in politics that even the Hungarian events [i.e. the Soviet invasion of 1956: R.P.] (now I'm ashamed to admit it) passed me by and I didn't show the least interest in them.
>
> Now I realised that events were occurring which concerned me directly. Today Sinyavsky and Daniel are on trial, and tomorrow they would try me for something or other or even for nothing at all.[12]

At a mass meeting of the writers with the judge Smirnov, Voynovich felt that the authorities had realised they had made a mistake, given the outcry inside and outside the country over the arrests. Voynovich sent up a note to the praesidium of the meeting with a suggestion that the writers themselves could stand bail for Daniel and Sinyavsky, as there existed the practice of re-educating criminals who were not completely hardened. The response of the establishment writer Mikhalkov from the platform was to throw up his hands in horror and exclaim 'What bail! . . . Thank God we have the KGB to protect us from these Sinyavskys and Daniels!'[13]

12. V. Voynovich, 'Voynovich o sebe', in *The Third Wave* (see note 4), p.140.
13. Ibid, p.141.

A few days later a letter appeared with whose composition Voyno-vich had had nothing to do, but which took up his suggestion. This famous letter was signed by sixty-two writers including Voynovich, but to no avail. Daniel and Sinyavsky were despatched to labour camps. Yet there were no immediate consequences for the signa-tories. However, this letter unleashed a flood of open letters and the government responded by, in Voynovich's words, 'trying to turn back the wheel of history', insisting that Stalin was not such a villain after all. Voynovich signed these new open letters, but since they had no effect, he became disillusioned. In this frame of mind, however, he signed the letter in support of the protesters Ginzburg and Galanskov. This was when Voynovich ran into trouble:

> The Writers' Union issued me with a severe reprimand. I should have had a book come out with a publishing house — but it didn't. My plays which had been running successfully in fifty theatres in the country, the film scripts which were to be used, were banned. Even my song, which had become almost the official anthem of the cosmonauts, which it would be difficult to delete from the Soviet repertoire, was either not sung or sung without reference to the author. Party propagandists disseminated all sorts of slander about me right down to saying that I was connected with foreign intelligence and was a smuggler.[14]

It was at this stage that Voynovich tentatively tried his hand at a different literary genre, in its way age-old, but in Russia in the twentieth century enjoying a new lease of life: the open letter.

> I wrote a letter to the secretariat of the Writers' Union roughly as follows: 'I, the undersigned, together with other writers signed a letter in defence of Ginzburg and Galanskov, considering that they had been wrongly sentenced. Various official personages and organisations, demanding that I remove my signature from this letter, have banned my books, plays, film scripts, songs and separated me from my reader, and deprived me, my family and my children of our daily bread. Well, their argument has convinced me, and so I am removing my signature from the letter in defence of Ginzburg and Galanskov. However, as I can't be certain that the present letter won't cause me new repression, I'm removing my signature from this one too.' I wrote my signature and then crossed it out.
>   I have to confess that I didn't send this letter, but contented myself with reading it to a few close friends.[15]

About a year later there was some movement, and Voynovich's star began to rise a little. There was talk of publishing one of his

14. Ibid, pp.142–3.
15. Ibid, p.143.

books. He published a novella in a 'not very prominent journal' and film studios became interested in his scripts again. However, the renaissance was short-lived. 'Either Kosygin and Podgorny or Kosygin and Polyansky, I don't remember now' saw a play of his at the Soviet Army theatre and the performance was banned. Then the first part of Voynovich's *magnum opus, Private Ivan Chonkin*, was published abroad in the émigré journal *Grani*.

'Seeing that events were taking a menacing turn I wrote a protest to *Grani*, which *Literaturnaya gazeta*, with a few additions of its own, printed.'[16] Voynovich was not imprisoned or expelled from the Writers' Union, but given another severe reprimand and a last warning. His work was banned until the end of 1972. Though to the outside world his situation was quite happy, in fact he was in limbo, blacklisted and his older works being removed from libraries.

> During my countless conversations with the Party and literary bureaucrats 'working me over' [*prorabotat*' is the Russian verb here: R.P.], I realised these people defended the interests of the state and Marxist ideology (in which I personally had never believed) only as a gesture. In actual fact they were malicious and devious cynics who were serving only their own selfish interests and nothing else, and any kind of demagogy they fostered while doing it was only a smoke screen. I decided to behave more cautiously and kept quiet for three years. I conducted myself loyally and did not sign any letters . . . I wrote a book during this time about Vera Figner, the member of the 'People's Will' [a nineteenth-century revolutionary group: R.P.] and continued my work on *Chonkin*, now not doubting that one day I would publish it.[17]

A Degree of Trust (the book about Vera Figner) and a collection of Voynovich's stories were published and it seemed as though the authorities had forgiven him — but he had not forgiven them and anyway: 'I did not want to write about ardent revolutionaries, but about bandy-legged Private Chonkin'.[18]

In 1973 the Soviet Union finally signed the international convention on copyright and seemed to tidy up what hitherto had been a very unsatisfactory state of affairs in publishing. Foreign works had until then been translated and published in the Soviet Union without any royalties having to be paid, or if they were paid, they were generally in roubles to be spent inside the country. Many leading Western writers had been deprived in this fashion: Graham Greene, Kingsley Amis, Michael Frayn. Similarly, Western publishers had

16. Ibid, p.144.
17. Ibid, p.144.
18. Ibid, p.144.

simply pirated Soviet works and felt no obligation to pay the Soviet authors anything. Perhaps more important than the money was the question of misrepresentation, of an author being published when he did not want to be, or in a form of which he disapproved. This issue became a vital one for Solzhenitsyn, for example, who engaged a Swiss lawyer to look after his literary interests in the West while he was still resident in the Soviet Union. Even the Czech writer Milan Kundera, when he was widely acclaimed in Moscow and Prague in the early 1960s, was unable to prevent a bowdlerised version of his play *The Owners of the Keys* running in the Soviet Union.

Clearly the situation did need to be rectified. The Soviet Union signed the Copyright Convention in May 1973, and later that year established VAAP — the All-Union Agency for Copyright. To many of those concerned, this seemed an ominous sign. All foreign publication of Soviet works had to be channelled through VAAP. Did this mean that writers in the Soviet Union who could only be published abroad would now be deprived of even this outlet, if Western publishers took fright at the prospect of litigation?

Given that Voynovich was, in 1972–3, back in good odour, and that his illicit publication abroad had been minimal, he had no motive of self-interest in opposing the new legislation. But his experiences at the hands of literary and political bureaucrats had given him the strong impression that there was more skulduggery than probity in the new copyright law and the establishment of VAAP. Having been, almost despite himself, drawn into the genre of the open letter by the Daniel–Sinyavsky trial and having been stung by the grotesque absurdity that followed it, Voynovich decided on his own open letter.

In writing his open letter of October 1973 on the subject of VAAP, one detects Voynovich's determination to keep open the channels of communication between himself and his reader. This is not quite the commonplace that it sounds, since in his writing one persistently senses the informal, familiar tone of the chance acquaintance, or of the *raconteur*, the teller of anecdotes. Time and again up till now, Voynovich's work had been subject to editorial amendment, to corrective assessment by reviewers, even to *Literaturnaya gazeta*'s additions to a letter he was ordered to write. When he had signed others' open letters he had been designated their author. Now, however, no one was to stand between him and his reader. Having written the letter, Voynovich tells us there came 'perhaps the happiest period in my life'.

Yes, they persecuted me, expelled me from the Writers' Union, my books

were banned again, they badgered [*travili*] me in various ways (sometimes not altogether metaphorically), I was threatened with all sorts of
punishments, my phone was disconnected, crowds of KGB men followed
me around, but I behaved as I wanted to, and wrote what I liked. I have
sometimes been called a fighter for freedom, but that's not correct. I
wasn't fighting for freedom, I was enjoying it. And freedom is the greatest
gift which a man can possess and to exchange it for the worthless
handouts which the bosses of Soviet literature can offer, from a trip to a
house of creativity to, at best, some Lenin prize, is simply stupid and
wasteful.[19]

In his address to the Los Angeles conference Voynovich records
that his next seven years were difficult ones but at least he lived them
according to his conscience. In the end though there was a limit to a
man's strength, he tells us.

The late 1970s were indeed a miserable time for many Soviet
writers, with political détente abroad, but ideological rigidity and
cultural cold war at home. Yet Voynovich enjoyed an inner freedom,
which allowed him to write more of what he liked. He was expelled
from the Writers' Union in February 1974, writing a satirical letter
to the Moscow Branch of the Writers' Union in response to a
summons to appear (and to be duly expelled). 'I will not come to
your meeting, because it will take place behind closed doors and in
secret from the public, that is, illegally, and I do not wish to take
part in any illegal activities'.[20] His fellow-writer Vladimir Kornilov
was expelled from the Writers' Union in March 1977. Vladimov
resigned from the Writers' Union. All the time pressure was growing
on Voynovich, and, now finding himself *persona non grata* in his own
country, he felt no compunction about expressing overt support for
civil rights campaigners. His own 'dissidence' was brought into
sharp focus by the publication in Paris of the first two parts of
Chonkin in 1975. There were two interviews with KGB agents in
May of that year, during the second of which the writer was
threatened with sudden death, and after which he was seriously ill
for several days. He was convinced he had been given a poisoned
cigarette during the meeting.[21]

One of the greatest acts of intimidation of the late 1970s visited on
the intelligentsia was the murder of Konstantin Bogatyrov, the
translator. Bogatyrov was widely known in literary circles in the
Soviet Union and abroad, especially in Germany. His father, a

19. Ibid, p.145.
20. Voynovich, *Putyom*, p.249.
21. See *Index on Censorship*, 1975, Vol.4, No.3, p.89. *The Sunday Times*, 29 June 1975,
    p.6; and Yu. Maltsev, *Volnaya russkaya literatura*, Possev, Frankfurt, 1976, p.352.

leading expert on Czech and Slovak folklore was the Russian translator of Hašek's *The Good Soldier Švejk*. 'Kostya' Bogatyryov translated Rilke into Russian, was well acquainted with Lev Kopelev, the prominent memoirist and scholar of German literature, and he was also a friend of Heinrich Böll. In April 1976 he was attacked outside his flat one evening and later died of his injuries. He was buried on 20 June 1976. Lidiya Chukovskaya's account of his death[22] includes some illuminating remarks on Voynovich and endorses the truism that comedy is a serious business. At the burial, which was attended among others by Andrei Sakharov, 'only Voynovich mastered his grief by his anger, and in expressing his sorrow over the loss, answered with anger the insult which had been dealt to him and friends'. Chukovskaya was grateful that Voynovich accentuated 'we' in his funeral address, and she went on: 'Was it true that the intelligentsia really did still exist? That it had not all died out, been put in prison or was abroad?'

Disgraceful acts of harassment were perpetrated on Voynovich and his family. In 1976 his telephone was cut off. In 1978 his father was taken to a police station and told his son was missing, believed dead. Shortly afterwards his mother died, having been fed the same false information. In early 1980 he was told he would be allowed to emigrate. All sorts of delays and backtracking ensued, during which he had several heart attacks, his parents-in-law died, the mother of heart trouble, the father the same day at the shock of the news.[23] Finally, the authorities honoured their promise to let him leave, and he and his wife and daughter moved to West Germany in December 1980. At customs there was an incident which so typically summed up Voynovich's fate. As a condition of his leaving he had insisted on permission to bring all his books with him. According to the samizdat *Chronicle of Current Events* (*Khronika tekushchikh sobytiy*) the customs officials confiscated a copy of *A Degree of Trust* (the most conformist of the writer's books).[24] He insisted that the work be returned, or at least handed over to the friends who had accompanied him, and eventually the authorities did so. Voynovich's own version of the incident is rather different: at Sheremetevo airport he was asked to sign a form acknowledging the confiscation of a manuscript, which

---

22. L. Chukovskaya, *Protsess isklyucheniya*, YMCA, Paris, 1979, pp.171–82. See also: W. Kasack (ed.), *Poet-perevodchik Konstantin Bogatyryov*, Otto Sagner, Munich, 1982.
23. B. Levin, 'The Tragedy of Comrade Voinovich', *The Times*, 23 December 1980, p.10.
24. *Chronicle of Current Events* No.60, 31 December 1980, Amnesty International Publications, p.82.

he thought was a discarded chapter intended for an earlier book and which he had probably already sent abroad. He created a scene, refused to leave, and the faded manuscript was then returned to him.[25]

Ostensibly Voynovich was in the West as a visitor for a year, but in July 1981 he was duly stripped of his Soviet citizenship, and joined, willy-nilly, the third emigration.[26]

Novyy mir's Unknown Soldier

In the early 1960s, Voynovich was a popular and respected Soviet writer. In the heady days of 1963 *Novyy mir* happily proclaimed that it proposed to publish in 1964 his 'novella *The Life of Private Ivan Chonkin*' which was about 'the warriors [*voiny*] of the Soviet Army'.[27] No doubt Voynovich would have enjoyed the unintended irony in this statement, and in his work being listed next to 'The memoirs of the General of the Army, A. Gorbatov'. The Soviet reader is still waiting for the official publication of Voynovich's masterpiece, whereas A. V. Gorbatov, 'of peasant origin, defender of Soviet Power after the October Revolution, illegally repressed in the 1930s, rehabilitated, one of the Russian commandants in Berlin', did indeed have large extracts of his memoirs published in *Novyy mir* in 1964.[28]

Bearing in mind Voynovich's view that the formative years of a writer's life are childhood and youth and that these provide enough material for later years, clearly his stint in the armed services has been of crucial importance. Voynovich's military service lasted from 1951 to 1955, during which time he was stationed in Poland. In addition to *Chonkin* the following stories are concerned directly with army life and the Second World War: *Putyom vzaimnoy perepiski* ('By Means of Mutual Correspondence'), *V krugu druzey* ('In a Circle of Friends'), and four autobiographical pieces: *Uncle Volodya, Major Dogadkin, Captain Kurasov* and *Lieutenant Pavlenko*.

Discipline and authoritarianism, those pillars of military life, beget their own antibodies. At the age of twenty-two Voynovich decided to become a writer and to start by writing his memoirs — so he tells us in a short preface to his autobiographical pieces.[29] Such

25. V. Voynovich, *Antisovetskiy Sovetskiy Soyuz*, Ardis, Ann Arbor, Mich., 1985, pp.175–9.
26. 'Soviet Satirist loses Citizenship', *The Times*, 18 July 1981, p.5.
27. *Novyy mir*, 1963, No.10, p.286.
28. *Novyy mir*, 1964, No.3, pp.133–56; No.4, pp.99–138; No.5, pp.106–53.
29. Voynovich, *Putyom*, p.193.

an attitude denotes confidence and even impudence. If one considers
the enormous amount of Soviet literature devoted to war memoirs —
for example those of Gorbatov as cited above — and the reverence
with which the war effort is viewed, Voynovich's effrontery is breath-
taking. There is, in fact, a surfeit of material on the war theme in
Soviet literature and an enormous deficit of literature about ordinary military life, of the role of the Soviet military in peace time. The
prose works of Vladimir Kornilov, who was expelled from the
Writers' Union in March 1977 and subjected to harassment similar
to that meted out to Voynovich, gives glimpses of military life in
peace time, following Stalin's death in particular, so unorthodox as
to ensure publication only abroad.[30]

Voynovich has expressed special admiration for Vasiliy Grossman,[31]
whose major work *Life and Fate*, had until 1987–8 appeared only
abroad and a long time after his death. It is interesting that this
work should capture Voynovich's imagination, because it is utterly
in the style of traditional, realistic prose and deals head on with the
Second World War, particularly the battle of Stalingrad. It has none
of the lightness or irreverence of Voynovich's work and might more
easily be compared with the epics of Tolstoy or Solzhenitsyn. It
depicts in stark terms the dark side of the Russian war effort, the
debilitating machinations of the security forces, the careerism and
selfishness of the high command, and in particular the novel puts
over the idea that Stalin's victory meant also the victory of Russian
nationalism with all the consequences that that entailed for the
non-Russian victors, primarily the Jews.

Voynovich's regard for such serious treatment of the war theme
helps one gauge the seriousness of his own comic writing. It may
well be the case that the theme of the Second World War is
'inexhaustible', as a hack writer in Solzhenitsyn's *The First Circle*
puts it, but what is dead from exhaustion is the routine glorification
of the Soviet war effort, regardless of whatever moral ambiguity may
have been present among individuals and whole sections of Soviet
society. Certainly since Stalin, several prominent writers, such as
Yuriy Bondarev, Bulat Okudzhava and Vasil Bykov, have drawn
attention to genuine moral dilemmas generated by the war. However, no one until Voynovich had ever gone in for a wholesale
debunking of the Soviet war effort, of depicting Russia more at war
with herself than with the Germans, of making mock of heroic

---

30. Chukovskaya, *Protsess isklyucheniya* p. 182. See, for example, Kornilov's novel
Demobilizatsiya, Possev, Frankfurt, 1976.
31. Voynovich, *Antisovetskiy Sovetskiy Soyuz*, pp.201–4.

individuals and, more pointedly, of the historical process itself.

Voynovich's autobiographical pieces are disappointing, but they do give us a disconcertingly fresh picture of life in the Red Army, with all the absurdities and conflicts generally associated with military life anywhere. Voynovich and his comrades-in-arms emerge as a difficult and insubordinate bunch with little regard for the lofty ideals propagated *ad nauseam* by the authorities. Of rather more interest to an understanding of *Chonkin* are the two short stories 'In a Circle of Friends' and 'By Means of Mutual Correspondence', both of which could have been incorporated into the fabric of *Chonkin* with little difficulty. The theme of both stories is power.

One way of measuring the impact of 'In a Circle of Friends' is to compare it with the official version of the events in the Kremlin on the night that Hitler launched operation Barbarossa. Aleksandr Chakovsky's mammoth novel *Blockade* (1968–73) attempts an 'objective' view of Stalin, pointing to his weaknesses as well as his strengths, emphasising the corporate strength of the Party and the people, over mere individuals. That Stalin was guilty of certain 'excesses' was true, but the Party itself had been the first to highlight this fact after his death. Likewise, in the run-up to the war in some ways Stalin was prepared; in other ways his arrogance had led to blindness. He went into a state of shock for some days when the Germans invaded, but the machinery of government ran smoothly until he re-emerged, once again the man of steel, and now the generalissimo.[32]

'In a Circle of Friends' (1968) could hardly be a more piquant response to such a view. Dubbed by the author, in a typically self-deprecating way, 'a not very authentic story' and bearing a disclaimer at the end about any similarities with real persons being purely fortuitous, the work explodes many of the official myths about Stalin — going to grotesque extremes to do so. Officially sponsored myths have left intellectuals so sceptical in the Soviet Union that there is a tendency to 'over-compensate' and always assume that the opposite of what the propaganda machine turns out must be true. Voynovich mocks this phenomenon too. In his story even Stalin's moustache and pipe are fake, as well as the solitary lit window in the Kremlin, the sign to passers-by that the great man works on while his people rest.

Stalin is only happy when he too can shed the outer trappings of power: 'He loved this room where he could be himself: not have to

---

32. See M. Crouch and R. Porter, *Understanding Soviet Politics through Literature*, Allen and Unwin, London, 1984, pp.43–54.

smoke a pipe, nor wear a moustache, but just live simply and modestly'.[33] As elsewhere in Voynovich, we see that simple, authentic life is a surer road to happiness.

Few tyrants in history can have been depicted in fiction more frequently than Stalin. In Russia the fictional Stalins fall readily into two categories: the officially sponsored portraits which engulfed every art form in the Soviet Union throughout the reign, and the dissenting pictures of Stalin, which actually began to appear before the cult of personality really got under way. The most famous of these include Osip Mandelshtam's poem of November 1933 (Stalin's 'grub-like fingers and cockroach whiskers'); but, interestingly, one of the earliest examples occurs in Pilnyak's *Story of the Unextinguished Moon*, published in 1926. On the whole the dissenting portrayals veer towards the monstrous or grotesque, though there are more straightforwardly realistic depictions (e.g. in Victor Serge's *The Case of Comrade Tulayev*). In recent times we have, in addition to Voynovich's work, Solzhenitsyn's *The First Circle* (1968), A. Zinoviev's *The Yawning Heights* (1976) and A. Gladilin's *Rehearsal on Friday* (1978). Solzhenitsyn's novel is a work very much in the realistic tradition, yet, in the opinion of many, flawed by the caricature portrait of Stalin. It seems difficult for the Soviet dissident to depict Stalin in anything other than grotesque terms. Anatoliy Rybakov's novel *Children of the Arbat* does attempt a realistic but thoroughly negative portrait of the dictator.

'In a Circle of Friends' relishes the monstrous. All the characters have warped names: Molotov becomes Molokov ('Hammer' becomes 'Milk'). Adolf (Hitler) becomes Adik ('Little Hell'). Khrushchev is Borshchev ('Cabbage Soup'), Zhdanov is Zhbanov ('Jug') and so on. People are turned into objects and diminutivised. The purpose of this is not simply 'knock-about' comedy, but rather to disrupt the value system created by tyranny. People lose their names and their identities. Incidents lose their scale of importance. The night is first of all taken up with Koba — Voynovich prefers to use Stalin's pre-Revolutionary alias in this story — trying to solve a crossword. He terrifies a leading academic into providing him with the answer to a clue, and such triviality is placed on a par with the outbreak of a world war. As power advances, reality recedes and the real becomes the chimeric. The 'circle of friends' in fact turns out to be one of enemies, far more suspicious and fearful of one another than they are of the enemy.

The disunity between the characters goes much further, since it

33. Voynovich, *Putyom*, p.166.

emerges that Stalin is divided against himself. He confronts himself in a mirror and shoots his own image. Given this degree of dislocation there can hardly be any unity within the Party or between Party and People as, say, Chakovsky would have his readers believe. The minor figures in Voynovich are often highly significant, and this is so with the old woman who waits on Stalin. He can fool himself that he has sympathy for the people in providing her with a voucher for millet and butter, but he does not know that she will sell the piece of paper with his autograph for a fortune. The whole comic episode illustrates again the social disunity and the lack of mutual comprehension engendered by power.

'By Means of Mutual Correspondence' depicts the exercise of power in a minor way of one individual over another, an exercise of power that becomes possible because human communication is so poor. Letter-writing plays a vital role in Voynovich's work. Thanks to him and several other Russian writers, the open letter has become once again an art form. The conventional, private letter becomes in Voynovich's fiction a springboard for pomp and fantasy, for self-delusion and calculated deception. The act of writing in Voynovich is fraught with danger, and actions always speak truer than words. The hero of 'By Means of Mutual Correspondence', Ivan Altynnik, a junior sergeant, gives free rein to his imagination in replying to 'lonely hearts'. 'It would not be just to say that Altynnik lied, he merely gave his hand its freedom, knowing that it would not let him down.'[34] As it happens, his epistolary talents embroil him with Lyudmila Syrova, whom he marries after she has plied him with drink and slept with him; then later he has to cohabit with her, having fathered her child. The closing scenes of the story show Lyudmila to be a violent and uncouth wife, belabouring her downtrodden husband. The story is a highly comic illustration of the unpredictable power of the written word to change people's lives. Altynnik the manipulator is hoist with his own petard.

'In a Circle of Friends' and 'By Means of Mutual Correspondence' demonstrate that, all its instability notwithstanding, fiction can be the only effective antidote to wanton power. The narrator of the latter story makes an entry at the end to record Altynnik's downfall and thus triumphs in his story-telling over the hero and his letter-writing. At his most optimistic Solzhenitsyn declared in his Nobel Lecture: 'Lies can prevail against much in the world, but never against art. And no sooner will the lies be dispersed than the repulsive nakedness of violence will be exposed — and age-old

34. Ibid, p.98.

violence will topple in defeat.'[35]

Solzhenitsyn's only weakness (and a constituent of his great strength) as a writer has been that he has a limited sense of humour and no degree of self-scepticism. Other well-meaning, disaffected writers coming from the Soviet Union could find Solzhenitsyn, as well as the Soviet establishment, a butt for some of their criticisms (witness Zinoviev, Limonov, and Voynovich himself in *Moscow 2042*). Voynovich's display of a literary *persona*, a device as old at least as Chaucer, and intriguingly back in fashion in the twentieth century, makes him ultimately less vulnerable than some utterers of a *prima facie* truth. *Chonkin* has some profound truths in it. The comedy of the work gives those truths armour-plating.

'The future of Russian literature, if it is destined to *have* a future, is being nourished by jokes [*anekdoty*], just as Pushkin grew up imbibing the tales his nanny told him. The joke is a pure demonstration of the miracle of art, which thrives on the savagery and rage of dictators . . .'[36] Thus Sinyavsky. Voynovich dubs his *magnum opus* 'a novel-joke' (*roman-anekdot*) which rather understates the powerful jolt that the work gives one, even on a superficial reading; it also demonstrates exactly Sinyavsky's contention. As we have seen, after the first part of the book was published in Paris in 1975, the author's life was endangered. Clearly the book had aroused the 'rage of dictators'. At the time Voynovich wrote to the KGB: 'Murder too is no mean estimate of a writer's works — I am not afraid of threats, Private Chonkin will avenge me.'[37]

At first sight Chonkin hardly seems to be the sort of character to avenge anyone. But his qualities have attracted Voynovich repeatedly and work as the most effective antidote to the evil he sees around him. These qualities, for the sake of convenience, may be called collectively 'innocence', though they comprise elements of the Tolstoyan 'simple-hearted man' (*prostoy chelovek*), the 'Ivan the Fool' or 'village idiot' (*Ivan-* or *Vanya-durachok*) of folk tales, and an instinctive moral awareness, unashamedly devoid of intellectual basis. The possessor of 'innocence' is usually a simpleton, by no means at odds with the system, but always a thorn in its side, because of his ostensible incompetence. It is not that he does not want to, he simply cannot. In this, he differs from the more notorious — under-

35. J. Dunlop, et al. (eds), *Aleksandr Solzhenitsyn: Critical Essays and Documentary Materials*, 2nd edn, Collier Macmillan, London, 1975, p.575.
36. A. Sinyavsky, 'Literaturnyy protsess v Rossiyi', *Kontinent*, 1974, No. 1, pp.143–224, p.166.
37. Maltsev, *Volnaya russkaya literatura*, p.352.

ground — men of Soviet literature like Yuriy Olesha's Kavalerov and Yevgeniy Zamyatin's D–503, who consciously set themselves up in opposition to the establishment, and in this, he would seem to be rather a phenomenon of post-1945 Russian literature, than of Soviet literature as a whole.

Voynovich's predilection for 'innocence' in his characters can be traced back to some of the stories he published in *Novyy mir* in the 1960s. 'We Live Here' opens with a *Vanya-durachok*. In 'At a Distance of Half a Kilometre' one reads 'Nikolai had one peculiarity. He gave human names to things he made himself and he spoke to them. He chose their names to harmonise with the names of the product'.[38] Thus a box (*yashchik*) is called Yasha and so on. Timofei, in the same story, has the reputation of being a book reader (i.e. an 'intellectual', a dubious phenomenon in Voynovich) and, in recounting to Nikolai Tolstoy's views of Chekhov and Shakespeare, says:

> 'Shakespeare — he was an English writer.'
> 'And he wrote badly?'
> 'Not so much badly — more illiterately. In our language, of course, we corrected him, but in his own he was on the weak side.'[39]

If a character in Voynovich acquires nothing but 'base authority from other people's books' he is hardly to be relied on.

In *Chonkin* there is the author's 'assumed innocence', which operates through the mode of narration, and the natural innocence of most of the main characters, which manifests itself in their various reactions to events. The two kinds support each other, and clear the ground of established myths and stereotypes for authentic existence. In this way the novel is truly subversive to any society. If it were to be read simply as a satire on peasant backwardness, the shortcomings of collectivisation, and Russia's unpreparedness for war in 1941, it might just be accommodated, as the satirists Ilf and Petrov have been; but even if it were published officially in the Soviet Union, attempts to assess it using conventional Soviet literary criticism would fail, as orthodox Soviet criticism has in some measure failed to come to terms with that other comic gem, *The Master and Margarita*.

The full title of the novel *The Life and Extraordinary Adventures of Private Ivan Chonkin*, and *Pretendent na prestol (Pretender to the Throne)* suggests an episodic, picaresque novel, and the book has been, justifiably, compared with Hašek's *Good Soldier Švejk*. The émigré

---

38. *Novyy mir*, 1963, No.2, p.191.
39. Ibid, p.196.

critic Yuriy Maltsev[40] feels that the comparison goes no further than the titles, and while one might disagree with such a bald dismissal, there are important differences. Unlike *Švejk*, *Chonkin* is not repetitious or episodic. It has a strong plot-line throughout; the initial event — the crash-landing of an aeroplane — animates all the characters throughout. In one sense, the characters, particularly the hero, have a ring of authenticity about them, being self-sufficient and familiar. Chonkin himself, the military drop-out, has a long literary pedigree. Minor characters like Baba Dunya and Ninka are the stock-in-trade of village life. Golubyov, the harassed book-cooking chairman of the collective farm is a type common enough to be known to everyone, and easily enough presented as an aberration rather than an everyday and inevitable phenomenon, to be ridiculed in the pages of the Soviet satirical magazine *Krokodil*. On several occasions the novel is deliberately derivative. The first exchanges between the pilot of the plane and the collective farm chairman parallel closely the conversation between the mayor and Khlestakov in Gogol's *The Government Inspector*. When rumours start to circulate about Chonkin and his band, one is reminded of the rumours surrounding Chichikov in *Dead Souls* and the legend of Captain Kopeykin. When Chonkin is arrested Nyura runs from office to office and all the bureaucrats she encounters blur into one 'personage' (*litso*), hardly different from the one that Akakiy Akakiyevich in *The Overcoat* had to deal with. Frequently metaphors gain the ascendancy over facts, as in Gogol.

The author constantly interrupts his strong plot-line with digressions and interjections: by appealing to the reader not to read on if he is irritated, by apologising for his characters when they refuse to submit to any external authority, even their creator's. In his very first chapter the author asks us not to read what must surely be one of the most readable novels of recent times:

> As for me, I got together all that I'd heard of the matter in hand, added a thing or two myself, perhaps even more than I'd heard. Anyway, this story struck me as so amusing that I decided to put it down in writing, but if you think it's not interesting, or boring or even stupid, then just spit and pretend I haven't told you anything at all.[41]

If the reader objects to the author's unedifying hero then there is an answer:

---

40. Maltsev, *Volnaya russkaya literatura*, p.347.
41. V. Voynovich, *Zhizn' i neobychaynyye priklyucheniya soldata Ivana Chonkina* (hereafter *Chonkin* I) YMCA, Paris, 1975, p.5.

I'll have to admit that I haven't seen him anywhere, I thought him up in my own head and not as a good example for people, but simply because I had nothing else to do . . . Couldn't the author have taken a real, noble warrior from life, a tall, fine figure, a disciplined paragon of scientifico-military and political background? I could have, of course, but I didn't get a chance. All the paragons got grabbed first and I was left with Chonkin. At first I was upset but I came to terms with it. You see a hero of a book is like a baby — whatever way he turns out, that's what he is, and you're not going to chuck him out the window. Maybe other people have got better, cleverer babies, but yours is dearer to you than all them, just because he's yours.'[42]

The author creates situations which the characters fail to see the relevance or importance of. The very first chapter is built on a series of digressions and misunderstandings. Being literate, Nyura knows that superstitions are just remnants of the dark past, therefore she tries not to believe in the 'iron bird' that has just landed by her vegetable garden. Borka the pig is digging in the ground and there is nothing supernatural in that, as she tells herself. But there is nothing particularly logical or scientific about it either, since he digs whether he has found a suitable place or not. Christianity seems to be the best way out of her predicament, but she cannot make the sign of the cross lying on her stomach. Nyura finds it difficult to take in this piece of modern technology, even when she does realise what it is — she uses the word *aeroplan* instead of the modern *samolyot*.

Moreover, understanding what it is in abstract terms hardly helps the locals communicate with the pilot. Plechevoy 'was not surprised, not afraid',[43] and launches into a long diatribe on the history of the name of the village and its environs. The women take a lively interest in the pilot's clothing. The collective farm chairman is not surprised at the plane's arrival, it is the long-expected and feared *inspektsiya* or *reviziya*. The banalities concerning pregnancy, the brewing of *samogon* (home-distilled liquor), the machine-tractor-station (MTS), all crowd out the one fact that should, by the laws of historical determinism and the consensus of orthodox Soviet litera-ture, be absolutely central — the year is 1941. The pilot, by his status in Soviet society, should enlighten and direct the *kolkhozniki*, but he lapses into embarrassed speechlessness. The locals might all be dismissed as variously ignorant, superstitious, cowardly, im-pressionable, or pushy; but their common trait is spontaneity. Casting aside all preconceived notions, be they from the dark, superstitious past or the new, scientific present, they confound the

42. *Chonkin* I, p.21.
43. Ibid, p.7.

newcomer by their very naturalness. This first chapter then gives the first round to 'the people' (the *narod*) who, as Golubyov with fine unwitting irony and truth tells us, 'see everything and know everything'.[44]

Chapter II simply reverses the situation. Chonkin, the peasant, is defeated by the unnatural life he is forced to lead in the army. Once he is slotted back in where he belongs, the illusions, the false fabric of social life, collapse and the *narod* really comes into its own. 'With the sort of folk who live here — they don't even lock up their huts' Nyura tells him to his surprise,[45] and once in the village, Chonkin is able to give full vent to his instinctive morality and his intuitive sense of duty, which depend on his day-to-day existence rather than on an artificially constructed hierarchy. Without any external stimuli, he becomes an efficient farmer, a good husband, even something of a sensible businessman and, most astonishingly, a fine soldier. None of these activities involves him assuming a one-dimensional role; he simply takes events as they come and reacts in much the same way as the peasant women reacted when they saw their first airman. It is important to note that he flouts not just Soviet conventions, but all social conventions. While Nyura goes out to work, he stays at home to do the cooking and cleaning; and in his spare time he takes up embroidery. In this remote village with the singularly inappropriate name of Krasnoye (meaning 'red' or historically 'beautiful'), Chonkin becomes a total human being, liked, loved, feared, respected by others — not simply written off as an incompetent and unwilling army recruit, as he was before.

At the same time, he preserves all the weaknesses and inconsistencies of the human kind. Stereotypes are impossible to achieve because they are illusory, absolute and passive. By contrast, Ivan Chonkin's versatility involves the use of salty language, occasional laxity in doing the cooking, getting drunk on *samogon* and sometimes falling out with his friends and loved one. As much as anyone else, he is prey to gossip and jealousy. Like the good soldier Švejk, his only constants are his amiability and his talent for survival.

One of the most salient features of Chonkin's make-up, and something that gives the novel as a whole a wider perspective, is the occasional dream sequences. Chonkin's dreams define the tensions in the hero's psychology; they also allow the author to indulge in blatant ridicule of Soviet sacred cows — Stalin appears as a transvestite, human beings are turned into animals. However, the dreams

44. Ibid, p.14.
45. Ibid, p.48.

go far beyond this. It is clear that most of the protagonists are constrained by officially sponsored illusions. Golubyov is trapped by an economic system that just does not seem to work, Milyaga is in pursuit of a band of cut-throats that does not exist, and more than all the others Gladyshev is shaped entirely by a bogus scientific ambition; it is in the nature of things that he, misguided by a spurious example imposed from above, should eventually clash with Chonkin, who has managed to liberate himself and achieve total inner integrity and self-realisation.

Gladyshev's experiments with *Puks* (an acronym meaning literally 'the path to Socialism'), the hybrid potato-cum-tomato plant, and with various types of excrement, are a transparent parody of Lysenko's scientific activities, which held back the science of genetics in the Soviet Union for perhaps three decades. At the same time, Lysenko had something of a popular following and was undoubtedly effective on the practical level in agriculture, particularly in the war years.[46] Gladyshev is likewise revered by the locals, and at first Chonkin befriends him.

Chonkin's dreams stand in opposition to the illusions that already exist. They provide a counterweight to them and hint at a fundamental philosophical objection to them. In his waking moments they provide harmless escape from boredom (usually induced by political indoctrination classes); in his sleep they annihilate all the laws of nature.

In the first dream[47] a horse tows the aeroplane across the sky, and Yartsev, the political instructor, turns into a beetle and then back into a human again. Trofimovich becomes a horse and paws the ground. Just before he wakes up, Chonkin is about to be shot for desertion, having spent most of the dream trying futilely to catch the aeroplane. In Chonkin's second dream[48] Plechevoy takes Chonkin to Nyura's wedding, where the guests turn into pigs and the hero is forced to grunt like a pig, and even made to enjoy grunting like a pig. The guests are served human flesh (*chelovechina*)! Chonkin's waking meditations are at worst harmless, at best, suffused with charming, benign nonsense: it's usually warm in summer and cold in winter; if it were the other way round summer would be called winter and

---

46. See Zh. Medvedev, *The Rise and Fall of T. D. Lysenko*, Columbia University Press, New York, NY, 1969. Though Lysenko is the most obvious target here, Voynovich's satire is hardly original. There are similar experiments and activities to be found in Swift (*Gulliver's Travels* Pt.III Ch.5) and Rabelais (*Gargantua and Pantagruel*, Bk. V. Ch.XXII). I am grateful to Margaret Hardwidge for drawing this to my attention.
47. *Chonkin* I, pp.50–2.
48. Ibid, pp.88–99.

winter summer.[49] His dreams proper may take on the semi-harrowing, semi-humorous world of Kafka, but they are kept firmly in their place and the hero always wakes up in time to be saved. Yet these innocent fantasies form a definite system of cross-references with the real world that Chonkin has entered on arriving in Krasnoye, and the two spheres tend to validate each other. In this way man gains at least as much as he loses by being repeatedly compared with animals.

In *Cancer Ward* Solzhenitsyn uses the world of animals in the zoo scene as an allegory of man's various qualities, life styles and moral standing. Earlier in the novel, Shulubin has mentioned Kropotkin's *Mutual Aid*, a work designed to refute Darwin and to point out that man can learn from the example that higher animals give us in the way they offer each other mutual aid. In Voynovich's work there is not a trace of didacticism, but the same notion is nonetheless there. Until she meets Chonkin, Nyura's relations with other people have been unsuccessful in the extreme, but there are compensations:

> Loneliness had made a special mark on Nyura. Take for instance her relations with the cattle. With other people a cow, say — is just a cow. You feed it, milk it, herd it, and that's all there is to it. But Nyura really fussed over her cow, washed it, picked the thorns out of its hide. And spoke kindly to it, as if to another person, and shared and shared alike with it if there was anything tasty to be had (sometimes a lump of sugar, sometimes a pasty), and likewise the cow treated her as one person treated another. When they drove the herd into the village it would break away and run home as fast as its legs would carry it — homesick, you see. . .
>
> And Borka the pig was always running after Nyura like a dog . . . Nyura had nursed him like a baby . . . And so he too lived with Nyura instead of a dog, skinny, dirty, running around the yard, chasing the chickens, following Nyura when she went to the post office, and going to meet her when she came back . . .
>
> Even the chickens weren't like other people's . . . One would perch on her shoulder, another on her head, as if roosting, stock-still. Because of this a lot of people in the village took the mickey out of Nyura; still, she never took offence, but kept thinking that if some man were to come her way, maybe ugly, or not too bright, as long as he was a good man and treated her well, she'd return the compliment and open up her whole heart to him.[50]

Here the equation between man and animal is made in a sentimental way, but it frequently occurs in a humorous or mildly ironic

49. Ibid, pp.26–7.
50. Ibid, pp.44–5.

guise. It is Borka the pig who wakes Chonkin up from his second dream and thus saves him from Stalin's clutches. When war is declared and the villagers are fighting in the market place, brigadier Taldykin, not for a moment suspecting the irony of his statement, shouts 'This isn't a menagerie'.[51] Predictably, Gladyshev's experimental plants meet their end because of the most basic and vital of actions: eating. Chonkin says ' . . . you know yourself, a cow isn't a human being, it can't reason out in its head what's yours and what's somebody else's, if it sees something green then it eats it'.[52] Again the irony is that neither can the human beings decide on who owns what, since they have just caused a minor riot over hoarding salt and soap. When the security man Svintsov is 'wounded', he is pitied as one would pity a wounded animal.[53]

Whilst both men and animals seem totally indiscriminate in their moral choices, it is significant that the only characters to be actually hurt by the animals' actions are those furthest from the authentic life of the village. The Christian ethic that man can choose morally and animals, not having a soul, cannot is hardly stated in positive terms; on the two occasions when a Christian gesture is contemplated Nyura is unable to implement it, and Gladyshev's crossing himself comes through more as a final capitulation of his rationalism than as new-found faith.[54] The moral message, if any, is rather that one should discover one's own authentic existence first and then morality will naturally fall into place. All the moral lectures that the army and the media hand out are totally irrelevant; rather than nurture popular morality, they tend to destroy it. 'With the sort of folk who live here — they don't even lock up the huts' says Nyura, but her words convey more truth at the start of the story than they do at the end.

The newspaper editor Yermolkin could hardly be further removed from real life. He has not been home for so long he thinks his son is still three years old, when in fact he has just been called up. He has forgotten the way to his own home and passes through a so-called rogues' market (*khitryy rynok*), populated by tricksters and prostitutes. The narrative here takes on an overtly Kafkaesque quality — the news hound finds himself in a disorientating and unfamiliar world; he is almost in a trance and has lost all sense of reality.[55] Yet

51. Ibid, p.123.
52. Ibid, p.171.
53. Ibid, p.209.
54. Ibid, p.287.
55. V. Voynovich, *Pretendent na prestol: Novyye priklyucheniya soldata Ivana Chonkina*, YMCA, Paris, 1979 (hereafter *Chonkin* II), pp.76–83.

the reader knows this is the real world, and that Yermolkin, in debasing the Russian language and publishing highly selectively, has been under an illusion. The old Jew called Stalin sells him a horoscope warning him against horses. As it turns out nothing could be more prophetic. Firstly, Yermolkin allows the only professional mistake of his life, a misprint in his newspaper which has Stalin as a 'gelding' (*merin* — the Russian word has connotations of stupidity and mendacity), instead of a criterion (*merilo*).[56] Later on, Yermolkin is knocked down by a coffin containing a horse's bones and this precipitates the disintegration of his identity, and his death. In the hilariously confused circumstances of the state-sponsored funeral of what is supposed to be a national hero, the newspaper editor imagines he is a foal, and he pleads for his mother just before he expires.[57]

The morality exuded by man in his natural state, when he is animal-like, stripped of abstract theories and superimposed moral norms (often depicted in the novel as norms of etiquette rather than virtue), is at the centre of Chonkin's innocence. Any attempts to categorise, generalise, or attribute this quality are severely censured. When Golubyov and Chonkin get drunk on *samogon* they both end up crawling around on all fours.

> 'Jean-Jacques Rousseau said that man should get down on all fours and go back to nature.'
> 'And who's this Jean-Jacques?' asked Chonkin, struggling over the peculiar name.
> 'Sod only knows. Some Frenchman or other.'[58]

The attempt by Gladyshev to differentiate between man and beast not only fails, but works directly in favour of the innocent and to the detriment of the abstract thinker. Gladyshev tries to instil some crude Darwinism in Chonkin by explaining that toil turned the monkey into man. It takes Chonkin some time to voice his objection, but when he does Gladyshev is found to fall back on popular oaths rather than enlightened debate. Chonkin argues that the horse works more than the monkey and therefore he should be the true ancestor of man.

---

56. *Chonkin* II, p.88. The incident is based on fact. During and after the war Stalin was always referred to as *glavnokomanduyushchiy* (Commander-in-Chief). Voynovich knew of one editor who committed suicide when the 'l' was omitted in one edition of his newspaper, making Stalin out to be a 'shit-commander'. *Antisovetskiy Sovetskiy Soyuz*, p.214.
57. *Chonkin* II, p.248.
58. *Chonkin* I, p.239.

Gladyshev's rationalism fails to make headway with Chonkin; but Chonkin's wild, unbridled dreams infect the village scientist, and bridge the remaining gap between innocent, benign fantasy and the destructive illusions of rationalism. Gladyshev's horse visits him in a dream, having achieved human status through toil; he now has human ambitions of going to Moscow, yet retains his moral superiority — he cannot fight for either the Germans or the Russians since he still has hooves and cannot pull a trigger. Later on Gladyshev finds the horse's shoe, the horse runs away and is killed. When Gladyshev finds one Lieutenant Bukashin's note, 'If I perish, I wish to be considered a communist', by the carcase, he abandons rationalism entirely and attributes this plea to the horse. Thus the 'real' world of Krasnoye with its man-made illusions and neurotic bigwigs is ousted by the sweet, innocent dream-world of Chonkin, with its natural morality. The clearest example of this process is the funeral, where even in death the horse destroys a self-deluding biped.

Chonkin's triumph by proxy over Gladyshev still leaves a great many square pegs in round holes. There are a number of passages where a natural rhythm and order predominate, where characters are at one with their environment and situation, and any implicit violence in the air is as nothing compared to the uproarious scenes of psychological and physical conflict — one recalls the evening scene where war is announced on the radio while Chonkin's attention is turned more to the snatches of popular song, accordion-playing, and domestic altercation;[59] all this occurs immediately after his row with Nyura. However, these scenes of serenity are rare. Voynovich's business is more with the nature of social conflict and its causes. There seems to be a contrast between the authority of spontaneous human response which persists in confounding the system, and the naked power of this system, which operates without any authority, through a rigid hierarchy and a gradation of threats and sanctions. Sergeant-major Peskov can write to his fiancée about the advantages of military life, drawing analogies with bringing up children and pointing to the perils of capitalist encirclement, and yet the main thrust of his letter is that in the army you have more subordinates than in a factory and you have them for twenty-four hours a day. This conclusion is reached by his being able to make Chonkin's life a misery; but he does not get a chance to finish his letter, as a second-lieutenant comes in at that point to make his life a misery. While military life is clearly the best example of this power devoid of authority, the same factors are present in all sections of society. The

59. Ibid, pp. 86–8.

power of the MTS, with its political section, allowed for little rationalism in agricultural economics, and as an institution was widely resented. This, plus the *raikom* and the local NKVD, would be enough to put the average collective farm chairman in a position not much different from an NCO. Moreover, the official language of the media throughout the thirties was militaristic in the extreme.

It is in language particularly that one sees the discrepancies between what is officially expected and what actually happens. Whilst one finds a good many earthy expressions in the work, Voynovich is also adept at elaborate euphemism and mock pedantic circumlocutions. Arguably he is the most successful Russian writer at steering a middle course between the broadest obscenities of, say, Aleshkovsky or Limonov and the anodyne officially sanctioned expletives. One of the finest examples of the dichotomy between language as it is and language as the establishment would like it to be is the title of the hybrid plant Gladyshev is trying to perfect — *'Put' k sotsialismu'* — Puks, which is a children's word for 'breaking wind'. However, the argument goes beyond bawdy puns.

The whole area of official language, the radio, newspapers, lectures, and even literature, comes in for bitter indictment. One of the main reasons for the prerequisite of 'realism' in official Soviet literature has been to 'get the message across', to make art comprehensible to the masses. Yet the over-simplified, high-sounding jargon of the news flashes and political lectures drives Chonkin and his kind to either boredom or total confusion. As World War II breaks out the local newspaper devotes its columns to a discussion on Soviet etiquette in which the local bard, Serafim Butylko, joins, writing a poem which is not exactly on the theme of the discussion. In the context of the novel this may seem like little more than good *feuilleton*; it only takes on a serious and grotesque aspect when one recalls the lack of psychological and military preparation with which the Red Army faced operation Barbarossa. The lack of communication brought about by the manipulation of the language is refined to its most comic state in the scene between Milyaga and his interrogator; perhaps the upshot of this passage is not so much the inevitable incomprehensibility of official jargon as the inevitable limits that all language has when it comes to communication. Chonkin's animal-like seduction of Nyura, almost wordless, reflects far more mutual understanding than dialogue ever can.

The manipulation of language leads to greater problems than comic misunderstandings. Ultimately it leads to distorted conscience and morality. In *Chonkin* language would seem either to strip the characters of all conscience and morality, or deform conscience to an absurd degree — one thinks of Revkin, the first secretary of the *raikom* who, suffering from 'unhealthy moods', turns himself in to the NKVD, while his wife promises to bring up their son as a true bolshevik so that he will forget even his father's name.[60] The most striking examples, however, occur in the figures of the newspaper editor Yermolkin and Yevpraksein, the public prosecutor. The former has so debased language in his indiscriminate use of metaphor that on one occasion he is forced to run a headline announcing the discovery of 'ordinary gold'. For fifteen years or so he has lived in the realm of metaphor — a few days in the real world leads to his death. In a delightful parody of a show trial, Voynovich has Yevpraksein, in rotund waves of officialese, accuse Chonkin of every imaginable crime. Immediately afterwards, in his cups, he repents, tries to commit suicide, changes his mind and kills himself by accident. In his case, distorted language has engendered distorted morality and ultimately complete loss of control over his own actions. Free-will and personal identity have no dominion in the madhouse that rigid linguistic and social norms give rise to.

Chonkin's conscience is certainly troubled from time to time, but it is always by domestic things — even the aeroplane, which gains a certain symbolic meaning as the novel progresses, has to be domesticated, i.e. dragged into Nyura's garden, before it presents an authentic moral issue. (Even then, at one point its wings are still described as 'absurd'.) Conscience only becomes valid when it springs from inner harmony and complete self-realisation. The fact that these two conditions are so rarely fulfilled gives Private Chonkin all the fire-power he needs.

Chonkin remains unfinished. Parts three and four were published in 1979. Five parts had been promised in all. Voynovich has dropped some, possibly tongue-in-cheek, hints as to how the work will progress, but has devoted his energies to other projects. It may be that like some other picaresque novels the book is ultimately unfinishable. Indeed, there are suggestions in the text we have so far that the events are still unfolding to this very day. The *perpetuum mobile* one associates with Chonkin is barely confinable to a finite narrative. Voynovich tells us that 'getting rid of Chonkin isn't so simple'.[61] Similarly Shakespeare could not shake off Falstaff.

The very plethora of events and characters in *Chonkin* implies vitality and exuberance belying the fundamental tragedy that shadows most great comedies. Far from all of Voynovich's characters

60. Ibid, p.215.
61. *Chonkin* II, p.94.

are 'dead souls' — they will find their salvation. Moreover, there is a good deal more emphasis on births than on deaths in *Chonkin*. Ninka's and Nyura's swelling bellies have as much obstinacy about them as any of the other absurdities that the novel can muster. While there is persistent reference to families, lineage and marriage, once these are formalised, they too bring trouble and misunderstandings. A lot of the comedy relies on the resonances of such names as Golitsyn, Stalin, Chonkin. Is Chonkin a prince or a peasant? Could Stalin have Jewish blood? Stalin himself, as opposed to his Jewish namesake, wonders if 'Chonkin' might have something to do with ChON (*Chast' osobogo naznacheniya* - a 'specially designated unit', possibly the equivalent of the British SAS!). The more outlandish the posturing of the character, the more outlandish the name: 'Kuzma Gladyshev' is perfectly standard, but his wife and offspring have acquired Greek names, as has the Soviet bigwig billeted on Nyura. An unvarnished Russian diminutive with all its connotations of familiarity and affection is more likely to be a sign of approval on the author's part (Dunya, Ninka, Nyura, Vanya) than is a florid name-patronymic-surname. That Milyaga cannot recall his beloved Stalin's patronymic at a crucial time contributes to his death.

When Yevpraksein has heaped calumny on Chonkin, the defendant is struck dumb, but Voynovich speaks up for him, blending sentimentality with modesty and simplicity, and soon working his monologue round to the subject of birth and growing up:

> Chonkin was silent. What could he say in his defence? That he was young, that he hadn't seen life, that he still hadn't taken delight in food, water, freedom or a woman's pulsating body? He had no understanding that he was an inimitable miracle of nature, that with his death there would also die the whole world which was accommodated inside him. Possessing a concrete, not a vainglorious imagination, he knew for certain that when he disappeared nothing around him would change. The sun would still rise and set, night would follow day, and winter summer, it would rain and the grass would grow, cows would low, goats bleat, and some people would handle horses, sleep with their womenfolk, keep things and do all the things they were supposed to. It would have been easier for him, if only once in all that time he had met Nyura and she could have spoken to him, so that he would have learnt that his seed had stuck somewhere inside her body, had put out shoots and like a tadpole had entered a period of secret development after which it would turn into a human creature, maybe bow-legged, maybe lop-eared, but anyway resembling Chonkin.[62]

62. Ibid, p.318.

'A concrete not a vainglorious imagination' — these words are the key to *Chonkin*. Chonkin's fantasies flow directly from his own psyche. The self-deluders all apply their intellect to create their fantasies and we have seen the results: moral and physical destruction. Here the transmission belts of life frequently involve all forms of communication: the media as already discussed, but often letters, rumours, and telephone calls, not to mention the discussions which are undertaken on a given set of assumptions that go awry because the assumptions are false. The invocation of decades of friendship, or of loyalty, devotion or ideological purity is often the futile act of a doomed man, rather than an illustration of real human communication.

It has been argued that the dialogues in *Chonkin* have the effect of speeding characters up, of making them into cartoon types.[63] This is indeed the case, especially when one considers the pace of the action, the scenes of mindless violence that leave the hero and his kind relatively unscathed physically, the ridiculous names and the exaggerated physical descriptions. Yet there is in *Chonkin* a degree of earthy authenticity, an obstinate truth about mankind, a suggestion that his state is essentially absurd. There is an abundance of familiar satire in the novel, in which historical personages are ridiculed, show trials and economic failings parodied. And at times one detects a deliberate anachronism: Chonkin's trial echoes more exactly the stage-managed dissident trials of the 1960s and 1970s than those of the 1930s and 1940s. The alleged superstitions of people in high places accords with the rumoured faith-healing that Brezhnev was inclined to in his final years, and the cigarette case with the timing device which someone wishes to give to Stalin was a gadget that Brezhnev actually possessed.

Fantasies oust realities; animals upstage human beings; Chonkin teams up with the security man Svintsov (a reassuringly animal name); Nyura's belly swells. Such matters as these are a bracing re-statement of life's absurdity and of the necessity of recognising it.

Soviet Conformist, Russian Émigré

Voynovich's most conscious attempt to be a conventional Soviet writer is his novel *A Degree of Trust*, a biography (in the 'Ardent Revolutionaries' series) of Vera Figner. It is a routine and largely

---

63. M. Kirkwood, 'An Aspect of Humour in Voynovich's . . . "Chonkin"', *Essays in Poetics*, 5, No.2, 1980, pp.43–65.

tedious piece of work, but in two respects the real Voynovich breaks through, and the work is, in any case, worthy of some attention for being at the antipodes of the author's out and out 'dissident' works: *Ivankiada (The Ivankiad)* and certain open letters, produced in the Soviet Union; and his two major works to date written in emigration, *Antisovetskiy sovetskiy soyuz (The Antisoviet Soviet Union)* and *Moscow 2042*.

A Degree of Trust concentrates on the 1870s and the assassination of Alexander II by the People's Will in 1881. Vera Figner develops from liberal to propagandising radical and then to terrorist, without affording the reader any insights into her psychology. Her many years in prison, and her subsequent years of freedom under Soviet power are dealt with briefly and perfunctorily. Voynovich shows his true colours in his portrayal of a minor figure, the writer Skurlatsky, who falls victim to his own fantasies. He maintains, contrary to the truth and to all the evidence, that he was one of the key conspirators of the People's Will. The authorities are driven to the opinion that even if his statements are just a product of his imagination, they too must be dealt with. Pobedonotsev concludes that Skurlatsky's fantasies must be punished, just as real, dangerous criminals are.[64] While it is fair to assume that this is another example of Voynovich's self-deluders getting their come-uppance, it is also an example of the power of imagination, the miracle of art over 'real' life. In this way Skurlatsky is able to lead the authorities by the nose and, through an albeit debased art, make a gesture of freedom.

Thus one comes to the second way in which the real Voynovich manifests himself. Ostensibly about a *freedom* fighter, *A Degree of Trust* rather suggests that the heroine has precious little idea what freedom is. Deliberately, without providing a context and without interpreting her words in the prescribed revolutionary way, Voynovich records what Figner wrote a few months after her twenty-year imprisonment ended: 'My freedom is like a wooden apple, only on the outside it has been made to look like a real one: my teeth sink into it, but there is nothing resembling the taste of fruit'.[65] The Tsarist police on occasion sound uncomfortably like the revolutionaries, in their assertion that personal feelings must be suppressed for the good of the cause. Vera concurs with a ludicrously detailed picture one of her comrades-in-arms paints for her of the bright future: 'Life will be quite unlike present-day life. Everybody will be

---

64. V. Voynovich, *Stepen' doveriya*, Politizdat, 1972, pp.328–9.
65. Ibid, p.382.

healthy, beautiful and graceful. Everyone will take part in physical work on an equal basis and in moderation. People will devote their free time to the sciences and art'.[66] The diatribe continues with a fanciful description of the towns of the future, the entrances, balconies and so on, all identical. Suchlike gentle mockery of the wildly utopian ideas of the early revolutionaries is permissible in modern Soviet literature; indeed it was encouraged under Brezhnev to counter the extravagant claims of the now discredited Khrushchev and the embarrassing orthodoxy of such Stalinist die-hard writers as Vsevolod Kochetov.

Against such bold and grandiose schemes of the future, the 'real' Voynovich sets much humbler aims, aims ostensibly concerning himself and his immediate well-being. In addition to his open letter complaining about his telephone being cut off, there is the account of his battle to obtain a flat, as retold in *The Ivankiad*. *The Antisoviet Soviet Union* with its personal discourses on life, literature and politics may be seen as an exercise in self-explanation and justification. The time-travel fantasy *Moscow 2042* has the hedonistic hero indulging himself, just as keen on the limitless supplies of free drink on the trip to the future as he is on whatever he might find when he gets there. Paradoxically, in contemplating the self, Voynovich's heroes frequently arrive at a position morally superior to that of their antagonists. More often than not, the 'selfishness' of the hero is a spontaneous act, devoid of mental calculation or a programme. We have seen that Voynovich once said that he enjoyed freedom, he did not fight for it. His insistence on small freedoms for the self quickly becomes a subversive act with wide ramifications. Chonkin is caught in the eternal conundrum of whether the system or individuals are to blame and Voynovich is too subtle a writer to come down on one side or the other.

Notably in *The Ivankiad* Voynovich's identity (his *zamysel*) emerges in clear opposition to the 'flexibility' of Ivanko, who at times even enjoys the reputation of being a liberal, of being instrumental in the publication of Bulgakov's *The Master and Margarita*, for example. However, for Voynovich he represents elitism and opportunism. The narrative is sprinkled with references to Gogol, with a view to both pointing up the illogicality of modern life and suggesting that in social attitudes little has changed since the Revolution. However, Ivanko is not quite a Very Important Person, and Voynovich is a very different creature from Akakiy Akakiyevich.

In *The Ivankiad* a relatively trivial issue becomes a matter of

66. Ibid, pp.199–200.

principle and this in turn allows Voynovich to erect a formidable moral case against the Soviet establishment. At times he speculates, invents conversations, or embroiders on characters and events, but the essential facts remain, and the message to emerge is that Ivanko's values and attitudes *are* the Soviet Union. The Russian title of the work 'Ivankiada' is difficult to render properly — possibly 'Ivankery' would convey better the notions of underhand activity. Readers of Russian literature will also note the echoes of Bulgakov's collection *Diavoliada* (1925), with all its irrationalism and evil-doing.

The Antisoviet Soviet Union provides us with more details of Voynovich's biography and affords us more insights into his perception of things. The paradox in the title is maintained throughout. Even in the autobiographical section the author delights in the paradoxes of his own origin: one distant relative was a founder of the Black Sea Fleet and has the main harbour in Sevastopol named Grafskaya in his honour. Many relatives, as his name suggests, were warriors. Yet he is pleased to record that the Serbian dissident intellectual Milovan Djilas is also a relative. His father was a journalist and his mother a school teacher, but before becoming a professional intellectual himself, he was a jack of all manual trades. His father was arrested in Stalin's purges, but released before the war broke out. He was urged to rejoin the Party, refused and astonishingly escaped punishment. The implication of Voynovich's account of his own origins is that social patterns and historical orderliness simply do not exist. A man from a long line of warriors has produced one of the most successful anti-war novels of modern times.

An old soldier's war memoirs will never be as stirring as his exploits, and it is true that *The Antisoviet Soviet Union* is an uneven mixture. Some of the episodes are worthy of *Chonkin* in their humour and zest. For example a high-ranking official in a Moscow hotel dies of a heart attack while various categories of medics argue over the degree of privilege the patient enjoys, and over who should take charge of him. Such purportedly true stories are the very stuff of Soviet life and give credence to the widely held belief that the anecdote is itself a literary genre in the Soviet Union today. Elsewhere in the book, Voynovich displays his device of taking supposed axioms of Soviet life to their logical extreme to expose their falsity; or he fills in the lacunae in Soviet press reporting, or bridges the gaps in Soviet *non sequiturs*. The book is also a useful companion to Voynovich's fiction.

The 'straight' passages on Voynovich's beliefs and philosophy support the contention of this chapter that Voynovich is fundamentally a new voice in Russian literature, though hardly in the way that the writer Vladimir Tendryakov had in mind when he reviewed Voynovich's early work.[67] Voynovich's delight in the absurd and irrational never becomes a cult as, arguably, it does in Pilnyak, Bulgakov and Sinyavsky. Rather there is a powerful tendency in Voynovich towards rational scepticism, and here one perceives closer affinities with the literature of Central Europe than with that of Russia. At his best Voynovich is able to synthesise the best of the Russian cultural tradition with an existential awareness of the absurd.

> I know an elderly lady who when she was a little girl fought so frantically in her college against ideological heresy that even the Party organisers stopped her. In 1953 she accused her friend at a Komsomol meeting of not weeping on the day of Stalin's death. And now, when this one-time young girl writes 'we Christians' in the émigré press it really grates on me. For me the concept 'a Christian' has always been connected with the concept of a 'man of conscience', but far from all of our new converts can be categorised as such.
>
> I am not at all against people changing their convictions. On the contrary, I fully agree with Lev Tolstoy when he said something like: 'They say it's shameful to change your convictions. But I say: It's shameful not to'.
>
> It is stupid and sometimes even criminal to stick to convictions which have started to contradict the experience of life and history. Incidentally, I personally (forgive my being categorical) do not trust *any* convictions unless they are accompanied by doubts. And I do not believe either that any one teaching can be acceptable for everybody.[68]

The reference to Tolstoy notwithstanding, these sentiments are more likely to be found among disaffected intellectuals in Czechoslovakia or Poland than in Russia. Voynovich's matter-of-fact philosophy is in stark contrast to the messianic pronouncements of the Soviet establishment or of some sections of the émigré community. Voynovich's philosophical and political pronouncements may not be especially penetrating or original, but their enactment in his fiction assures him a special place in European literature.

The novel *Moscow 2042*, which appeared in full (parts having been printed in the émigré press earlier) in 1987, raises, perhaps *malgré soi*, the key question that faces the émigré writer: To what extent can the creative writer operate successfully outside his native environment? The futuristic *Moscow 2042* is Voynovich's first real work of

---

67. V. Tendryakov, 'Svezhiy golos — yest'!' *Literaturnaya gazeta*, 25 February 1961.
68. Voynovich, *Antisovetskiy Sovetskiy Soyuz*, p.283.

fiction produced abroad, and while one can readily detect affinities with the author's other fiction in terms of quality and approach, there is, of necessity, a tendency towards overkill in the reference to the phenomenon of the third emigration. Is the third emigration now so large that it can exist culturally without the Soviet Union? Vladimir Nabokov single-handed more or less managed. Is the third emigration now so much an accepted fact of life in a century that has produced so many émigré intellectuals generally that its self-consciousness is more of a burden than an asset? In *Moscow 2042* Voynovich addresses his fellow exiles at least as much as he addresses the Soviet system. More pertinently, he confronts his own predicament and uses his own trusted ally — his sense of the absurd — to come to terms with it. As he affirms at the close of the work:

> Maybe future reality will turn out to be dissimilar to that which I have described. Of course, in that case my reputation as a thoroughly veracious person will be somewhat tarnished, but I'm prepared in advance to live with such an eventuality. Who cares about a reputation! Just as long as living is a bit easier.
> That's what it's all about, gentlemen.[69]

These words suggest that the author is writing as much as for himself as for a readership, yet at the same time they reflect the irreverently modest philosophy at the back of much of Voynovich's work — the notion that entertainment is therapeutic and scepticism is healthy.

While the title of the work reliably hints at a political satire directed against the Soviet system, the author's starting point is really the Russian émigrés. In emigration Voynovich has certainly maintained a dialogue with his expatriate colleagues (note his attendance at prominent émigré conferences and his publication in a variety of émigré journals), but it is not without significance that he has kept a certain distance too. He has settled in the small town of Stockdorf in preference to gravitating towards the larger capital cities that traditionally accommodate so many émigré Russians.

It is tempting to read *Moscow 2042* as a *roman à clef* and identify several of the leading characters with prominent members of the third emigration; thus the narrator–hero Kartsev becomes Voynovich himself, Sima Simych Karnavalov is Solzhenitsyn. Moreover, the name Karnavalov also recalls Kornilov, Voynovich's contemporary, but this hardly accords with the 'sixty pieces of rubble' (*glyb*) that Karnavalov has written, an impudent reference, of

69. V. Voynovich, *Moskva 2042*, Ardis, Ann Arbor, Mich., 1987, p.339.

course, to the many 'knots' (*uzly*) of Solzhenitsyn's historical cycle *The Red Wheel* and to the collection of nationalist essays he contributed to entitled *From under the Rubble*. The denunciations of Stepanida Zueva-Dzhonson take the form of 'letters to a friend' (a transparent reference to Stalin's daughter's work *Twenty Letters to a Friend*). However, the interpretative exercise cannot be taken too far without doubts or qualifications creeping in, and anyway the work should not be treated solely as parody.

The author is in fact adopting a manner which was much in evidence in Aleksandr Zinoviev's first 'fictional' (as opposed to philosophical) work, *The Yawning Heights*. In this amalgam of dialogue, bawdy and anecdote, the reader is persistently tempted to identify some of the leading characters: Chatterer, Truth-teller, the Boss and so on, yet it would be nigh impossible to identify all the cast and the task would be pointless. Zinoviev's (and Voynovich's) purpose is to imply a generalisation, to suggest that the so-called 'Soviet' system is organically linked with the pre-revolutionary Russian system, that while externals may change, some traditional values and attitudes do not. Zinoviev has his characters conducting their discourse in the urinal or in other sordid circumstances, swamping the Russian language with meaningless verbosity and ludicrous acronyms: not just rendering the simple difficult and the sensible ridiculous, but also showing how damage can be done to our perceptions, indeed implying that the very function of language in the Soviet Union is to destroy a sense of reality.

The Russian language is in even more danger in emigration. It can be destroyed by its own garrulity — Karnavalov's sixty 'pieces of rubble' never see the light of day and he is utterly forgotten by the year 2042. Moreover, daily exposure to foreign influences will annihilate the language. Voynovich seems to derive a certain amusement from having to use words like 'floppi disk' and 'kompyuter' in Russian, given that there are no handy Russian equivalents, but he balks at wholesale importations: *zarentovat kar, khaivey, ekzit, mail, shulder* and even *folovat* (to follow) are packed into one message the bemused author receives from Toronto, and he has to provide a glossary for the reader's edification.[70] The other extreme is on display no less. Karnavalov resists any loan words at all, and in his vocabulary a television is *glyadelka*, aeroplane is *letalka*, and he reads Dahl's dictionary from 10.30 to 11.30 each evening.[71]

An insight into Voynovich's own 'middle-of-the-road' approach

70. Ibid, p.39.
71. Ibid, pp.72–3 and p.85.

to the Russian language can be glimpsed in a passage from *The Antisoviet Soviet Union*. Two alcoholics are waiting for the liquor department to open and one asks impatiently the question that no lesser personages than Chernyshevsky and Lenin had posed in their time: 'What is to be done?' His companion replies, 'Mooch around a bit, mooch around! They'll lift the blockade in half an hour, and we can get two bottles right away.'[72]

'Oh the great, mighty, truthful and free Russian language!' exclaims Voynovich (quoting the celebrated words from Turgenev's *Senilia*), noting in particular the two words 'mooch' (*kruzhitsya*) and 'blockade' (*blokada*). Both terms are well established in Russian, the first being somewhat homely and colloquial, the second of foreign origin but thoroughly legitimate in modern Russian, yet connoting major disaster associated usually with war and deprivation. Voynovich's approval of the language of two alcoholics stands in clear preference to the distortions the language undergoes at the hands of ideologues, be they nationalist dissidents, Soviet wordmongers or any people who strive to dispense with their linguistic origins. The exchange between the two alcoholics has a richness and resonance of which the Russian language, when appropriated by the vainglorious, is sadly bereft.

Voynovich's depiction of the Russian nationalists in emigration is hardly subtle in its caricature. Corporal punishment, asceticism, arrogance amounting to messianism are all on display. Arguably, the case against the nationalists is weakened by the lack of any close allusion to their programme. When Karnavalov returns to the Soviet Union, has the head of the church there crucified and establishes his own regime, farce supplants satire.

Voynovich's thoroughly outlandish picture of the monarchy being restored in Russia and some patriarchal system of government re-introduced in fact supports Zinoviev's fundamental thesis that the Soviet system as it stands is essentially 'normal', that the adoption and application of a form of Marxist ideology have been quite in keeping with the Russian tradition. The natural conclusion to draw from such a position is indeed pessimistic — that Russia is doomed to boorish governments of whatever colouring, to absurd contradictions and injustice, to economic backwardness and isolation.

The eagerness with which some Russian nationalists look to the past is at least as worrying as the way the ideologists strive for the future. *Moscow 2042* is at its crudest in its caricature of political

72. Voynovich, *Antisovetskiy Sovetskiy Soyuz*, p.279.

nostalgia, but it is probably at its best in its ridicule of those who fabricate a future by the manipulation of existing resources, economic, cultural and linguistic. That Russia seems incapable of fundamental change was the crude position expressed by Zinoviev in an interview in June 1987 — in the midst of Gorbachev's campaign of 'restructuring', 'openness' and 'acceleration'.

> Gorbachev made his career as a party apparatchik in the Brezhnev years. He bears full responsibility for all that was done in those years. He is a demagogue and a chatterer [*boltun* — incidentally the name of one of the characters in *The Yawning Heights*: R.P] possessed with vanity. There is nothing fundamentally new in his initiatives — it has all been tried many times before. That his 'reforms' are meeting opposition is explained not by the fact that the 'old guard' is afraid for its privileges, but the 'silent work-horses' [*prostoye bydlo*] don't want to change their customary way of life, and by the fact that the Gorbachev 'reformers' are in principle alien to the communist social system. They are doomed to failure in advance. Gorbachev is playing the role of a kind of 'dissident on the throne'. A hypocritical role. He himself belongs to the 'old guard' and the 'work-horses'.[73]

Voynovich's view of the Soviet Union in the next century would seem not just to endorse such sentiments but to imply that the conscious striving to the future by the demagogues leads back to the past. When the hero arrives in Moscow in the year 2042 he discovers that in almost every area of technology the country has slipped back from the position it held in the 1980s. As the technology has receded so the jargon has accelerated. Excrement ('the secondary product') has to be recycled to obtain food ('the primary product'), and there are human interpreters to facilitate communication between people not of different languages but of different ideologies. The high style persistently masks the sordid. A 'self-service' brothel is a 'Palace of Love'.

Ideological jiggery-pokery has led in the twenty-first century to a situation that looks uncomfortably like Ivan the Terrible's Muscovy, when the state was divided administratively into the Oprichnina and the Zemshchina. There has been an 'August Revolution' and Communism has been established in Moscow, while in the surrounding 'zone' there is still only 'socialism'. The hero soon discovers the difference when he is moved out of the 'Communist Hotel' where he can just about survive into the 'Socialist Hotel' where there are none of the basic amenities and the concierge steals his boots. Karnavalov's triumphant return (after sixty years of suspended animation in

73. A. Zinoviev, in *Russkaya mysl'*, 26 June 1987, p.13.

a Swiss bank) has not a little of the Time of Troubles about it.

The comic devices in the novel, some more successful than others, add up to little more than a *feuilleton* with all the ephemeral qualities that this term implies. Yet *Moscow 2042* does have some enduring strengths. Firstly, one detects Voynovich's penchant for parading a literary ancestry. The work purports to be not so much science fiction (the author exhorts those who are interested in the technical details of time travel to read science fiction)[74] so much as an anti-Utopian work in the mode of Zamyatin, Huxley and Orwell. Yet here too, the expectation is not quite fulfilled: the future turns out to be like the past, not so much a horror to which we are all heading, rather a harsh joke that has been played on us before. A number of émigrés have tried their hand at political fantasy — Vasiliy Aksyonov in his *Island of Crimea* (1981), which treats the Crimea as a kind of Soviet Hong Kong, eventually to be repossessed by the mainland; or Gladilin's story, already noted, *Rehearsal on Friday*, where Stalin awakes from the dead; additionally there are numerous passages in Zinoviev's books which can be classed as political fantasy.

Unlike these writers, Voynovich adopts a more conscious literary persona, as he does in some of his other works. The disclaimers and direct addresses to the reader, so reminiscent of pre-nineteenth-century prose fiction and the epistolary genre, serve in *Moscow 2042* to establish the author's identity and role. An exile in space and time, in language and in culture, the hero needs all his common sense and self-awareness to retain his sanity. The vicissitudes of a literary career are only too plain, given Kartsev's idolisation and Karnavalov's obscurity in the twenty-first century. One abiding quality of *Moscow 2042* is that it offers no hostages to political fortune. For a work that has little reverence for anything, the spectacle of the Generalissimo towering over the statue of Pushkin while the author clutches at the dictator's boot demonstrates at least a respect for great literature — consistent, enduring and with a sense of proportion.

In subtler ways the novel also confronts the perennial dilemma of Russian literature — is there one Russian literature or does it divide into the authors published at home and those who survive in exile? In the Moscow of the twenty-first century there are two kinds of literature: that which is spoken, and the superior variety which is written down. The perplexed hero recalls that in his day there were also two kinds of literature: Soviet and anti-Soviet, both written

74. Voynovich, *Moskva 2042*, p.92.

down.[75] The absurdity of such divisions hardly needs comment. There is a hint at the back of this exchange that the author believes the opposite to be true, namely that there has only ever been one Russian literature and that superior quality may well reside in oral literature — the anecdote and the conversation. In this connection one might note Kartsev's amiable and essentially unserious relationship with word-processors and floppy disks. The implication appears to be that all the technology in the world cannot alter the quality of literature — only the human mind can do that.

As we have noted earlier, Gogol is never too far away in Voynovich's best works, and in *Moscow 2042* one detects the affinity between the two authors, particularly in the preoccupations that society has for rank, position and identity. Seasoned by the vagaries of public opinion and official grace in real life, Voynovich's writing on such matters is a form of self-defence, and also a cautionary tale for literary and political pundits. The appearance of grandeur frequently connotes utter banality. Flattery is perceived by the narrator for the comforting lie that it is. And from such considerations, just as in Gogol, the work progresses to becoming an intermingling of dream and reality, as in *Chonkin*. Kartsev has a dream in which communism in its pure state is achieved, there is an abundance of material and spiritual wealth and perfect happiness. All this contrasts pointedly with the sordid and run-down future in which the hero finds himself; and this future of course contrasts in turn with the present (1982) from which the hero has journeyed.

The banality of Western affluence in 1982 has its drawbacks and dangers: spies, bribes, materialism, political extremists of all persuasions certainly sully the relatively quiet life that the exiled writer leads. Moreover, the West is depicted as a cultural wasteland — Kartsev cannot even understand the American soap opera 'Dallas', that seems to enjoy so much popularity.

Finally, in contrast to the philistinism of the West, there stands *Moscow 2042* itself. The unsubtle literary and political references, the *feuilleton* humour, the sometimes laboured comedy apart, the novel ultimately succeeds because of its modesty and good sense. The manner in which the work feeds on itself re-opens all the possibilities for the novel that Cervantes discovered when he wrote *Don Quixote*, and which the twentieth century has rediscovered. The genre of metafiction in which one story begets another is traceable from Leonid Leonov's *The Thief* (1927), through Mikhail Bulgakov's *The Master and Margarita* and on to Yuriy Galperin's *Bridge over the Lethe*

75. Ibid, p.214.

(1982). In *Moscow 2042* the metafiction does not play a central role, but it does, as in the other works cited here, affirm the autonomy of fiction, the triumph of art over the exigencies of the moment.

* * *

1987 was certainly a year of extraordinary new freedoms in literature, but the embargo on living exiled writers was, with the qualified exception of Brodsky, still not lifted. Voynovich was a case in point. He entered into a correspondence with the new editor of *Novyy mir*, Sergei Zalygin, in March and the exchanges were later published in the émigré press, in *The New York Times Magazine*, and the West German press, as well as being broadcast by the BBC Russian Service.[76]

Voynovich offered Zalygin 'By Means of Mutual Correspondence' for publication: 'It was written for *Novy Mir* almost 20 years ago, prepared for publication and typeset (I still have the very yellowed page proofs).' Voynovich recalled that he had even been paid an advance for the work. If Zalygin did not like the story, Voynovich could offer other things including *Chonkin*, which had also been under contract to *Novyy mir* at one time. Zalygin declined the offer: 'Our *main* tasks are here. All our resources are directed toward resolving these tasks, and we hope to make do with our own resources.' Exceptions, according to Zalygin, could be made only for 'a few works that are particularly successful from an artistic point of view'.

Voynovich replied:

> In sending you my story, I cherished no hope that you would publish it, even though I would have considered its publication a small, but important step on the road to correcting in literature what are euphemistically called 'mistakes of the past'. I had hoped to see this story stand in contrast to the slander that is still being heaped upon persons who share my fate.

The correspondence continued, with Zalygin citing authors now rehabilitated and Voynovich pointing out that all these authors were dead: 'Like Pasternak I was publicly called a "pig in clover". This is a rare distinction, even more uncommon than the Lenin Prize. But unlike Pasternak, I am still among the living, and therefore I will continue to be banned.'

Voynovich the campaigner was very much in evidence in these exchanges. Voynovich the comedian was more apparent in a public

---

76. 'Where Glasnost has its Limits', *The New York Times Magazine*, 19 July 1987, pp.30–1. The correspondence dates from 7 March to 17 May.

address he made pointing out the real truth about all the Soviet leaders over the years: they alternated between bald men and those who had a head of hair. This was true from Lenin right through to Gorbachev; and the bald ones were idealists and reformers, while the others were realists and conservatives.[77] As with all good comedy there was some truth in this.

Voynovich's pronouncements in 1987 rather echoed the ambivalence that many Western observers felt towards the new order of things in the Soviet Union. On the one hand there was sympathy for *glasnost* and *perestroika*; on the other hand there was a sense that it was to a degree mere window-dressing, or wildly quixotic. Perhaps any expatriate has to justify his circumstances by a negative view of whatever happens in his homeland. To Voynovich's credit he appears to have kept his mind remarkably open, while never ceasing to be sceptical. His impudence earned him a place in *Literaturnaya gazeta's* short list of 'most malicious and intransigent renegades', when it renewed an attack on Vladimov in September 1987.

77. Published first in the émigré press, the piece was given prominence in *The Guardian*: 'The Bald and the Hairy', *The Guardian*, 28 December 1987.

–4–

Georgiy Vladimov
The Dissident

There are two words in Russian for 'dissident'. One is *inakomysl-yashchiy* (literally, 'one who thinks differently'), and the other, much more common, is *dissident*. This term has been used in the Soviet media with the deliberate intention of stigmatising individuals who are openly at odds with the regime. Frequently, the disparaging phrase 'so-called dissident' has occurred. In practice, such terminology is not particularly helpful or accurate, and a good many disaffected East European intellectuals reject such categorisation. Dissenters are by their nature apt to dissent from each other as well as from any given social system. We have chosen to dub Georgiy Vladimov a 'dissident' because he, more than many other Soviet writers who have suffered censorship, harassment and banishment (witness Voynovich) conforms to the Western stereotyped image of the 'dissident', an image that has perhaps been reinforced by the widely known example of Aleksandr Solzhenitsyn (convict, writer, moralist, hero).

Vladimov writes realistic prose that bears a vigorous moral awareness. He, like Solzhenitsyn, might be termed an inverted Socialist Realist. In all his major works he displays a faith in man's basic decency, even if grotesque moral distortions take place. As a Soviet writer he challenged the system. As a proscribed writer he had his differences with other 'dissidents', notably the historian Roy Medvedev.[1] In emigration he has fallen out with the émigré journal that championed him and which for two years he edited.[2] Vladimov's moral stance and robust honesty, like Solzhenitsyn's, have not made for uniformly good relations and intellectual comfort.

---

1. R. Medvedev and G. Vladimov, 'Controversy: Dissent among dissidents', *Index on Censorship*, 1979, Vol.8, No.3, pp.33–7. Also, a letter from Zhores Medvedev (Roy's brother), *Index on Censorship*, 1979, Vol.8, No.5, pp.76–7.
2. See 'Vmesto kolonki redaktora', *Kontinent* 1986, No.48, pp.353–4, and supplement pp.i–xxi in *Grani*, No.140.

Georgiy Vladimov

The Great Ore

'He stood on the surface of the earth, above the gigantic oval bowl of the quarry. He was wearing a ruddy-coloured velvet zipper coat and off-white canvas trousers soiled with lime and black oil. His hand held his cap low over his brow so that the wind would not blow it away.'[3] 'He' is Viktor Pronyakin, the hero of Vladimov's first novel *Bol'shaya ruda* (*The Great Ore*), and the way we are introduced to him is familiar to the point of tedium. He is looking for work commensurate with his skills; there are no openings for him apparently, but given half a chance, he proves himself, and becomes a truck driver on the Kursk Magnetic Anomaly. Countless novels of socialist construction begin in a similar vein. Marietta Shaginyan's classic of the genre *Hydrocentral* (1930–31) opens with a scene at the equivalent of the labour exchange and with discourses on how different things are now there is no unemployment as in Tsarist times.

Interestingly, Shaginyan's job applicant is referred to as an eccentric (*chudak*) and a circus-performer (*tsirkach*) at the outset;[4] Vladimov's hero has to wait only a little while to earn precisely the same epithets.[5] If the positive hero is to set an example to the people he must seem in some way out of the ordinary to them. Vladimov's hero is brash and self-centred, and he eventually dies showing off as much as fulfilling some lofty mission. In this he is hardly the conventional positive hero we have been led to expect.

Pronyakin is quickly plunged into the world of work and the reader is given lengthy and genuinely enthusiastic technical descriptions of trucks and mine-workings. Work is seen very much as a series of problems to be solved, or aims to be achieved. One can recall another classic of construction fiction, Valentin Katayev's *Time, Forward!* (1932). Likewise something of an eccentric, Katayev's hero faces the day ahead:

> Margulies sat there, wrapped in a soiled sheet and looking like a Bedouin . . .
> Much was not clear.
> The labour part? Transportation? The capacity of the machinery? The number of men? The distance to the place where the concrete must be poured? The height to which the scoop would have to be lifted?[6]

3. G. Vladimov, *Bol'shaya ruda*, Possev, Frankfurt, 1984, p.5.
4. M. Shaginyan, *Gidrotsentral*, Izvestiya, Moscow, 1965, pp.6–7.
5. Vladimov, *Bol'shaya ruda*, p.26 and p.51.
6. V. Katayev, *Sobraniye sochineniy*, Khudozhestvennaya literatura, Moscow, 1969, Vol.3, p.132.

Pronyakin can have a driver's job if he can repair the truck: 'The MAZ-200, a two-axle, wide-winged vehicle was really in a terrible state. It would need some careful, really expert work on it so as to straighten the springs, beat out the cab, beat out the wheel rims.'[7] The catalogue of technical problems continues, but very soon Pronyakin has his truck on the road.

As in the two classics of Socialist Realism cited above, *The Great Ore* concentrates on characters' physical details (scruffy clothes, colour of hair, build) and makes reference to the natural elements (wind, rain, terrain). The purpose is straightforward enough: to portray real, credible characters in difficult but familiar circumstances and then to show the people imposing their will on nature. It is here that Vladimov's story differs from the traditional formula, for the hero is eventually defeated, but not before the author has treated us to some socialist rhetoric and dubious philosophising. It is open to conjecture to what extent these are presented to us tongue-in-cheek. A girl at a dance says: 'Our girls are always moaning: there's none of this, none of that, just dying to get back to Moscow. But after all, what have we come here for? Wasn't it so that we could feel that we are participants in a great, real cause? Isn't that joyful? That's what I tell them every day.'[8]

Of a fellow worker: 'He was taciturn and gloomy, and a vertical wrinkle cut across his forehead with its widow's peaks. Anyway, Pronyakin understood him. Having three kids and a pregnant wife disposes you to deep thinking.'[9] This kind of facile philosophical aside is not unknown in another Socialist Realist classic, Mikhail Sholokhov's *The Quiet Don*.

A closer point of reference for *The Great Ore* would be the early stories of Vladimir Tendryakov. It would be natural for reviewers to draw attention to his novella *Potholes* of 1956, which, like Aitmatov's *My Little Poplar* (see page 60), dealt directly with lorry drivers, the difficult terrain that they operated over and their conflicts with bureaucracy. Tendryakov's more profound *Three, Seven, Ace* (1960) is in some ways closer to *The Great Ore* in that it depicts a newcomer introducing himself into a working collective. The common factor in these post-thaw stories is that they describe the new relationship between an individual and a new situation; at the same time the writer is using well-worn stylistic devices and patterns to handle a new freedom. If nothing else, *The Great Ore* is an interesting illustration of the cross-roads at which Soviet literature found itself after

7. Vladimov, *Bol'shaya ruda*, pp. 17–18.
8. Ibid, p.30.
9. Ibid, p.51.

Khrushchev's 'secret' speech. That Vladimov, in emigration, twenty-three years later should republish the work without any changes might suggest that the Socialist Realist elements in the book should never have been taken at face value. However, Vladimov added an illuminating afterword to the émigré edition:

> This novella was written by a 29-year-old author at the best time of 'the thaw'; re-reading it now with quite different eyes, I find nothing in it to correct, to enrich with subsequent experience; the illusion of the time imprinted in it, in my view, is no less valuable and instructive, than the wisdom of recent sobriety . . . Show our people just a flicker of beneficial changes, give them just a whiff of freedom, fulfil just one of the masses of promises, just the least lightening of their endless burdens, and then see the enthusiasm, the songs at the railway stations, and the trains taking the romantics off to tame the Asiatic virgin lands or the Altai mountains, and people throwing up their careers and breaking their necks, dreaming of new towns built with their own hands, falling asleep by campfires and being eaten alive by swarms of midges in the *taiga*.[10]

There could hardly be a better indication of the genuine impulse to civic-mindedness which is also at the back of Socialist Realism. In Vladimov's biography there could hardly be a better illustration of how the authorities, in constantly exhorting writers (and everyone else) to high-mindedness, open a Pandora's box for themselves. Mikhail Gorbachev, in utterly orthodox fashion, reiterated the moral duties of literature at the twenty-seventh Party Congress: 'Only literature . . . educates people to be honest, strong in spirit, capable of taking upon themselves the burden of their time'.[11] The orthodox critic Starikova, in reviewing *The Great Ore* was unable to resist reproducing Marx's dictum, now become a slogan in the Soviet Union: 'Being determines consciousness', and in analysing Pronyakin, she went on:

> He is a brave and capable man, and his desire that his abilities should receive recognition is legitimate and understandable. But at the same time he is a very ignorant [*tyomnyy*] person and has a very poor vision of what is needed to deserve that recognition and what is needed for him to feel he is recognised. A television? A motorcycle? A house with a fence? His picture in the newspaper? Actually, it is not so easy for a man to understand and decide what is best for him, what is essential for him, what he lacks in life . . .
>
> Collectivism in opposition to individualism is the generally recognised basis of communist morality.[12]

10. Ibid, pp.149–50.
11. *Literaturnaya gazeta*, 26 February 1986, p.9.
12. Ye. Starikova, 'Zhizn' i gibel' shofyora Pronyakina', *Znamya*, 1962, No.1, pp.206–14, p.211.

This opposition between the collective and the individual is the key to Vladimov's fiction.

Three Minutes' Silence — A Soviet Novel?

I

Vladimov's other 'Soviet' novel *Tri minuty molchaniya* (*Three Minutes' Silence*) is an excellent example of what processes Russian literature can go through in its pilgrimage to the reader. The work was serialised in *Novyy mir* in 1969 and there was a book edition in 1976. In 1982 the definitive version, following the French language Gallimard edition, appeared in West Germany. There have been many other instances of works being published in the Soviet Union in one form and in another abroad. Anatoliy Kuznetsov's documentary novel *Babiy Yar* was published abroad in a different version after his defection in 1969. Solzhenitsyn has undertaken the re-publication of all his works in the West since his expulsion in 1974; the results are most dramatically seen in *The First Circle* and *August 1914*. Other works that have until recently achieved only partial publication in the Soviet Union, but full publication abroad, include Fazil Iskander's *Sandro from Chegem* and Andrei Bitov's *Pushkin House*. Not until 1988 was the prose part of Boris Pasternak's *Doctor Zhivago* published, whereas all the poems that form its last chapter had been printed, though without any mention of the novel.

On one level Vladimov's writing could, as we have seen, easily pass for Socialist Realism of the most conventional kind. His heroes are ordinary workers, yet they strive to complete or exceed production norms; they are utterly credible characters of flesh and blood, who do battle with the elements. Vladimov seems to delight in descriptions of the work situation where the technical details of day-to-day life for people on 'the shop floor' are spelled out, but such episodes are nearly always seen as just part of a broader spectrum. The author neither denies nor extols the virtues of manual work. It is rather the case that work is seen as an integral but not exclusive part of man's existence. 'Grandad', the ship's chief engineer in *Three Minutes' Silence*, tells Senya, the young wayward hero:

> I've seen you on deck, you're good. But you don't love your work, it doesn't do anything for you. That's why you're always swaying about, can't find a place for yourself . . . I can't teach you how to live, I don't know myself, but you will learn to love your work . . . You'll feel a different person. Because people will deceive you, but a machine is like

nature, what you put into it, that's what you'll get out, it won't cheat you.[13]

The details of life at sea are recorded with a regard for correct terminology that even some Soviet reviewers have found irksome: 'Gradually, though with difficulty, one gets used to the many professional phrases, one is not put out by these *"kepy"*, *"kapy"*, *"drify"*, *"kandei"*, *"rokana"*, *"tryama"*, *"smainat"*, *"virat"* etc. — one feels literally drawn into the conveyor belt of workdays, of activities, one almost suffers with sea-sickness — the uniform, stereotyped details piled on one another like waves.'[14]

The narrative style of *Three Minutes' Silence* might be described as sophisticated *skaz*, the device of recounting a story in the language of the participant in the story. *Skaz* is most frequently used in Russian literature for comic effect: colloquialisms, coarseness and even poor grammar are appropriated by the author to create immediacy, to draw the reader into the reality being recorded, and to point up the absurdity of life. Vladimov feeds his reader nautical technical terms and nautical slang, the better to convey a reality far removed from everyday experience. Senya may not love his work, but he obviously loves telling a story. He addresses the reader directly, pauses to explain to him various maritime customs, to describe working conditions or to recall previous voyages and acquaintances. He initiates the reader with the same mixture of concern and harshness as he does the two newcomers, Alik and Dimka. He educates his reader as Socialist Realism demands.

Moreover, in a sense, the lessons that Vladimov imparts through his hero are acceptable, even desirable in Soviet terms. Any peruser of *Literaturnaya gazeta* will be regaled with photographs of writers in earnest conversation with welders, milkmaids and navvies. The vigorously sponsored contact between intellectuals and workers for mutual edification is an aspect of Soviet life that Vladimov took one stage further. He worked *incognito* as a simple sailor on a trawler, No.849, 'The Horseman' (*Vsadnik*), out of Murmansk for three and a half months. The result was the last full-length novel that Aleksandr Tvardovsky, the liberal editor of *Novyy mir*, was able to publish before he was removed in 1970. Here then was a book based on first-hand experience with Soviet workers, which depicted in graphic and racy terms the dangers and hardships of their life, and saw them

13. G. Vladimov, *Tri minuty molchaniya*, Possev, Frankfurt, 1982, p.81. This is the author's authorised version.
14. D. Tevekelyan, in *Literatura i sovremennost'*, Sbornik, No.10, Moscow, 1970, pp.354–61, pp.354–55.

triumphant in adversity. Here was an impressive array of positive heroes and a clear civic-minded message. One émigré reviewer wrote:

> Unfortunately this work does not bear comparison with *The Great Ore*. Although the author is similarly concerned with problems of humanity, of the attitude of the hero to his work, of the interrelationship of personality and the collective, and the meaning of life overall, the outcome is not a fully artistic work . . . The actions of the hero are poorly motivated and the false ending of the novel (as if written by the hand of the editor) is not at all like Vladimov — a love 'happy ending' and the decision to return to sea: 'After all, the country needs fish . . .'.[15]

Elsewhere in the same review there are again complaints about the technical jargon and a criticism that the work does not rise above the level of a 'journalistic sketch' (*ocherk*).

Significantly, when the author published the uncensored version abroad in 1982, the hero's decision to return to sea still stood, as did the phrase (repeated) 'the country needs fish'. Clearly, Vladimov was not kowtowing to a Soviet editor in incorporating elements into his work which could be construed as official rhetoric. Likewise, all the nautical jargon stayed in the uncut version. On his emigration to the West Vladimov, when asked what had been expunged by the Soviet censor, replied:

> Well, maybe, the main thing, the pivotal thing, what people suffer for, why they rush about, why they give themselves bumps on the head, go to sea in search of adventure and especially: the thinking about oneself, about the meaning of life, about the destiny of man on Earth, about the link between generations, and then the completely seditious — about our country's past, about her present and her future. That is, every time there appears some spirituality, some sort of let's not say plight, but glimmer of independent, hard-won thought, then the censor's pencil immediately flies over, hovers over your text. For it's all, in their terminology, rotten 'god-seeking' and is to be rooted out . . .
> i think that the deeper our literature goes into the spiritual world of man, and the more it seeks to widen the framework of what is permitted in ideology, the sharper becomes the conflict with the censorship. Who will win out, only time can tell.[16]

In this long and somewhat episodic novel, the essential plot is quickly told and hardly varies between the Soviet and uncut, émigré versions. Senya is a young, brash and violent sailor, who is forced

---

15. V. Chernyavsky, 'Gibel' geroyev', *Grani*, 1977, No.106, pp.204–28, pp.212–13.
16. G. Vladimov, 'KGB protiv literatury', *Posev*, 1983, No.3, pp.37–43, p.42.

back to sea by his drunkenness and the bad company he keeps. His ship *The Galloper* (*Skakun*) is damaged but has netted a huge haul of herring. Senya cuts the nets, allowing his vessel to limp to the rescue of a Scottish trawler and save the lives of the sailors on it. Senya and his captain may well face severe legal proceedings over the loss of the catch.

It should be emphasised that there is nothing particularly seditious or new in the work's indictment of the crassness of Soviet law and the suggestion that the individual may perform a highly moral action which the Soviet system is likely to condemn. Rasputin's *Money for Maria* is in like vein. Nor is *Three Minutes' Silence* unacceptably frank about everyday Soviet life — the drinking, the promiscuity, even the criminality. What officialdom found so uncomfortable in Vladimov's novel was the far subtler quality of 'spirituality' of which the author spoke. What does the spirituality consist of?

II

The epigraph to the novel is taken from Kipling's 'Tomlinson', a poem that derides second-hand morality, acquired through hearsay and books rather than from authentic existence: 'the God that you took from a printed book be with you, Tomlinson!' the pathetic hero, rejected by God and the Devil, is told. These words reflect not only Vladimov's own approach to literature, writing from first-hand experience, but also his disdain for the notion that books which simply exhort people to be better will actually make them better. More pertinently, the epigraph urges the reader of *Three Minutes' Silence* to consider the work as an objective investigation of a man's soul. Kipling's 'hero' hardly has a soul at all, indeed 'has no soul of his own' as the Devil's minions declare, so keen is he on mouthing proprieties. Vladimov's hero is made of other stuff.

Geoffrey Hosking has argued that Vladimov in *Three Minutes' Silence* is, along with many of his contemporaries, redefining the spiritual side of man and moving away from the established Soviet view: 'Now, in the received Soviet view of man (formulated by Chernyshevsky and passed on by Lenin), the 'spiritual' is not more than the sum total of the sensations and thought processes taking place in the individual. Man is seen as a creature of matter, wholly explicable, at least in principle, in terms of biological and social laws.'[17]

17. G. Hosking, 'The Search for an Image of Man in Contemporary Soviet Fiction', in C. Barnes (ed.), *Studies in Twentieth-Century Russian Literature*, Scottish Academic Press, Edinburgh, pp.61–77, p.61.

Yet, argues Hosking, in *Three Minutes' Silence* and other Soviet novels, the spiritual element is autonomous and implies a sphere of freedom which Marxism cannot cater for.

One might cite many Soviet works which to non-Marxist critics seem to fit awkwardly into Soviet-made patterns, but what is particularly interesting in Vladimov's case is that, as we have seen, on the surface, his works — at least those published in the Soviet Union — can be construed as quite conformist. The central paradox in *Three Minutes' Silence* is that all the characters behave credibly though at times their actions may be difficult to explain in rational terms. It is this which presumably led the émigré reviewer cited above to speak of Senya's 'poorly motivated actions'.

In his discussion Hosking says that Senya 'constantly, even obsessively, seeks human contact'.[18] Yet one might add that his purpose in this is really to assert himself, to impose himself on others. This explains the first person narration and the bold addresses to the reader. He foists himself on the various women he meets, Lilya, Nina and Klavka; he invites conflict with the cooper, the captain and others. At the same time people are drawn to him and have great affection for him. Young, tough and a high wage earner, he has little trouble attracting female companions. The men's regard for him is more difficult to explain, but in the chief engineer Grandad, for whom Senya has a lot of respect, one might detect traces of Senya's own character.

Grandad was a war hero, who scuppered his ship when attacked by the Germans and managed to swim to an island. His shipmates were captured, so there was no-one to corroborate his story when he was picked up and he is punished with exile by his own side. When Senya asks if he would like to get even with the person who denounced him, he says no, since 'that was just the way things were at that time'.[19] Grandad then is rather fatalistic about moral questions; he does not so much actively forgive those who do him evil, as shrug off the injury done to him. Senya shares Grandad's energy, but more especially his propensity to self-containment. Beaten up and robbed by Askold and Vovchik, two chance drinking companions, Senya first refuses to give the police the full version of events (having been in prison once himself, he is reluctant to visit it on others); and then towards the end of the novel he encounters the two good-for-nothings once more. Senya is content to remind them of their theft but tells us 'It was comic, I thought. I felt no malice

18. Ibid, p.64.
19. Vladimov, *Tri minuty molchaniya*, p.40.

towards them. But no pity [*zhalost'*] either'.[20] And he refuses to invite them to the 'Arctic' restaurant, to celebrate with his ship-mates: 'I would invite you, mates. But you weren't with us. I'm very sorry but you weren't with us'.

At the outset of the story Senya was hardly better than Askold and Vovchik, or at least, he himself could barely distinguish between himself and them, but now he has come to set more store by himself and his shipmates. Significantly, Senya refers to Askold and Vov-chik as 'oddballs' (*chudaki*) when he sees them; he now has a greater sense of community and is, in his own mind, less of an outsider than they are. This is not to say that he has simply become part of the collective and made the 'right' rational choice, contributing to a conventional ending.

The tension between the individual and the collective is one of the main themes of *Three Minutes' Silence*; as Dimka puts it, referring to the ship's company: 'A family! Spiders in a jar, not a family'.[21] The subsequent actions on the ship are characterised by alternating hostility and comradeship, with neither coming out on top. Senya's spiritual dimension is part of this dichotomy running throughout the novel. He is actually in tune with the spirit of the work, even though the overall result may not be a harmonious symphony. Senya has a tendency to spontaneous action and herein resides his freedom.

There is one episode where one sees clearly how spontaneity and instinct win out over cerebral processes. Senya overhears Dimka explaining to Alik that they should use the deck as their horizon, not the sea and that way they'll keep their sea-legs. They are both pleased at this apparent discovery, but still have to hold on when walking. Consequently, Senya tries to monitor what he looks at as he walks, and stumbles.[22]

This passage is immediately followed by Grandad and Senya conversing over a bottle and Senya sneering about Alik and Dimka seeking 'the meaning of life', and reading books. Grandad's response echoes Vladimov's words about his novel being concerned with the link between generations and the past:

Today good youngsters must do well, I've got great hopes for them. My generation — it's terrible to think about it — some laid down their lives, some lost an arm or a leg, some lost 15 years of their life, like me. And even those who weren't affected, you wouldn't envy them either. Look someone straight in the eye and you'll see he's nothing but an invalid. But

20. Ibid, p.394.
21. Ibid, p.90.
22. Ibid, p.101.

there might be something obstinate there, and you want to touch it all the time.[23]

This is the sort of sentiment in Vladimov that illustrates his ability to take at face value a Soviet shibboleth and then use it to sow the seeds of dissent. The *Novyy mir* version omits any reference to Grandad's fifteen lost years, thus giving a much clearer impression that the war was Russia's only blight, while emphasising the customary buoyant optimism about youth. Another specific instance of the past recalled in *Three Minutes' Silence* occurs when Senya throws a marlinspike at the trawlmaster (*drifter*). The trawlmaster says: 'Why are we so merry, Senya? Who's made us like this? None other than Khrushchev. Always thinking up something. But in the Boss's [i.e. Stalin's: R. P.] day, you remember, there was order . . .'[24] Again, the references to Khrushchev and Stalin are omitted from the *Novyy mir* text with not a little damage done to the underlying notion. In the trawlmaster's view Senya's wanton acts and his general attitude are attributable to history. We are uncomfortably close here to Marx's dictum that 'being determines consciousness' — as we have seen, words that occurred to a reviewer of *The Great Ore*. With the same indifference that Senya lets Vovchik and Askold off the hook he throws the marlinspike: 'I didn't want to kill him. It was all the same to me'. Senya's irresponsibility is his freedom.

There are no intellectuals in *Three Minutes' Silence* and any sense of history that the characters have is based on personal experience rather than comprehensive knowledge. Senya records for us his initial attraction to life at sea, recounting how his father was killed, three sailors assisted at the scene of the accident and gave the young boy the idea of joining the navy and thus one day meeting them. Senya was forced to leave full-time school after seven classes to feed his mother and sister.[25] Yet, born during the war, Senya would have experienced Nazi occupation in his native Oryol, the deprivation during the post-war years and the renewed strictures of Stalinism, then the political thaw of 1956 and the resultant permissiveness in all walks of life. He refers to none of this directly and is, in effect, cut adrift from history. His attempts to impose himself on others and on a given situation, to establish his freedom when he has no knowledge of history, provide the basis for his anti-social behaviour. It seems safe to speculate that the excision of such passages as the one cited

23. Ibid, p.102.
24. Ibid, p.155.
25. Ibid, p.142.

above can only create more disaffected personalities like Senya in the long run.

In the way he drifts from girl to girl, from aggression to solicitude (at one point he is mockingly called 'a humanist' for throwing back a fish, elsewhere 'an enemy of the people'), the manner in which he rejects the chance of a career, his rejection of books, in his constantly changing plans for settling down on shore, Senya is in a long line of seekers that one finds in Russian literature. The truth he is after concerns a definition of himself, and if it is to be found it is not in a teleological sense — in the future, finite and ultimately tangible — but in isolated moments. In this above all he differs from the standard positive hero. The reader will find it hard to picture Senya settling down with Klavka at the end of the book, and Vladimov has his hero tell us, somewhat uncertainly, perhaps rather diffidently, that this is 'another story'.[26]

There are no genuinely traumatic moments in *Three Minutes' Silence*, i.e. that will change a character and conceivably save him; there are only isolated islands of respite from a disorientating modern world. The three sailors who tended Senya's father did it silently: 'Some day we'll understand that the best things are done in the world without speaking' (*molcha*).[27] Senya's most important action is of course his cutting of the nets and the conventional interpretation of this episode must be that he committed a good deed, saving the lives of others at the expense of material considerations and the rule-book. There is no little danger to himself either, since when the cable whips back it could easily kill him. However, this action is accompanied by some conversation with Alik, which Senya is reluctantly drawn into. Afterwards, the hero reflects: 'I don't know what kind of action I had performed — good or evil. But I did it'.[28] Alik, who has witnessed this destruction of state property, has offered to help and has sworn himself to secrecy. The other sailors must know Senya has done it because, we are told, they would have felt the jerk as the cable snapped. The officers seem unaware of the nets being cut and Senya supplies the information himself, so the ship can get under way and rescue the Scottish sailors.[29] This confession occurs in one of the hourly three-minute periods when radio silence is maintained by all ships so that distress signals can be picked up. Vladimov, through Senya, comes back to the novel's title at the end of the book. This passage, reproduced in

26. Ibid, p.403.
27. Ibid, p.144.
28. Ibid, p.308.
29. Ibid, p.323.

full here, was heavily cut in the *Novyy mir* version:

> Yet it would be good to understand what we are living for, why we go to sea. And as for those Scots, why we went to save them and didn't save ourselves. And how things would be with me in the future, as 'Grandad' used to say: maybe I would go and take lessons from him, or pluck up the courage and apply to naval college, become a 'sharp man' with a mac and a white scarf! — or was I really just going to break my life in two?
>
> Or did it really matter how I arranged my fate even without Klavka. Whatever happened, I wouldn't find peace anywhere: why are we alien to one another, all enemies? Probably someone gets some benefit out of it — but we're just all blind, we can't see where we're going. What disasters do we need to make us come to our senses and recognise our own kind! After all, we're good people, that's what you have to understand; I wouldn't want to think that we aren't people at all. But we carry bastards around on our backs, and we're as obedient as sheep to those who are more stupid than we are, and we hurt each other pointlessly . . . And that's the way it will be, as long as we don't learn to think about our fellow man. Not about how you can keep ahead of him, how you might outdo him, no we won't save ourselves that way — no-one will! And life won't be put right all by itself. What each and every one of us needs is three minutes a day — to be quiet, to listen and see if someone is in trouble, because it's you who are in trouble! — just as all the radio operators listen to the sea, as we get alarmed about far-off things on the other side of the Earth . . . Or is all this pointless dreaming? Is it so much, altogether three minutes! You know, you become a man little by little . . .[30]

Senya as moral philosopher may be a little hard to credit, especially when we recall his earlier discussions with Grandad ('I didn't fancy getting on to moral questions with him. Neither he nor I were up to it'),[31] and it is true that in this instance we see the disadvantage that Vladimov has given himself in adopting first person narration. The rhetorical note, particularly in concluding passages, has, moreover, been the stock-in-trade of the Socialist Realist writer. Be that as it may, Senya's reflections sum up most poignantly the spiritual quality in man that Vladimov depicts in this novel. It is unfortunate that the rhetoric here is dangerously close to drowning out the silence that the novel as a whole is pleading for.

Vladimov's call for 'silence' ('not speaking' is a more accurate translation of the Russian *molchaniye*) amounts to a plea for the inner voice to be heard. Solzhenitsyn, of whom Vladimov was the most vigorous supporter in 1967, has written at length on the need for the voice of conscience, as opposed to the falseness of ideology, to be heeded. Vladimov is at pains in *Three Minutes' Silence* to avoid

30. Ibid, p.396.
31. Ibid, p.102.

expatiating on what the inner voice might be; his characters rely on instinct rather than conscious acts — Senya does not know whether he has done good or ill — the important thing for him is that he has (again) asserted his own personality, in a situation which has rendered all the other characters passive — even Alik, who contemplates fleeing in the life-raft, does not go through with his plan in the end. Vladimov, in his concentration on momentary acts, 'moments of truth', would seem to be in tune with the existentialist notion of man as a product of his choices. With each act man transcends himself. Vladimov does not depict a facile moral progression. Rather he suggests, like Voynovich, that morality may well ensue, if, at the outset, a greater comprehension of one's own existence is achieved.

III

Each of Vladimov's major works superficially owes something to some well-worn tradition. In the case of *The Great Ore* it is, naturally, the Soviet production novel. *Faithful Ruslan*, as we shall see, springs from an older and broader tradition, the animal as hero. *Three Minutes' Silence* is similarly in an old and familiar genre — the seafaring yarn. Vladimov delights in taking the familiar and standing it on its head. The eternal struggle of man with the wind and the waves recalls Hemingway's *The Old Man and The Sea*; at one point Vladimov cites from Melville's *Moby Dick*; most Soviet readers would be bound to make comparisons with Second World War classics that recounted the vital work that the Murmansk convoys carried out. Yuriy German produced a number of highly conformist works, his two major pieces about the war being *The Cold Sea* and *Far in the North*. Leonid Sobolev's key work of the war was a collection of stories called *The Soul of the Sea*. To give an idea of what impact *Three Minutes' Silence* could have on the Soviet reader and on the literary establishment, it is instructive to recall Sobolev's own words: 'The soul of the sea is decisiveness, resourcefulness, stubborn valour and unshakeable firmness. The soul of the sea is unhypocritical friendship in arms, a preparedness to support a comrade in battle.'[32]

As we have seen, this is hardly the life of Senya and his shipmates. In his preface to the 1982 'restored' edition of the novel, Vladimov records some of the headlines in the Soviet press which appeared when the work was first published: 'A distorted mirror', 'Off course',

---

32. Quoted in *Istoriya russkoy sovetskoy literatury*, Izdatelstvo Nauka, Moscow, 1968, 2nd edn, pp.40–1.

'Through dark glasses', 'The shallows and reefs of thought', 'Are Murmansk sailors really like this?', 'No-one needs a book like this', 'Whom are you saving, Vladimov?'[33]

To the Soviet critic with a keen eye for 'typicality' and 'objectivity', the pronounced individualism of *Three Minutes' Silence* would hardly be acceptable.

In choosing Murmansk and the Arctic ocean in which to set his novel Vladimov is not so much dealing in travelogue as matching his backcloth to his characters, particularly to Senya. Murmansk is further north than Archangel and lies some two hundred kilometres inside the Arctic circle. Yet unlike Archangel it is ice-free all year round, because of the Gulf Stream (hence the importance of the port in the Second World War). So Murmansk has, like Senya, certain contradictions.

Vladimov makes no bones about the harsh conditions of life in Murmansk and at sea ('We had one weird guy, got pissed and started taking his footcloths off in the street, and he fell asleep in the frost, and afterwards they had to cut half his leg off'),[34] but he is irritated by official attempts to make virtue out of a necessity as the popular culture tries to, witness the snatches of popular song on Vovchik's and Askold's lips: 'The harsh North is dearer to us than Caucasian palms and Crimean warmth'.[35] This comes shortly after the other man in Nina's life has told Senya how unsuperstitious he is and that: 'man is the master of nature, of a whole world outlook, he must keep a steady course in his behaviour. And not pay attention to anything on the side'.[36] Senya, of course, is in a far better position than is his interlocutor to pontificate on what man can and cannot do to nature.

Rather strikingly there is little nature description in *Three Minutes' Silence*. Max Hayward has observed: 'There is a strong undercurrent of nature symbolism in a lot of Soviet writing. Whether consciously so intended or not, it tends to contradict the belief in historical "victory" ... Nature, as a symbol for something at once pure and invincible, plays a large part in the "new wave" post-Stalin fiction (notably Kazakov and Tendryakov).'[37]

One might take this further and suggest that in some Soviet writing nature actually mocks man's puny endeavours and in fact suggests that he would be wiser at very least to treat it with respect.

33. Vladimov, *Tri minuty molchaniya*, preface.
34. Ibid, p.44.
35. Ibid, p.57.
36. Ibid, p.52.
37. M. Hayward, *Writers in Russia 1917-1978*, Collins, London, 1983, footnote, p.159.

This would be the 'bottom line' that all the village writers would insist on. Vladimov takes his characters through a process of self-identification by means of their interrelationship with the natural elements. At times that interrelationship involves a struggle for survival; at other times there is a degree of harmony between man and nature; similarly human beings are alternately in accord or at loggerheads. In doing battle with nature man is unlikely to defeat nature, but he is likely to transcend himself and learn more about himself.

Senya is not the sort of man to verbalise this process, or, when he does, he sacrifices some of his autonomy and credibility as he becomes Vladimov's vehicle. However, in his spontaneous conversations, reflections and actions he displays an authentic interest and regard for the natural world. When Grandad tells him about laying an asphalt road and states that the machine did no evil, Senya is concerned about the wildlife that was driven away.[38] The hero also has a pet fulmar, and he recalls an incident where a baby blue whale was caught in the nets. Grandad in conversation with Senya early on in the story uses a (presumably) seaman's proverb that implies man is left to his own resources ultimately: 'Out there no angel will appear, nor seagull come' (*Tam uzh — ni angel ne yavitsya, ni chayka priletit*), and the hero pointedly uses the same phrase near the close of the novel when discussing with Klavka how her life will be in future.[39] The phrase is charged with meaning: it contributes to the indeterminate ending of the novel; it emphasises the isolation of man, his state where neither metaphysics nor the physical world can solve all his problems. It reflects Senya's new spiritual state. It echoes too the hero's accord with the animal world. Moreover, the words are reminiscent of lines in Pushkin's famous poem about the legendary Upas-tree, so poisonous that it destroys all life around it: 'To it no bird flies / nor tiger approaches.' Pushkin's lyric is generally understood as a statement about the evil in mankind and the power of life and death that one man may have over another. Vladimov's choice of words rather points up the notion that may also be at the back of Pushkin's work: that all men, whether nominally masters or slaves, are ultimately at the mercy of greater forces.

Senya the philosopher has his weaknesses. His strength as a story-teller is in his attention to detail and his powers of observation. On several occasions the natural descriptions imply a panhumanism beyond materialist philosophy.

38. Vladimov, *Tri minuty molchaniya*, p.82.
39. Ibid, p.30 and p.401.

Ninth day and since morning we've been trawling. The same water, blue and green, and the shorelines the same about 30 miles away, like a mountain ridge under snow, and the Norwegian cruisers blinking — on the edge of the territorial waters. But there's no room, there are so many fisher folk there — English, Norwegians, French, Faeroese — all roaming the sea, like balls rolling over a billiard table, making zigzags under each others' noses. [But looking at them was nice, at those foreigners]: the little vessels might be lighter than ours, but they were nicely rigged out, [the sides shining with varnish — blue, orange, green, red, the deck cabin snow white,] the motorised lifeboats hanging so neatly. And then one of ours comes long — black, nasty, everything hanging off it in all directions. But true, none of theirs was out for more than three weeks, home was nearby, no problem looking after a vessel, whereas ours were 105 days and nights from home — they got so battered about they were ashamed to go into port [for getting chased away like mangy cats].[40]

The differences between the *Novyy mir* version and the 1982 version are of passing interest. 'Danes' has been omitted from the list of fisher folk in the later version — this could be a misprint. More significantly, one can see that in 1969 it was indeed possible to draw comparisons with foreigners which did not altogether flatter the Soviets, but such comparisons could not be taken too far. Hence the excisions, marked in square brackets above, and hence the detriment, not too serious here, to the novel's wider implications concerning a common humanity, and general diversity and variety.

Fortunately, the spiritual aspects of the novel are in evidence more plainly elsewhere. Senya refers on several occasions to the Gulf Stream, at least twice as the 'merry (or jolly) Gulf Stream' (*vesyoloye techeniye — Gol'fstrim!*)[41] and the novel closes with the word *Gol'fstrim* when Senya resigns himself to having lost his expensive coat in it. The Gulf Stream comes from the warm climes of the Straits of Florida and, breaking down into various tributaries reaches the northern shores of the European continent. It is to the Gulf Stream that Murmansk is indebted for its *relatively* mild climate. To Senya's mind the Gulf Stream breaks you in gently for the cold of the Arctic north, and then speeds you on your way home at the end of the voyage. Nature as a benign force linking continents and helping man is only half the picture, since frequently men are at the mercy of the elements, and not always are they united in their struggle. Senya's frequent clashes with the cooper bring this out graphically: 'We

---

40. Ibid, p.122.
41. Ibid, p.87 and p.381.

were alone on deck, alone on the whole sea, and the wind was whipping us, and we were doing the same job, yet there were no worse enemies than we.'[42]

Just as Senya adopts Grandad's dictum about angels and sea-gulls, so too, in bequeathing his coat to the sea, he enacts Grandad's philosophy about giving to nature what you get out of it. What Senya has obtained from his voyage is a greater authenticity. The raw, naked moments of violence, danger, action, passion leave social norms of etiquette, social and power structures barely relevant. For all his faults Senya has a greater grasp of reality than his captain, or more pointedly still, Grakov, the production chief, whose mind is fixed on quotas and who gets drunk when faced with danger.

The crew of the *Skakun* may not be intellectuals, but they are all vulnerable to the power of fiction and themselves indulge in yarn-spinning as well as listening. Vaska has an aptitude for inventing fairy stories (*skazki*), and when they are broken off his audience is genuinely disappointed. Many of the seamen have stories of previous voyages, whether they concern promiscuous women or the sailor who tried hard never to return to land — the so-called 'Flying Dutchman'.[43] No-one ever discerns why this man never wanted to return to the shore or what he would do with all his earnings. He retains in Senya's mind a mysterious, ineffable quality and a root-lessness which evokes some of the novel's main themes. Interestingly, we have a brief insight into Senya's tastes in reading. Grandad has lent him a book about ship engines in the vain hope of giving him a practical skill. However, Senya rejects this in favour of a collection of short stories by Richard Aldington. This poet, novelist, biographer and critic became very popular in the Soviet Union (he celebrated his 70th birthday there in 1962). The novel which Senya has read, *All Men are Enemies*, was written in 1933 (Russian translation 1937), a sequel to *Death of a Hero* (1929); together, these books illustrated the disillusion prevalent after the First World War, and the hypocrisy of the modern, industrialised world. In his poetry Aldington attacked the encroaching mechanisation of the twentieth century. No wonder Senya finds the English author appealing. Significantly, Senya and his shipmates seem to have scant regard for their home-grown culture in the form of the occasional spy films and so on that are brought aboard for their entertainment.

42. Ibid, p.216.
43. Sadly, this episode and the episode mentioned previously concerning the baby whale were, for reasons of space, omitted from the first English language translation of the novel, *Three Minutes' Silence*, trans. by Michael Glenny, Quartet, London, 1985.

Three Minutes' Silence retains all the virility of the seafaring yarn, while discarding the residual romanticisation of that genre. Moreover, in its literary references and its unashamed narrative postures it endeavours to illustrate the power that all good fiction exercises over the human imagination. In this, in terms of Socialist Realism, it out-Herods Herod.

Faithful Ruslan — A Thoroughbred in Samizdat

I

Often the manner of a work's debut proves to be one of the least reliable indicators of the work's ultimate worth. Russian literary history is punctuated with dramatic accounts of gems being discovered. One is familiar with the story of Dostoyevsky's *Poor Folk*: Grigorovich and Nekrasov woke up the young author at about 3 o'clock in the morning to tell him, on the strength of this one short manuscript, that he was a genius. The literary bombshell of Solzhenitsyn's debut with the publication of *One Day in the Life of Ivan Denisovich* is itself an exciting yarn. Since 1956 several Soviet writers had been producing, but not publishing, accounts of life in Stalin's labour camps. Anna Berzer at *Novyy mir* bypassed her immediate superiors to get Solzhenitsyn's manuscript to Tvardovsky the editor-in-chief. He started to read the work in bed, as was his custom, but very quickly got up, dressed and read all through the night. By morning he was bursting with excitement: 'a wonderful, pure and great talent'.[44]

The story of the appearance of *Vernyy Ruslan* (*Faithful Ruslan*) is very different from that of *Ivan Denisovich*, though the works have much in common. It is worth reproducing in full Vladimov's own account of what happened for the light it sheds on literary practices and politics in the 1960s:

> *Ruslan* was written three times, the first time in 1963 when I saw that not only the gates of the labour camps were opening a bit, but also the gates of the labour camp theme and *Ivan Denisovich* had squeezed through them. Incidentally, this novella was not a sensation for me; in 1956–57 Aleksei Kosterin brought his labour camp sketches to us in the Prose Section of *Novyy mir*, Varlam Tikhonovich Shalamov came with his *Kolyma Tales*; we read them with horror and admiration — but what could be done at that time? The most revolutionary leap that we were able to allow ourselves

44. M. Scammell, *Solzhenitsyn: A Biography*, Hutchinson, London, 1984, p.414.

was Dudintsev's *Not by Bread Alone*. And that brought us a packet of trouble, as a result of which the editor-in-chief Simonov had to leave.

At the same time I myself wanted to have my say on the subject of labour camps; I had run into it enough when my mother was repressed and I used to visit her in a camp near Leningrad, and afterwards I heard her stories. At that time I lived under fear of arrest; they were also preparing a case against me, but Stalin's death cut it short (one day I'll write about that separately). However, in the spirit of the good old Russian tradition, I had to find a hero, find a figure who would contain all the philosophy of the thing. The Gulag had its victims and its executioners, but who was its real hero, the one who believed in the justice and the sacredness of that monstrous undertaking? Not Abakumov and Beria; those cynics knew what they were creating and there was no philosophy at the back of them.

But one day the essayist [*ocherkist*] N. Melnikov, a *Novyy mir* author, came from Temirtau, where there had formerly been a camp and told me, among other things, of some unfortunate dogs left to the will of fate, so emaciated they had to stand sideways to be seen, since they were not taking food from anyone and were not picking up anything edible from the ground; and when a column, a demonstration, went by they accompanied it, chasing back anyone who stepped out of line. And I realised — there was my hero!

Quite quickly, I wrote a story of about sixty pages, in the spirit of a light-hearted satire on a Stalinist camp guard who was still serving 'in his soul' with dog-like loyalty. I took this story to *Novyy mir* and showed it to Tvardovsky. They were on the point of deciding to print it, but at the same time Tvardovsky told me of his dissatisfaction. That is, he was fully prepared to 'squeeze' the story through, as he put it, but in his opinion, the author had been too keen on satire and had made police shit out of a dog, whereas there was a sense of tragedy here, of great, but alas, unrevealed possibilities of plot. In short, with regard to superfluous anthropomorphism, I had not 'played up' [*razygral*] this dog, and maybe it would be worth thinking the thing over a little more and 'caninising' it.

Reluctantly, I took the manuscript away, quite incapable of imagining how to play it up and caninise it, and meanwhile it lay around at the editorial offices, the typists typed it out and let it do the rounds in *samizdat*, only they cut off the author's name so as not to get him into trouble. For some time the story was attributed to Solzhenitsyn, but soon this history of a dog became an oral legend [*izustnaya legenda*], a stray plot [*brodyachiy syuzhet*], on which to my knowledge a dozen people wrote variations, including Aleksandr Yashin. As it happened I turned out to be the thirteenth person to take up this plot, and, I dare say, was more successful than the others. Incidentally, that goes to show that borrowing others' plots is fruitless. (I know Pushkin gave Gogol plots, but they were ones he did not need himself, and Gogol thought they suited him well.)

So, about eighteen months later, I broadened the thing, played it up as best I could: however by that time they had dropped Khrushchev, put the lid on the labour camp theme completely, and all that the people of *Novyy mir* could do was shrug their shoulders when I brought it to them. The curious thing was, the second version, close to the way the novella looks now, did not get distributed in *samizdat*, the 'market' was already glutted by the first version. Again I put the manuscript away, right at the farthest corner of my desk, with no hope of coming back to it in the future.

But I did. At the start of the 1970s a correspondence was struck up between me and one of the employees of 'Possev' [the prominent Russian émigré publishers: R.P.]; it arose fortuitously and on a fortuitous matter. I requested some information from the German library in Frankfurt. When it came to light that I was corresponding with 'Possev', I reacted to it, I won't say, indifferently, but calmly, given that I was in despair after the defeat of *Novyy mir*[45] and at a time when some of my friends had gone into emigration. I reacted equally calmly to the suggestion that they publish *Ruslan*; however, I decided all the same to re-read it — what I had written in 1965. Years had gone by and I had pretensions regarding my text, so I re-wrote it from start to finish, but I deliberately put an earlier date on it, not for reasons of security, but so as to put myself back into that frame of mind which had governed us in 1963–1965. It would have been impossible to work on the thing in a different frame of mind; after all, I was describing the camps closing down, and how the end of a terrible epoch had come — whereas that epoch was still continuing and gathering strength again . . .

That's how the third and last version of *Ruslan* came about, the one which came out in 1975 in *Grani*[46] and at the same time as a book with Possev.[47]

II

The theme of the dog in literature is as old as literature itself, and it is still very much with us in sentimental books and films as well as cartoons. The popularisation of the theme though should not make one lose sight of the very rich pedigree behind works of the calibre of *Faithful Ruslan*. It is highly likely that the school of ancient philosophers known as Cynics derived their name from the Greek word for 'dog' and were in their unconventional life styles and their rejection of material values keen to 'lead the life of a dog'. When the Cynic Diogenes died the Corinthians erected in his honour a pillar on which a dog rested. Browning alludes to the satirist Lucian as 'some Greek dog-sage, dead and merry' (*Pippa Passes*). Thus Vladimov was hardly innovatory in first conceiving his dog story as a satire. Given the vulgarisation of the word 'cynic' and its etymology, there is also a latent irony in Vladimov's title: a conflict between belief, faith and goodness on the one hand, and a sneering rejection of sincerity on the other.

The key elements in the canine tradition in literature are that the

45. This refers to Tvardovsky's resignation in 1970.
46. *Grani*, 1975, No.96, pp.3–173.
47. G. Vladimov, 'KGB protiv literatury', *Posev*, 1983, No.8, pp.37–43; pp.40–2.

dog can speak and that he is frequently of a philosophical bent, able and anxious to comment — as it were, from the outside — on human conduct. It was Cervantes who brought the form to perfection in his *Colloquy of the Dogs* (1613), where all the social ills and falseness of seventeenth-century Spanish society are perceptively noted by the canine hero. Cervantes's work inspired many imitations throughout Europe, including Francis Coventry's *History of Pompey, the Little; or The Life and Adventures of a Lap Dog* (1751). Incidentally, this work was dedicated to Henry Fielding and in the fashion of *Tom Jones* is a picaresque novel, allowing the author much social comment as he traces his hero's fortunes.

Twentieth-century European literature provides us with many illuminating points of reference for *Faithful Ruslan*. However, before discussing some of these one should not ignore the Russian ancestry of the theme as present in, for example, Gogol's *Diary of a Madman* (1834); the hero, a lowly clerk driven to insanity by unrequited love, is privy to the conversation of two dogs. We will refer to Gogol at greater length in due course. Yet we should remember that he owed much to Hoffmann — as did Franz Kafka.

In Kafka's *Investigations of a Dog* one notes that the traditional form of the dialogue has now been replaced by a monologue. Moreover, it is typical of Kafka that we are drawn into accepting the illogical rules of the author's game — of thinking that we understand the language of a dog, a dog which is alienated, but which by implication is 'talking about human society and the limits of human understanding'.[48]

Theodore Ziolkowski concludes a penetrating study of the canine theme in literature with comments of particular relevance to *Faithful Ruslan*:

> Despite all characteristic differences these treatments of the philosophical dog since Kafka display several basic similarities. First, they all represent inversions of the conventional form: it is easier to understand the works within the tradition than completely independent of it. Indeed, the authors often count on our recognition of their sources as the necessary background for their humour. Second, the inversions of form reflect an inversion in the nature of the philosophical dog. These canines are no longer detached witnesses, standing apart and passing judgement on mankind: they have become troubled participants who suffer from all the afflictions of mankind. Yet despite all deformations the philosophical dog

---

48. T. Ziolkowski, *Varieties of Literary Thematics*, Princeton University Press, Princeton, NJ, 1983, p.113. The article in the collection, on which my remarks on the history of the dog in literature are largely based, is entitled 'Talking Dogs: The Caninization of Literature': pp.86–122.

is still being used for the purpose of cynical social comment that has been conventional since Lucian. For these dogs . . . exemplify modern society and its discontent, an image that is all the more shattering when we see it manifested in animals whose natural innocence has been corrupted by the pernicious influence of mankind.[49]

A Soviet reader of *Faithful Ruslan* might not be aware of its long pedigree and his immediate points of reference could well be rather different from the ones discussed above. Before revealing his own views on *Faithful Ruslan*, Sinyavsky in his article on the novel comments routinely that there is a lot of literature on dogs, from Jack London's *White Fang* to Chekhov's *Kashtanka* (1887).[50] Chekhov's children's story (and his slighter *Whitebrow*) is a perfectly realistic story of a pet dog and displays themes, traditional in the genre, of loyalty, devotion, talent, exploitation, observation and philosophy. Kashtanka 'divided all mankind into two very unequal parts: masters and customers; between the first and the second there was a very real difference: the first had the right to beat her, and the latter she had the right to seize by the calf'.[51] London's *White Fang* and other major works have been adopted by the Soviet establishment as fine examples of Socialist Realism abroad. No doubt London's humble beginnings, his left-wing views, notably his support for the Russian Revolution of 1905, and his action-filled biography showing man surviving against all odds, are as much to do with his canonisation in the Soviet Union as any intrinsic qualities his writing may have. *The Great Soviet Encyclopaedia* entry on Jack London states: 'The positive hero of J. London's northern stories is a resolute, courageous man, ready to come to the aid of a comrade, capable of great and genuine love'. In 1919, three years after London's death, Mayakovsky was to direct and star in a film version of London's *Martin Eden*. London had written a glowing review of Gorky's *Foma Gordeyev*: 'The art of Gorky is the art of realism. But it is a less tedious realism than that of Tolstoy or Turgenev'.[52] Lenin had Jack London's *Love of Life* read to him on his deathbed.[53] In the late 1940s when it became very difficult to conduct serious studies in comparative literature, scholars were encouraged to research the

49. Ibid, p.122.
50. A. Sinyavsky (Abram Terts), 'Lyudi i zveri', *Kontinent*, 1975,No.5, pp.367–404, p.369.
51. A Chekhov, *Izbrannoye*, Khudozhestvennaya literatura, Moscow, 1974, pp.104–5.
52. P. Faner (ed.), *Jack London, American Rebel*, The Citadel Press, New York, 1947, p.516.
53. A. Starkov (ed.), *V. I. Lenin o literature*, Khudozhestvennaya literatura, Moscow, 1971, p.227.

influence of, for example, Gorky on Jack London.[54]

As was the case with *Three Minutes' Silence*, where one can also detect a very strong 'Jack London' dimension, in *Faithful Ruslan* Vladimov turns an established Soviet form inside out. At the same time, he manages to compress a millenia-old tradition into a tight framework to produce one of the most powerful pieces of fiction of modern times, with resonances that span eras and cultures. It became a truism that nineteenth-century Russian literature developed by decades rather than the centuries by which other more mature literatures developed. Could a work like *Faithful Ruslan*, being of such intensity, indicate the same pace of development for the second half of the twentieth century?

First of all, *Faithful Ruslan* is a work of conventional realism. It takes place in the winter to spring of 1956 to 1957, when Khrushchev was closing down labour camps and millions of ex-prisoners were released and were trying to adjust to a new way of life. *Faithful Ruslan* is less concerned with life in the camps, a subject more directly dealt with by Solzhenitsyn, Shalamov, Yevgeniya Ginzburg and several other realistic writers, than with the difficulties of readjustment, psychological and social, that Khrushchev's policy posed. Vasiliy Grossman's sadly neglected story *Everything Flows . . .* (1964) opens with precisely this problem. It was the poet Yevtushenko in his *Heirs of Stalin* (1962) who was able to raise the general issue of neo-Stalinism and to call for a 'doubling and trebling' of the guard around the dictator's tomb. Vladimov manages to get to the heart of the confusion and disorientation within the individual that lay beneath the simplistic historical sequence of Stalinism–thaw–neo-Stalinism through which the individual has lived from the end of the Second World War to the present. The descriptions of the camp that Ruslan gives us, the town and railway nearby, the terrain, the reported conversations between human beings (so well corroborated by the factual accounts one finds in Solzhenitsyn, Ginzburg etc.), all testify to a stark reality. When the work appeared in English there were plans for a film to be made of it.[55]

Secondly, though, the name 'Ruslan' is rich in connotations of folklore and Russian nationalism. Most readers will know the name from Glinka's *Ruslan and Lyudmila* based on Pushkin's first *poema*. Yet

54. G. Struve, *Russian Literature under Lenin and Stalin*, Routledge and Kegan Paul, London, 1972, p. 363.

55. G. Vladimov, *Faithful Ruslan*, trans. from the Russian by Michael Glenny, Penguin, Harmondsworth, 1979. Private conversation with the translator, who worked on a film script.

'Ruslan' is a corruption of 'Yeruslan', Yeruslan Lazarevich being the hero of many Russian fairy tales, folk songs and epic ballads (*byliny*). He was young and handsome, the archetypal knight errant (*bogatyr'*). At the core of the stories about him there is a battle between father and son. The first written versions of the Yeruslan legends appeared at the start of the seventeenth century. Pushkin makes a reference to the original stories when he has Ruslan encounter a *bogatyr*'s head. As far as Vladimov's work is concerned, it is instructive to recall the original features of the legend: a young, brave hero with a very clear sense of right and wrong, a conflict with the power that created him, a sense of national identity (Pushkin's and Vladimov's version of the name is bound to invoke notions of 'Rus', the pre-Petrine name for Russia); and finally there are the key themes of fidelity and love.

III

Sinyavsky gleefully points to the positive hero qualities that Ruslan possesses:

> So Ruslan is a *bogatyr'* of labour camp Russia (not for nothing is he called 'Ruslan'), he is the golden mean, the honest communist, of whom there are so few these days, the rank and file patriot, the fiery middle peasant, the conscientious guardian — the rock solid support of Soviet power. He's national [*naroden*] this Ruslan, but he's also party-minded [*partiyen*] and ideological [*ideyen*].[56]

With his sense of irony Sinyavsky, more than most, can appreciate the danger that Vladimov poses the authorities by acts of supererogation.

It is hardly surprising that Sinyavsky should be so effusive about Vladimov's novel, since both writers have a similar satirical method. In his early story *Pkhents* (1966),[57] Sinyavsky, like Vladimov in *Faithful Ruslan*, chooses the age-old satirical device of a non-human, essentially outside, observer to comment 'objectively' on human affairs. The (human) reader ostensibly knows more than his (non-human) informant, but, of course, gains new insights into his own condition by listening to the outside observer. Sinyavsky's work is essentially grotesque or fantastic (his hero is a sort of vegetable from the planet Pkhents, who crash-lands in the Soviet Union), whereas

56. A. Sinyavsky, 'Lyudi i zveri'.
57. A. Sinyavsky (Abram Terts), 'Pkhents', *Fantasticheskiy Mir Abrama Tertsa*, Inter-Language Literary Associates, 1967, pp.175–95.

Vladimov is at pains to maintain the realism of his novel. Here, one might venture to say that his 'omniscient author' approach in creating a credible dog works consistently well, whereas in *Three Minutes' Silence* the first person narrator occasionally sounds too philosophical or intellectual to be the coarse and violent sailor that he is generally presented as.

Reviewing the English translation of *Faithful Ruslan*, Henry Gifford[58] spoke of its 'Orwellian moral awareness' and likened the novel to Lidiya Chukovskaya's *The Deserted House*. Comparisons have understandably been made, too, with *Animal Farm*. However, Vladimov's purpose is not bald allegory; and the Orwellian touches might be more easily detected in the *1984*-style value-system which can be expressed in the manner of a slogan, often devoid of meaning: 'the delight of obeying', 'the Enemy', 'the best reward for Service was the Service itself'.[59] Of course, until recently Orwell has hardly been mentioned in print in the Soviet Union, but in 1984 the Soviet press, in part, did discuss his novel set in that year and concluded that it was a satire on capitalism.[60] While there is an émigré Russian edition of *Animal Farm*,[61] it seems unlikely that Vladimov would have been directly influenced by it, and we have his own account of how he came to write *Faithful Ruslan*; it seems to have been very much a case of 'being determining consciousness'. In its affinities with Gogol and Kafka, in the way in which it touches on the eternal questions of sanity and madness, freedom and slavery, rationalism and instinct, good and evil, *Faithful Ruslan* goes far beyond political satire.

Sinyavsky's interpretation of the story is that Ruslan really comes from Gogol's hero of *The Overcoat*, for both the guard dog and Akakiy Akakiyevich the government clerk are utterly devoted to 'Service'. If Gogol, through his hero, asked the key question 'Why do you offend me?' it was left to Dostoyevsky to develop the emotion of pity in his reader, to teach us to pity even the murderer Raskolnikov. Sinyavsky sees the two emotions of astonishment and pity as being at the heart of Vladimov's novel: when Ignus is whipped he looks at his master with 'astonishment' (*udivleniye*) and 'pity' (*zhalost'*). Given the historical points of reference and the realism of *Faithful Ruslan* it is startling that Sinyavsky should place the novel firmly in the tradi-

58. H. Gifford, *TLS*, 4 July 1980, p. 766.
59. G. Vladimov, *Vernyy Ruslan*, Possev, Frankfurt, 1975, pp.17–18.
60. M. Glenny, 'Orwell's *1984* through Soviet Eyes', *Index on Censorship*, Vol. 13, No.4, 1984, pp.15–17.
61. Dzh. Orvel, *Skotskiy khutor*, trans. by Maria Kriger and Gleb Struve, 3rd rev. edn, Possev, Frankfurt, 1971.

tion of the grotesque in Russian literature and focus on the emotional content in it. Yet the approach is justified and demonstrates how the work reflects the famous polemic between the nineteenth-century irrationalists, and rationalists, and how that debate has been carried right through to the present day. Ruslan becomes the bone over which the factions have fought, and the conflict can only be resolved by high artistry. It would be easy but wrong to see *Faithful Ruslan* as a sentimental story of a guard dog who continued to do his duty after his services were no longer required, and was then destroyed in the interests of public safety.

IV

One discerns throughout the novel a tension between motifs which can be broadly categorised as either 'rational' or 'irrational'. That everything is viewed through the eyes of a dog naturally loads the dice against the validity of the rationalists' assessment of the world; but the dog's probity is of the highest order, his morality and strength of spirit so great, that the reader is forced to question the very nature of morality (Sinyavsky asks who was ultimately to blame, Stalin, Lenin, Marx, Judas, Cain?).[62] If one wants a simplistic answer, and the artistry of *Faithful Ruslan* warns against such, it might be that morality resides in true individual freedom, which can only be arrived at through the inner promptings of conscience.

The first of the 'rational' motifs in *Faithful Ruslan* is the labour camp itself. Like Ivan Denisovich's, this camp is entirely self-sufficient, has its own internal logic, is governed by specific orders, and everything outside its perimeter and its jurisdiction is more or less beyond comprehension, an absurd wilderness that cannot afford man happiness. The camp is a monstrous enactment of all that Dostoyevsky felt was symbolised by the Crystal Palace. It is the embodiment of Zamyatin's vision in his novel *We*, where the people of a futuristic world are similarly surrounded by a Green Wall and are required to march in columns, just like Ruslan's charges.

It was not for nothing that in Ruslan's hierarchy the masters came first, they always knew what was good and what was bad; next came the dogs, while prisoners came last of all. Although they were two-legged, they were still not quite people. None of them, for instance, would dare to give orders to a dog, yet at the same time a dog partly controlled their actions. Anyway, how could they give sensible orders? They weren't clever enough; they thought there was some sort of better life beyond the forests

62. Sinyavsky, 'Lyudi i zveri', p.374.

and far from the camp — such stupidity would never occur to a guard dog. As if to prove their stupidity, they would go off and get lost for months on end, dying of hunger, instead of staying here and eating their favourite food — prison gruel, for a bowl of which they were prepared to cut each other's throats. And when they did return, heads bowed guiltily, they would still go on thinking up new ways to escape. Poor benighted fools! They didn't feel happy, wherever they were.[63]

The 'logic' of the camp is all-embracing. Ruslan's psychology is governed entirely by the camp from the day he is taken from his mother until his death. He has a memory, a culture and, of course, a faith which the camp seeks to master. Moreover, he has many colleagues, albeit with various nuances of character, who lend the work overtones of the epic. The judicious naming of characters we never get to know fully (Trigger, Breechblock, Era, Cartridge, Aza, Thunder, Bairam, Lady, Dick, Caesar, etc.) is a familiar enough epic device for conveying a sense of vastness and identity simultaneously.[64] The overall effect in *Faithful Ruslan* is to imply a generalisation rather than an aberration. Soviet critics had to strive hard with *Ivan Denisovich* to pass it off as an exposé of certain excesses, now thankfully in the past. One suspects that they would have had their work cut out even more to do the same for *Faithful Ruslan*, had they had the chance.

The camp takes in all of Ruslan's life-span and all the world he knows. It is also comprehensive in the temporal sense. One of the most striking phrases in the book is 'perpetual preservation' (*vechnoye khraneniye*),[65] concerning the length of time for which dossiers on prisoners were to be kept, even when the convicts are released. Ruslan first hears the phrase when listening to the Shabby Man and his ex-master talking. The Shabby Man suggests that the ex-guard's hands may go on shaking 'in perpetuity' too. The phrase has become a notorious commonplace in the literature of the camps. Lev Kopelev entitled the first volume of his memoirs *Khranit' vechno*, 'to be preserved forever', the words stamped on all prisoners' dossiers.[66] Solzhenitsyn was, after his spell in the camps, exiled to Kok Terek 'in perpetuity' and he has his exiled hero Kostoglotov in *Cancer Ward* reflect on this; he also wrote a ditty, in which he wonders if the security forces will last as long as his perpetual exile.[67] The phrase recurs late on in *Faithful Ruslan* when the author, in a rare instance of

63. *Vernyy Ruslan*, pp.66–7.
64. Ibid, p.32, and p.149 in particular.
65. Ibid, p.38.
66. L. Kopelev, *Khranit' vechno*, Ardis, Ann Arbor, 1975.
67. Scammell, *Solzhenitsyn*, p.314.

rhetorical address to his reader, describes Ruslan's dossier. Ironically referring to mankind in divine terms ('Masters of Life'),[68] he lists all the negatives in what is seen as a perfect record kept in perpetuity: Ruslan 'was not', 'did not take part in', 'did not have', and so on.[69] In this passage man's arrogance coincides perfectly with his distorted system of values, where negatives are seen as positive.

The next 'rational' motif, closely connected with the all-encompassing ethos of the camp, is the notion of 'order' (*poryadok*) and of the giving and obeying of instructions to maintain that 'order'. Like Kashtanka, Ruslan has an inclination to compartmentalise everything, but particularly living things: humans, dogs, prisoners and living food; there may be occasional subdivisions, as when Ruslan is recovering from being forced to eat mustard by his ex-master: 'On such occasions, mankind divides itself into two sorts: one sort walks around you with wary compassion; the other sort, of stouter heart, simply steps over you'.[70] Ruslan has a special talent for sniffing out murderers in the camp. He is only content when his assessment of humans coincides with the orders he is given. That this coincidence breaks down when the camp is closed is at the heart of Ruslan's tragedy. The actual commands that Ruslan responds to are significantly a corrupt and compressed form of human speech. (The English translator performed some ingenious tricks to get this across.) The language of the labour camps is a large and intriguing subject in its own right, yet in *Faithful Ruslan* the prisoners' slang, obscenities, ditties and jokes are hardly in evidence. We see instead just some of the officialese that went along with the camps. The crushing repetition of reveille call or the standard announcement before prisoners were marched out to work: 'A step to the left, a step to the right and we shoot without warning' have taken on the character of refrain.

There is nothing new in the notion that words lose their meanings when put at the disposal of politicians. The 'chicken-like' old woman in Blok's poem *The Twelve* stands bemused before the banner proclaiming 'All Power to the Constituent Assembly', and one might be reminded of this scene when Ruslan contemplates the banner over the camp gates, similarly lashed by the natural elements, and is unable to decipher the white markings on it.[71] Indeed, one of the major achievements of all Russia's writers since Stalin has been to

68. *Vernyy Ruslan*, p.143.
69. Ibid, p.143.
70. Ibid, p.33.
71. Ibid, p.8.

restore style and content to the Russian language. Isaac Deutscher writes:

> This anomaly, by which the style of the ruler became the ruling style of the nation, would perhaps have been less intolerable if the ruler had possessed literary talent. As it was, the national style degenerated into a peculiar lingo characterised by stiff, boring repetitiveness, plebeian coarseness mixed with pseudo-scientific pretentiousness, and grammatical and logic incongruity . . . Historians will wonder how a nation which had had Tolstoy, Dostoyevsky, Chekhov,Plekhanov, Lenin and Trotsky as its intellectual guides could have allowed the lights of its language and literature to be so thoroughly blacked out.[72]

One might contest some of the names on this Honours List, but the point remains a sound one.

It is not simply the case that language has been debased to the level of a few sub-human commands. Unlike many dogs in literature who pass on their experiences through conversation or even through writing (Bulgakov's canine in *The Heart of a Dog* writes denunciations to the police), Ruslan is effectively deprived of all means of communication. Like so many brave and honest spirits in Russian literature he is silenced. And his rational world of instant comprehension is a moral perversion.

This takes us on to another 'rational' motif, that of Ruslan's simplistic notions of good and evil. It is interesting that a moral dimension attaches itself at all to the carrying out of orders, but Ruslan is quite at home with words like 'good', 'evil', 'sin' and 'god'. Moreover, everything has to be seen in terms of 'good' and 'evil'. The moral ambiguity which pervades much twentieth-century literature, the 'secure realm somewhere between good and evil' as one of Milan Kundera's characters puts it,[73] is unknown to Vladimov's canine hero. In Ruslan's 'rational' world nothing is fortuitous: if a bakery is in his path to tempt him with its smell ' a secret, hateful enemy' must have put it there.[74] The canine logic is not distinguishable from Stalin's own style of argumentation. One of the dictator's favourite formulations was 'It is not by chance that . . .' when he wanted someone inculpated.[75] The Stalin connection is even more pronounced in the Russian text of the novel, given that the word for 'master' (*khozyain*) can also be translated as 'the boss' — the popular

---

72. I. Deutscher, *Stalin*, rev. edn, Pelican, London, 1966, pp. 363–4.
73. M. Kundera, *The Farewell Party*, trans. from the Czech by Peter Kussi, Knopf, New York, 1976, p.68.
74. *Vernyy Ruslan*, p.25.
75. R. Conquest, *The Great Terror*, rev. edn, Pelican, London, 1971, p.102.

way of referring to the General Secretary.

The impoverishment of human speech goes hand in hand with the manic insistence on only Good and Evil. 'Dogs understand such things, no matter how crude and inadequate was human speech'. This statement occurs at the height of the dogs' revolt when they savage the hose-pipe, unable to follow man 'to the extremes of Good and Evil' that he can attain. The dogs howl at their 'sin', at 'the poverty of a brain that cannot cope with madness'; at a certain point along men's path to Good or Evil the animal will rebel.[76] The rebellion — the Russian term *bunt* is used here (in clear preference to 'revolution'), implying spontaneity and in all probability failure — indicates the seed of instinctive freedom and individualism, the primeval rejection of indoctrination.

Ruslan persistently sees the guards as a divinity and this constitutes a final 'rational' motif. The key word in the Russian text is *bozhestvennyy* (divine); Ruslan sees the 'divine face' of the master,[77] hears his 'divine voice';[78] the commandant is a 'divinity';[79] near the end of the story we return to the 'divine face' of a master.[80] Ruslan's ability to identify, reify god in the way that he does is the last nail in his moral coffin. Aleksandr Galich's famous poem of the labour camps 'Poem about Stalin' has as its epigraph 'And ahead — Jesus Christ', the final line to Blok's *The Twelve*.[81] In inverting the enthusiasm of Blok's celebration of the Russian Revolution, Galich keeps alive the interpretation of the poem that has Christ very much ahead of the Bolsheviks, not with them. Similarly, the implication of *Faithful Ruslan* must be that deification, especially on the basis of a political slogan, can only lead to the destruction of ethics.

V

The specific images of 'divinity' that Ruslan has are in clear juxtaposition to the intangible, ineffable elements in the novel which make up its 'irrational' dimension. The dogs' revolt is the moment where the rational and irrational collide. Howling at their 'sin' and

---

76. *Vernyy Ruslan*, pp.100–1.
77. Ibid, p.40.
78. Ibid, p.52.
79. Ibid, p.98. Here the English translation has 'demi–god' — *Faithful Ruslan*, p.110.
80. Ibid. p. 169. Incidentally, on the occasion of the dogs' revolt the English translation is slightly misleading, having the dogs 'unable to understand man's god–like intentions' (p.112). The original has 'bessmertnyye zamysly' (p.101) — 'immortal designs'.
81. A. Galich, *Polnoye sobraniye stikhov i pesen*, Possev, Frankfurt, 1981; pp.269–81, p.269.

their inability to cope with 'madness', the dogs also howl at the 'infinite, cold sky'. The sky is the only thing that Ruslan fears:

> It was terrible how unwilling he was to set off on the long journey. Twilight was approaching, and he would have to come back in the dark, or worse still, by moonlight. In the dark he could see almost nothing, but moonlight drove him crazy, because it always aroused in him vague menacing forebodings. In this sense Ruslan was a perfectly ordinary dog, the legitimate descendant of that primeval Dog who was driven by fear of darkness and hatred of moonlight towards the fire inside Man's cave and forced to exchange his freedom for loyalty.[82]

An utterly irrational fear opens the door to Ruslan's emotional and intuitive side, and this involves a number of irrational motifs. From the outset one is aware that even Ruslan's emotions are far from governable. One cannot see in his eyes any sign of 'malice, torment or entreaty, but only humble expectation',[83] but from this vacuity he is quickly aroused to 'shame', 'despair' and 'longing'.[84] Paradoxically, the sky can also engender a degree of comfort: 'As the night thickened and became suffused with blackness and cold, more and more stars came out, glittering like the eyes of mysterious monsters. While he hated the moon so much that it somehow even smelled of a dead man, he felt these vital, twinkling little lights were closer to him.'[85] There are several other irrational motifs that impinge on Ruslan's psyche,the most important involving his imagination, memory and culture.

Ruslan's fantasies surface mainly in the second half of the novel after the reader has witnessed the Shabby Man's attempts to remake his life. We learn the ex-convict's history as a cabinet-maker, a craftsman, that he comes from Moscow, has (or had) a family. Memory, culture and tradition all play prominent parts in the Shabby Man's rehabilitation. Ruslan's dreams are, moreover, subsequent to the account of Ignus's character and behaviour. Ignus is the most intelligent of the dogs but has an unpredictable will of his own, so he lives on, for a time, with 'his incomprehensible dreaming', or as the instructor put it 'with the poetry of unaccountable actions'.[86] Ignus drives his instructor insane, he becomes like a dog himself and gives his charges visions of a perfect life, in freedom out in the forest where they will live according to the laws of

82. *Vernyy Ruslan*, pp. 33–4.
83. Ibid, p.13.
84. Ibid, p.20.
85. Ibid, pp.107–108.
86. Ibid, p.93.

brotherhood.[87] Ruslan envisages himself as a sheepdog or a pet or a hunter's dog. At the back of these dreams, and at the centre of Ruslan's character is the notion of the presumed innocence of mankind: 'For the whole truth and the whole solution to the riddle of Ruslan's character lay not in his believing that the rules of the Service might be wrong, but in that he did not regard his sheep as being *guilty* of anything as did the Corporal and the other masters.'[88]

Ruslan's innocent fantasies, concluded by this assessment of his character, are inaugurated by his looking at the town in the evening. In this description of the town special attention is paid to the church with its cross and the sunlight shining on it (so different from the connotations the moon has for Ruslan!). This restrained gesture towards religion is in marked contrast to the 'divine' image Ruslan perceives in his 'rational' world.

In Ruslan's visions 'love' appears as a spontaneous feeling, whereas outside these moments of reverie 'love' is one of the concepts most grossly perverted in the novel. The starting point for a better life in Ruslan's view is freedom, and from that all else flows. In inadequate human speech all concepts, including love, are debased. A prisoner about to be shot promises 'to love' his executioner in return for his life,[89] and Ruslan is so shaken and disobedient after the execution that his master ceased 'to love' him from that day.[90] He experiences 'love' for the Service;[91] but in death, at the very end of the novel, he knows not pain nor fear nor love for anyone.[92] Yet hitherto he has recognised the necessity for 'love' which 'no-one can live without'.[93] Ruslan's tragedy is that when close to death he can find happiness only in the perversion of morality, in picturing himself carrying out an inhumane command.

This distorted moral viewpoint is quite in keeping with the novel's approach as a whole. One cannot escape the fact that *Faithful Ruslan* started life as a satire, and that the age-old canine commentator is the central narrative device. His perception of the statues of Lenin and Stalin, men 'the colour of an aluminium feeding bowl' and 'obviously acting',[94] is a typical piece of bathos. Where Ruslan differs from his literary ancestors is in the strength and depth of his

87. Ibid, p.106.
88. Ibid, p.118.
89. Ibid, p.85.
90. Ibid, p.86.
91. Ibid, p.121.
92. Ibid, p.173.
93. Ibid, p.114.
94. Ibid, p.21.

personality, which without a trace of didacticism, inspires and enlightens the reader. It is perfectly possible to read *Faithful Ruslan* on the level of an allegory or a *roman à clef*. Indeed, Sinyavsky himself makes a perceptive, if somewhat exaggerated, interpretation along such lines: Styura is the Russian soil; Ruslan, like Russia herself, is capable of magnificent deeds but the potential is wasted; Ignus is the poet who shows Ruslan the way, and so on. Yet Ruslan, torn between loyalty and freedom, utterly compromised by other's sins, is as compelling and complex a character as many bipeds that walk the pages of modern literature.

The Path of the Dissident

Vladimov's first three novels, discussed here in ascending order of unacceptability to the Soviet regime (rather than in strict chrono-logical order), provide us with some notion of the author's 'dissi-dence'. However, his purely creative writing has gone hand-in-hand with wider concerns, and Vladimov's case is a prime illustration of how literature and human rights are frequently inseparable in a Russian context.

We should recall Starikova's words when reviewing Vladimov's first novel. Having quoted Marx on 'being' and 'consciousness' she states: 'Collectivism in opposition to individualism is the generally recognised basis of communist morality'. Until 1983 when he left the Soviet Union Vladimov's 'being' was entirely Soviet — he had known no other society. Moreover, until 1977 he was still, at least in part, working within the Soviet system — i.e. 'collectively'. One might assume that his 'consciousness' would not be something the authorities could take exception to, especially when one considers the explicit emphasis on moral issues in his work. However, Vladi-mov's highmindedness and ethical quest took him into a different camp.

He was born in Kharkov on 19 February 1931. He finished secondary school in 1948 and began to study Law at Leningrad University. His father had been killed in action during the war. His mother was arrested in 1952 and, given this situation, he was forced to study externally and support himself by menial work. He worked on a provincial newspaper and then began to publish literary criticism. From 1956 to 1959 he worked as an editor in the prose section of *Novyy mir*. *The Great Ore* brought him widespread success in 1961 and the work was staged, screened and widely translated. Vladimov wrote the first draft of *Faithful Ruslan*, and as we have noted this work went into *samizdat*, unattributed. Then came his incognito stint on the trawler 'The Horseman' which gave him material for *Three Minutes' Silence*. This experience was really very different from his 'study tour' of the Kursk Magnetic Anomaly, which he later claimed really had little to do with *The Great Ore*:

> As far as my trip to KMA is concerned, precisely nothing in particular came out of it, no plot occurred to me, I thought up the story of a hapless driver myself, putting into it all my previous personal experience — of course, not drivers' experience, I didn't drive a car then — Pronyakin's death arose out of a general tragic sense of Kursk Magnetic like the feeling of Moloch grinding down people's fates, and also from a sense of the shakiness of our happy and, it seemed, irreversible changes.[95]

Khrushchev's demise in October 1964 heralded a partial clampdown on what had proved to be a partial cultural renaissance. Daniel and Sinyavsky were arrested in late 1965 and tried in February 1966. However, it would be simplistic to view Soviet literature as being 'free' under Khrushchev and 'repressed' under Brezhnev. There was prosecution of certain writers under Khrushchev, notably the trial of Josef Brodsky in March 1964, and acts of 'liberalisation' under Brezhnev, for example the publication of Mikhail Bulgakov's *The Master and Margarita* (1966 and 1967): this novel, though heavily cut on its first publication, was very much in the grotesque, irreverent manner of the stories for which Daniel and Sinyavsky, less than a year before, earned sentences in labour camps. None the less, the period 1964–66 saw the locking together of literature and human rights. Vladimov was in the forefront of the process.

When Solzhenitsyn despatched his famous open letter to delegates to the Fourth Writers' Congress in May 1967, there were several powerful gestures of support for him, and a resounding silence from the Writers' Union's praesidium. Vladimov's open letter insisted on the 'social and moral life of the people', the 'legitimate demand of every honest, thinking artist', the 'freedom of creativity' with which the writer could 'influence his reader spiritually', 'develop his social conscience'.[96] This creative freedom existed only in *samizdat*, not in official literature. In *samizdat* there was 'the breath of talent', 'clarity', 'the radiance of emancipated artistic form', 'love of man', 'authentic knowledge of life'. Solzhenitsyn's reputation was assured for many years, whereas the names of the majority of the Congress delegates would not survive the end of the century.

95. Vladimov, *Bol'shaya ruda*. Afterword, p.152.
96. Vladimov, *Ne obrashchayte vnimanyya, maestro*, Possev, Frankfurt, 1983, p. 59.

Vladimov's outspoken support for Solzhenitsyn should be seen against a general background of widespread concern among the intelligentsia for human rights and freedom of expression. Many of the Soviet Union's most distinguished and established authors shared Vladimov's feelings. It is true that of the eighty signatories to a letter of support for Solzhenitsyn more than a few subsequently found themselves in emigration and/or clearly in the 'dissident' camp: Voynovich, Maksimov, Gladilin, Galich, Aksyonov. But others remained, to varying degrees and in some cases with serious qualification, on the side of the angels: Kaverin, Tendryakov, Trifonov, Mozhayev, Okudzhava, Iskander, Bykov.[97]

Just over two years after the Fourth Writers' Congress, Solzhenitsyn was fighting a last ditch battle to retain a toe-hold in the literary establishment, while Vladimov was publishing *Three Minutes' Silence* in *Novyy mir*. Solzhenitsyn was expelled from the Writers' Union in November 1969. At the same time, Vladimov was being chided in the press for his latest novel. His real turn was yet to come. Since the Daniel–Sinyavsky trial there had been a series of protests by some very brave young intellectuals against human rights violations. Ginzburg compiled his 'White Book' on the Daniel–Sinyavsky case and together with four associates was arrested in January 1967. A largish group of people, including Bukovsky, demonstrated against these arrests, and themselves were arrested. The whole process in the late 1960s of dissident intellectuals trying to haul back some of the ground which they felt had been won under Khrushchev has been wryly and aptly likened to the Russian fairy story of the old man trying to pull a carrot out of the ground. The only difference was that, after summoning sufficient help, the old man succeeds, whereas the human rights protesters are destroyed.[98] Vladimov was not directly concerned with the human rights issue pure and simple. At the time he maintained, like Solzhenitsyn, that literature, as the repository of truth and morality, might achieve much more than political demonstration. In his Nobel Prize Speech Solzhenitsyn was to write: 'A political speech, an aggressive piece of journalism, a program for the organisation of society, or a philosophical system can all be constructed — with apparent smoothness and harmony — on an error or on a lie ... But a true work of art carries its verification within itself: artificial and forced concepts do not survive

97. L. Labedz, *Solzhenitsyn: a documentary record*, 2nd edn, Penguin, Harmondsworth, 1974, p.117.
98. K. Van Het Reve, Introduction to Pavel Litvinov, *The Demonstration in Pushkin Square*, trans. by Manya Harari, Collins (Harvill), London, 1969, p.7.

their trial by images.'[99]

However, Vladimov maintained close links with writers and intellectuals, who, like he, found themselves increasingly debarred from official channels of communication because of their insistence on the autonomy of art. Two figures in particular, Leonid Borodin and Zoya Krakhmalnikova, became close friends of Vladimov. Both of them developed strong religious convictions and earned severe prison sentences. In 1973 Solzhenitsyn had the first volume of *The Gulag Archipelago* published in Paris. He was arrested and forcibly expelled from the Soviet Union in February 1974. In 1975 Vladimov had *Faithful Ruslan* published by Possev in Frankfurt under his own name. It seems likely that the blaze of publicity attaching to Solzhenitsyn's expulsion and the international scandal that it had engendered persuaded the authorities that in Vladimov's case a 'softer' approach might involve less political damage. Consequently he was invited 'to return to Soviet literature'. In February 1976 he published a lengthy, though of course uncontroversial, interview in *Literaturnaya gazeta*[100] and *Three Minutes' Silence* was brought out as a book — albeit with none of the passages re-instated that had been excised from the *Novyy mir* edition.

All seemed well on the surface, until Vladimov's Norwegian publisher brought out a translation of *Faithful Ruslan* and invited its author to the Frankfurt Book Fair, to be held in the autumn of 1977. The Writers' Union did not even forward the invitation to Vladimov, and it was clear that the price of a 'place in Soviet literature' was to be the renunciation of his most successful work. Vladimov's reaction was unprecedented and a sheer delight to his sympathisers: he *resigned* from the Writers' Union. In an open letter in October 1977 he 'expelled them' from his life and returned his membership card.[101] The moral outrage that had characterised his letter supporting Solzhenitsyn ten years before had not altered one iota.

On resigning from the Writers' Union Vladimov became chairman of the Moscow branch of Amnesty International, an illegal organisation in the Soviet Union. Prominent in support of leading human rights activists like Orlov, Ginzburg and Shcharansky during their trials in 1978 he was now beyond the pale himself. In May 1978 he wrote another open letter in support of the defendants. At the back of this current spate of dissent and persecution was the

99. J. Dunlop in *Aleksandr Solzhenitsyn — Critical Essays and Documentary Materials*, ed. John B. Dunlop, Richard Haugh, Alexis Klimoff, 2nd edn, Collier Macmillan, London and New York, 1975, pp.559–60.

100. Vladimov, 'Dialog o proze', *Literaturnaya gazeta*, 18 February 1976, No.7, p.6.

101. Vladimov, *Ne obrashchayte vnimaniye, maestro*, p.68.

1975 Helsinki Agreement between the Soviet Union and the Western Powers. This had made provision for respect of human rights, and freedom of thought and conscience. Various 'Helsinki monitoring groups' sprang up to publicise Soviet violations of the agreement. Along with many other dissidents Vladimov was subject to all manner of police harassment — his phone was tapped, then disconnected, there were poison pen letters and he and his wife and mother-in-law were occasionally accosted outside their flat. There were also anonymous death threats.

In November 1980 the novelist turned dissident was summoned to Lefortovo prison and interrogated, following which he suffered a heart attack.[102] In January 1981 he issued another open letter to 'The Released American Diplomats' (those held by the Ayatollah Khomeini in Iran) calling upon them to support other political hostages, notably Andrei Sakharov, who was then in internal exile in Gorky. The same month, on the first anniversary of Sakharov's exile, Vladimov together with several others issued another document describing Sakharov's circumstances and calling for a campaign for his release. In September 1981 the text of Vladimov's play *The Sixth Soldier*, fifty roubles and some papers went missing from his flat.[103]

The harassment continued in this petty fashion — Vladimov's car was periodically vandalised — but in general the period 1979–81 was relatively peaceful. However, in February 1982 the police raided his flat and carried out a search lasting some eight hours. His wife was detained at the Lyubyanka for four hours and then released. Many papers and documents were confiscated from their home. In his own words:

> After that our life in Russia lost its meaning — it's impossible to work in such conditions, when some ugly lout reads something you've written and deliberates on whether to take it away or not. I tried to answer them back with 'a stroke of the sword' — with the story 'Maestro' — but then they went completely bestial [*ozvereli*]: they broke in a second time and took the typewriters.[104]

This second search took place in December 1982. The following January Vladimov was summoned by the KGB for questioning about the cases of Borodin and Krakhmalnikova, and given until the 20th of the month to undertake in writing to desist from 'anti-Soviet

102. Ibid, p.77.
103. *Chronicle of Current Events*, English trans. by Amnesty International, No.60, p.94.
104. Vladimov, *Ne obrashchayte vnimanyya, maestro*, p.77. And Vladimov, *Posev*, No.8, p.39. See also the short biographical note appended to *Maestro*, p.77.

activity'.[105]

Vladimov's response was to appeal directly to Andropov to be allowed to emigrate. His open letter to the General Secretary was dated 12 January. He and his family finally arrived in Frankfurt on 26 May 1983.

The 'Maestro' that Vladimov referred to was the short story *Ne obrashchayte vnimanyya, maestro* (*Don't take any notice, Maestro*) written in 1982 between the two house-searches. The last known fictional piece that Vladimov completed in the Soviet Union, it is a thinly disguised account of police harassment of the author. Comic and barbed, the work is in the unmistakable genre of anti-establishment satire, with just a dash of the grotesque — the afterword to the book edition even says that the reader will find the work 'surrealistic'. The title is a line from Bulat Okudzhava's 'Song about Mozart', whose message is that art must retain its integrity and follow its own lights, no matter what the vicissitudes of life may hold: 'Mozart does not choose his homeland/ He just plays all his life through'. The words would have special relevance to Vladimov throughout 1982 and 1983.

The author reverts to the satirical device he adopted in the prototype of *Faithful Ruslan*, and chooses to examine the given situation 'from the side'. The dissident writer, the real object of the story, hardly figures at all in *Don't take any notice, Maestro*. The secret police invade the home of a middle-class intellectual family living opposite in order to keep Vladimov under surveillance. The behaviour of the three KGB operatives and the exchanges between them and the family whose flat has been invaded lead the head of the household to think that these people cannot be genuine security people, but common criminals. As a responsible citizen as well as an individual whose rights have been trampled on, he reports the matter to the 'regular' police. The police raid that follows has a good deal of slapstick comedy about it and clears up the immediate, superficial misunderstandings. The question that cries out for an answer at the end is why the police need to harass writers anyway. The KGB operatives have been so uncouth and cynical throughout that their answer is a moral obscenity: 'ideology' is the reason why such activities must be pursued — and they will keep the writer under surveillance 'all his life'.

These closing words to the satire echo the guard's statement in *Faithful Ruslan* about criminal records being kept 'in perpetuity'. But in *Don't take any notice, Maestro* such abstract concepts as 'ideology'

---

105. Open letter to Andropov appended to Vladimov, *Ne obrashchayte vnimanyya, maestro*, p.72.

hardly match the intellectual horizons of the characters who utter them, and the result is a grotesque comedy. The exchanges between the narrator's mother and the operational head sum up the clash of values:

> 'When your children grow up, they'll read his [the dissident writer's] books and ask you: what was so dangerous about a man just sitting and scratching away with a pen.'
> 'Oh, Anna Ruvimovna! They ask that now! But when they grow up, they'll stop asking. Because then they'll understand that it's because of ideology! You can't do that! Maybe that's the most dangerous thing there is — a man sitting and scratching away with a pen. And us not knowing what he's writing.'[106]

One notes an interesting progression in Vladimov's manner from *The Great Ore* to *Don't take any notice, Maestro*, from a conventional narrative that tested the aesthetic as well as the political boundaries of Socialist Realism to a work that at times reads like a fantasy but is grounded in facts. Sinyavsky advocated in his famous essay 'What is Socialist Realism?' 'a phantasmagorical art with hypotheses instead of an aim and with the grotesque instead of chronicle. This most fully answers the spirit of the present time.'[107] Vladimov's life in the early 1980s had certainly taken on a grotesque aspect.

No reader of *Don't take any notice, Maestro* will escape the parallel with the opening of Kafka's *The Trial*. Early in the morning unknown figures enter a house, treat the occupants as if they are under arrest, but they will not specify for what crime. Thus one wakes into a nightmare, into a situation that evokes guilt and questioning in the innocent. 'You yourselves know what for' is 'that delightful bulletproof answer of theirs!'.[108] Vladimov's biography and his literary manner up to his emigration could hardly be a better illustration of reality becoming Kafkaesque. One might recall the words to the Soviet air force's marching song: 'We were born to turn fairy tale [*skazka*] into reality';[109] many a Soviet intellectual in his more disaffected moments takes advantage of a fortuitous assonance and substitutes 'Kafka' for 'skazka'. In like manner, the author of *The Great Ore* abandoned promised production norms in favour of paltry reality and chose the grotesque as the best style with which to deal with it.

106. Ibid, p.58.
107. Sinyavsky, *Fantasticheskiy Mir Abrama Tertsa*, p.446.
108. Vladimov, *Ne obrashchayte vnimanyya, maestro*, p.11.
109. See G. Smith, *Songs to Seven Strings*, Indiana University Press, Bloomington, Ind., 1984, p.59.

* * *

From 1984 to 1986 Vladimov was the chief editor of the émigré journal *Grani*, which first carried his *Faithful Ruslan*. However, amid acrimonious exchanges which reverberated throughout the émigré intelligentsia he resigned.[110] He has to date published chapters of his latest novel *General i yego armiya* (*The General and His Army*) in the émigré journals *Kontinent* and *Grani*.

Literaturnaya gazeta launched two lengthy and uncompromising attacks on him in January and September 1987.[111] The Soviet reader was treated to a picture of Vladimov as an utterly mercenary employee of the CIA, who transmitted slanderous information to the West, and who was expelled from the Writers' Union. The vitriol hurled at Solzhenitsyn in 1973 and 1974 when he published *The Gulag Archipelago* in the West barely surpassed this. There was even a hint of anti-Semitism:

> Volosevich was his father's name, Zeifman his mother's, but the little son liked neither of these, and when he started out on the path of writer he called himself Vladimov. Well, so what ... call yourself what you like ... But under the surname Vladimov he made no great reputation for himself. He wrote two books which were, as they say, no worse than any others — *The Great Ore* and *Three Minutes' Silence*.

Why should there have been such an attack? The periodical *Grani* and the monthly *Posev* are organs of NTS, *Narodno-trudovoy soyuz* (The National Labour Union), the most conspicuous of the anti-Soviet émigré organisations. According to the Soviet authorities it was funded in former times by the Gestapo and is now funded by the CIA. Vladimov may have been ill-advised to have forged such close links with the organisation while still in the Soviet Union, and then to have become so prominent in it once he emigrated. Be that as it may, whatever was bad for *Grani* was good for the Soviet authorities. Here were some of the leading émigrés falling out in public; and the Soviet authorities had acquired Vladimov's correspondence with NTS dating back to the 1970s. The opportunity was too good to miss, especially as the Soviet establishment had tried and failed to

110. See for example: (1) Supplement to *Grani* 140.1986 p.I–XXI. 'Neobkhodimoye obyasneniye' by G. Vladimov and 'Vynuzhdennyy otvet' by the editorial board of *Grani*; (2) 'Seryye nachinayut i vyigryvayut' by émigré writers in support of Vladimov, *Kontinent*, 1986, No.48 pp.353–4.

111. (1) B. Ivanov, 'Otshchepentsy nachinayut i proigryvayut', *Literaturnaya gazeta*, 14 January 1987, p.15. (2) B. Ivanov, 'Yeshcho raz ob igrakh otshchepentsev', *Literaturnaya gazeta*, 30 September 1987, p.15.

bring Vladimov back into the fold in 1976 by the 'soft' approach. He was also the most recent prominent émigré. *Literaturnaya gazeta* duly regaled its readers with details of Vladimov's requests, despatched from the Soviet Union, to NTS for fees and fashionable clothes. This is what, in the eyes of Soviet officialdom, his chairmanship of the Russian Branch of Amnesty International, 'a well-known anti-Soviet, anti-socialist organisation' and his involvement with 'the self-styled Moscow Helsinki group' amounted to. According to the articles, he had planned his break with the homeland from the early 1970s. The current liberalisation ('strengthening of glasnost' and 'democratisation') in the Soviet Union was of no benefit to the émigrés; cuts in CIA funding would offer them a bleak future.

One looks forward to the day when the Soviet reader can measure these statements against the full facts, and against the sentiments expressed in Vladimov's fiction. So far he has been able to defend himself only in the émigré press.[112]

---

112. 'Kommentariy Georgiya Vladimova k vystupleniyu *Literaturnoi gazety*', *Kontinent*, 1987, No.51, pp.363–7.

Conclusion

A number of apparent anomalies emerge from our examination of these four writers. Vladimov's mother was imprisoned in the 1950s and Vladimov (understandably?) became a 'dissident'. Yet Vladimov, who in resigning from the Writers' Union placed himself outside Soviet literature with as much resolve as Senya hacked away the trawling gear on his ship, writes by and large in a manner that closely resembles classical Socialist Realism. Aitmatov's father fell victim to Stalin's purges, yet the son has become one of the Soviet Union's most established writers. However, in his revamping of folk legends and his mingling of fantasy and reality, he has redrawn the boundaries of Socialist Realism. Some commentators have dubbed him a magical realist and likened him to Gabriel García Márquez.

The two writers who have remained, and indeed have enhanced their position, within the Soviet system — a system that purports to be internationalist and atheistic — have in fact become increasingly interested in nationalism and religion. Rasputin has become a confirmed Russian nationalist and quasi-Christian (as well as a fervent conservationist). Aitmatov's ethnic origins have given him a more internationalist bent, but he is the very antithesis of, for example, the ludicrously orthodox writer in Vsevolod Kochetov's *What is it you want, then?* (1969). This writer 'believed in a system on earth whereby there would be no frontiers between states and then people with different languages would start to communicate more often and would produce a single language common to all mankind'.[1] Aitmatov, by contrast, has been far more sophisticated in blending national heritage with wider concerns.

In emigration Russian writers have, in the past, been notoriously insular and sectarian. However, the third emigration is now of such a magnitude that the situation may well have changed. We have noted the exchanges between Sinyavsky and Maltsev. Recently two leading Western scholars clashed publicly over the state of émigré

---

1. Quoted in M. Crouch and R. Porter, *Understanding Soviet Politics through Literature*, Allen and Unwin, London, 1984, p.82.

literature. Donald Fanger argued that the émigré journals were marked by 'clannishness, as much personal as ideological'. Gerald Smith responded that émigré writers had a great deal to say, and were no more 'ghetto-like than those of the United States'.[2]

Vladimov seems to have retained his conventional realistic style. The chapters of *General i yego armiya* (*The General and His Army*) published to date are set during the Second World War and deal with the machinations of SMERSH, the counter-espionage organisation that operated within the Red Army. Vladimov's quarrels with *Grani* seem to lend weight to Fanger's views. However, Voynovich has made every attempt to come to terms with his new situation. His ability to find comedy in the most unlikely places will ensure him a degree of universality. So emigration does not *per se* lead to sectarianism and/or introspection. Indeed, more rigidity and introspection might be detected in Rasputin's novella *The Fire* than in Voynovich's *Moscow 2042*.

Of all four writers, it appears that only Voynovich has developed a literary persona that accords with the irreverent attitude enthused over by Julian Barnes, which we alluded to at the outset. Rasputin, Aitmatov and Vladimov all wear their impulse to human decencies on their sleeve. In Voynovich's case the irreverent jocularity is very much a pose. We have seen that there is a man of high principle and urbanity behind the bawdiness and the fun. Scratch a Russian writer and you will find a moralist. The vicissitudes of political life in Russia present the creative writer with difficult and extreme choices sometimes. This is what gives Russian literature its power but also its weaknesses. Diverse circumstances are forced on writers who might otherwise live cheek by jowl rather than on opposite sides of a political divide.

All of which brings us to another apparent anomaly. Roughly speaking, all of the four writers produced better works in the 1960s than in the 1980s, despite the greater superficial freedom they have enjoyed either by their enhanced position within the Soviet system or by finding themselves outside the Soviet system. Well-being has not determined high quality. And so to a final anomaly: entitling

2. See D. Fanger, 'A Change of Venue — Russian Journals of the Emigration', *TLS*, 21 November 1986, No.4, pp.1321–2.
Letter from G. Smith, 'Russian Émigré Writers', *TLS*, 28 November 1986, No.4, p.1349. Letter from D. Fanger, 'Russian Émigré Writers'. *TLS*, 26 December 1986, No.4, p.1449. Smith did not reply directly to this rejoinder, but published a lengthy article in *TLS* the following spring demonstrating the real strengths of émigré literature: 'Another time, another place', *TLS*, 26 June 1987, pp.692–4. See also pp.694–6 of the same issue for further examples and discussion of contemporary Russian literature.

this section 'Conclusion', for it is clear that Russian literature is entering a new phase and that it will undoubtedly produce new talents. The writers whose time is yet to come will doubtless learn from (perhaps 'score off' would be a more appropriate phrase) the generation represented in this book. This will be true of both Soviet and émigré writers. Finally, if past history is anything to go by, in the fullness of time the most deserving works of all four authors examined here will be read both in the Soviet Union and in the West on an equal footing, and evaluated without the aid of such epithets as 'dissident', 'conformist', 'Soviet' and 'émigré'. Then the anomalies may well seem irrelevant.

Afterword

The developments outlined in the Introduction to this book have continued apace throughout 1988, so that this year is fast resembling an *annus mirabilis* in Soviet literature. The following major works referred to in this volume have now been published, or announced for imminent publication, in the Soviet Union: George Orwell's *Animal Farm* and *1984* (see p.154); Orwell's inspiration for *1984*, Yevgeniy Zamyatin's *We* (see p.8); the memoirs of Yevgeniya Ginzburg (see p.152). Pasternak's *Doctor Zhivago* (see p.7) did indeed appear in the first four issues of *Novyy mir*.

Josef Brodsky remains to date the one prominent living émigré to have been published in the Soviet Union — there was even a 'Brodsky evening' held in Leningrad on 12 April. However, another very notable figure of the 'third emigration', Aleksandr Galich (1919–78) (see pp.159 and 164) had poems published in the journals *Novyy mir* and *Oktyabr'*. As it turned out Yuriy Lyubimov (see p.9) did eventually pay a short visit to his homeland in spring 1988. More germanely, given the subject matter of this book, an extract from *Chonkin* was published in *Nedelya* (1988, No. 39, pp.18–19), and *Yunost'* announced publication of the full text for 1989. The writer Anatoliy Pristavkin wrote an affectionate article about Voynovich and Vladimov (*Nedelya* 1988, No.42, p.9).

All four of our authors have not been idle this year: Rasputin published chapters of a new book, *Sibir', Sibir' . . .*, in *Nash Sovremennik* (No.5, pp.3–40 and No.8, pp.3–54); *Novyy mir* announced new stories by him and a novel by Aitmatov, *Bogomater' v snegakh*, for 1989; Voynovich published a delightful short novel, *Shapka* (Overseas Publications Interchange, London, 1988); and in the article mentioned above, Pristavkin reported that Vladimov was laboriously 'finishing off' his novel *General i yego armiya*.

There has also been frequent speculation and discussion both in the Soviet press and abroad regarding the rehabilitation of Aleksandr Solzhenitsyn (see p.9).

All these events, whether actual or in prospect, should be viewed as part of a radically transformed intellectual and cultural climate. No doubt Gorbachev, like most politicians, will ultimately be judged by his success or failure in economics and international affairs, but he has taken the view that he can succeed in these areas only by winning over the writers and intellectuals. It is hard to see how the broader cultural parameters he has established can ever be totally abolished, no matter what may happen to his other policies.

A meeting between Soviet and émigré writers took place on the relatively neutral territory of Denmark in March. The conference, organised jointly by the Association of Danish Slavists and the Centre for East–West Research, was on 'Perestroika and the intelligentsia'. *Literaturnaya gazeta* reported the event as if it were simply a visit to Denmark by Soviet writers, though it added that some émigré writers were present. Some of these, it said, were greatly concerned with their motherland and should not be dismissed out of hand. The London-based journal *Index on Censorship* carried a much fuller account (May 1988, Vol.17, No.5, pp.7, 13–22, 36). The Soviet side included the head of Moscow's Historical Archives Institute Yuriy Afanasyev, and the writers and critics Grigoriy Baklanov, Galina Belaya, Vladimir Dudintsev, and Fazil Iskander. Among the émigrés were Vasiliy Aksyonov, Yefim Etkind, Cronid Lubarsky and Andrei Sinyavsky.

Afanasyev won the sympathies of both sides with his appeal to the émigrés to find common ground with their erstwhile compatriots: 'I think the use of the words "us" and "you" is unworthy of those who have met here. I think that everyone wishes the best for our homeland.' Sinyavsky spoke about recent developments in Soviet literature and greatly impressed the Soviet side, despite, or maybe because of, his opening words:

Last summer I read a story by a certain author in *Novyy mir*, and I suddenly discovered that socialist realism was dead or dying. This is surely a matter for congratulation. Socialist realism has done a great deal of damage to art. When I think about socialist realism in general, I picture it as a kind of heavy, metal trunk which came to occupy the entire living space allotted to literature. So that one either had to climb into the trunk and live beneath its watchful lid, or else do battle with it, get bruised bumping into it, trip over it, squeeze past it or simply slither underneath it. This trunk is still standing there, but either the walls of the room have shifted, or the trunk's been moved into more spacious and airy premises.

This is not an unfitting image with which to describe the unsettled but exciting situation in Russia today.

Bristol, 30 November 1988

Biographical Notes

Valentin Rasputin: Born in 1937 in the Irkutsk region. Studied at Irkutsk University and became a journalist. Literary reputation was established in 1967 with publication of *Money for Maria*. Since then publications have been sporadic but generally of a very high standard. Some works have been dramatised. Has become increasingly interested in ecology. Was severely beaten up by a gang of youths in 1980.

Chingiz Aitmatov: Born 1928. His father, a secretary of the Kirghiz regional communist party, was liquidated in 1937. Chingiz studied zoology and veterinary science, graduating in 1953. Later studied literature in Moscow. Became a journalist and published his first stories in 1950s. Joined the Communist Party in 1959. Member of the Supreme Soviet. *Dzhamilya, Farewell, Gulsary!* and *The White Steamship* established his world-wide reputation. Major works have been filmed and staged.

Vladimir Voynovich: Born 1932. Trained as a carpenter, though his background (mother a teacher, father a journalist) suggested more intellectual career. 1951–5 military service. 1960 worked for Moscow Radio, when he composed an 'astronauts' hymn'. Published stories in 1960s, some of which were dramatised. Supported repressed writers including Solzhenitsyn. Was expelled from Writers' Union in 1974. 1980 emigrated to West Germany.

Georgiy Vladimov: Born 1931. Studied law at Leningrad University but began a career as a literary critic. Fame came in 1961 with publication of *The Great Ore*. Supported Solzhenitsyn in 1967. Steadily increasing pressure on him. 1977 resigned from Writers' Union and became secretary of Moscow Branch of Amnesty International. More harassment. Finally emigrated to West Germany in 1983. 1984–6 edited journal *Grani*.

Selected Bibliography

General

Brown, Deming, *Soviet Russian Literature since Stalin*, Cambridge University Press, New York, 1978

Brown, Edward, *Russian Literature since the Revolution*, Harvard University Press, Cambridge, Mass., 1982

Clark, Katerina, *The Soviet Novel: History as Ritual*, 2nd edn, University of Chicago Press, Chicago, Ill., 1985

Hayward, Max, *Writers in Russia 1917–1978*, ed. and with an Introduction by Patricia Blake, Collins (Harvill), London, 1983

Hingley, Ronald, *Russian Writers and Soviet Society 1917–1978*, Weidenfeld and Nicolson, London, 1979

Hosking, Geoffrey, *Beyond Socialist Realism: Soviet Fiction since Ivan Denisovich*, Paul Elek (Granada), London, 1980

Shneidman, N., *Soviet Literature in the 1970s: Artistic Diversity and Ideological Conformity*, University of Toronto Press, Toronto, 1979. Contains lengthy discussions of Aitmatov and Rasputin.

Struve, Gleb, *Russian Literature under Lenin and Stalin 1917–1953*, Routledge and Kegan Paul, London, 1972

The following short bibliography merely draws attention to the major Soviet editions of the authors concerned or publication of separate books. By and large it seeks not to duplicate references made in footnotes. The books mentioned in the General Bibliography all have good bibliographical material relating to the four authors.

Valentin Rasputin

Editions used

1. *Povesti*: 'Proshchaniye s Matyoroy', 'Zhivi i pomni', 'Posledniy srok', 'Den'gi dlya Mariyi', Molodaya gvardiya, Moscow, 1980

Selected Bibliography

2. *Vek zhivi — vek lyubi*: rasskazy, Molodaya gvardiya, Moscow, 1982
3. *Izbrannyye proizvedeniya v 2-kh tomakh*, Molodaya gvardiya, Moscow, 1984
4. 'Pozhar', *Nash sovremennik*, No.7, 1985, pp.3–38

Criticism

1. Gillespie, David, *Valentin Rasputin and Soviet Russian Village Prose*, The Modern Humanities Research Association, London, 1986. This is the first monograph in English on Rasputin and itself contains a very extensive bibliography.
2. Shaposhnikov, V., *Valentin Rasputin*, Zapadno-Sibirskoye knizhnoye izdatelstvo, Novosibirsk, 1978
3. Tenditnik, N., *Otvetstvennost' talanta (o tvorchestve Valentina Rasputina)*, Vostochno-Sibirskoye knizhnoye izdatelstvo, Irkutsk, 1978

English translations of key works

Live and Remember, trans. by Antonina W. Bouis, Macmillan, London and New York, 1984
Farewell to Matyora, trans. by Antonina W. Bouis, Macmillan, London and New York, 1979
Money for Maria and Borrowed Time: Two Village Tales, trans. by Kevin Windle and Margaret Wettlin, Quartet, London, 1981

Chingiz Aitmatov

Editions used

1. *Sobraniye sochineniy v 3-kh tomakh*, Molodaya gvardiya, Moscow, 1982, 1983, 1984. This edition contains all the major fiction except *Plakha* plus numerous journalistic pieces.
2. 'Plakha', *Novyy mir* 1986; No.6, pp.7–69; No.8, pp.90–148; No.9, pp.6–64

Background reading on Kirghizia

1. Allworth, Edward, *Ethnic Russia in the USSR: The Dilemma of Dominance*, Pergamon Press, Oxford, 1980
2. Chadwick, Nora and Zhirmunsky, Victor, *Oral Epics of Central Asia*, Cambridge University Press, Cambridge and New York, 1969
3. Wheeler, Geoffrey, *The Modern History of Soviet Central Asia*, Weidenfeld and Nicolson, London, 1964

Selected Bibliography

Criticism

The three-volume edition of Aitmatov cited above has a good deal of critical comment. Note in particular:

1. Gachev, G., *Chingiz Aitmatov i mirovaya literatura*, Kyrgyzstan, Frunze, 1982
2. Levchenko, V., *Chingiz Aitmatov: Problemy poetiki, zhanra, stilya*, Sovetskiy pisatel', Moscow, 1983
3. Mirza-Akhmedova, P., *Natsional'naya epicheskaya traditsiya v tvorchestve Chingiza Aitmatova*, Fan, Tashkent, 1980
4. Voronov, V., *Chingiz Aitmatov: Ocherk tvorchestva*, Sovetskiy pisatel', Moscow, 1976

English translations of key works

'Jamila' and 'Farewell, Gyulsary', in *Tales of the Mountains and Steppes*, trans. by Fainna Glagoleva and Olga Shartse, Progress Publishers, Moscow, 1969

The White Steamship, trans. by Tatyana and George Feifer, Hodder and Stoughton, London, 1972

The Day Lasts More than a Hundred Years, trans. by John French, Macdonald, London, 1983

Vladimir Voynovich

In addition to the works in Soviet journals one should note the following separate books:

Soviet

My zdes' zhivyom, Sovetskiy pisatel', Moscow, 1963
Povesti, Sovetskiy pisatel', Moscow, 1972
Stepen' doveriya, Politizdat, Moscow, 1973

Emigré

Zhizn' i neobychaynyye priklyucheniya soldata Ivana Chonkina, YMCA, Paris, 1975
Ivankiada, Ardis, Ann Arbor, Mich., 1976
Putyom vzaimnoy perepiskoi, YMCA, Paris, 1979
Pretendent na prestol: novyye priklyucheniya soldata Ivana Chonkina, YMCA, Paris, 1979
Antisovetskiy Sovetskiy Soyuz, Ardis, Ann Arbor, Mich., 1985
Tribunal: Sudebnaya komediya v tryokh deystviyakh (a play), Overseas Publications Interchange, London, 1985
Moskva 2042, Ardis, Ann Arbor, Mich., 1987

Selected Bibliography

Criticism

There is to date no monograph on Voynovich.

English translations of key works

'I'd be honest if they'd let me', in *Four Soviet Masterpieces*, trans. and with an Introduction by Andrew R. MacAndrew, Bantam, London, New York and Toronto, 1965

The Life and Extraordinary Adventures of Private Ivan Chonkin, trans. by Richard Lourie, Cape, London, 1978

Pretender to the Throne: The Further Adventures of Private Ivan Chonkin, trans. by Richard Lourie, Cape, London, 1981

The Ivankiad, trans. by David Lapeza, Cape, London, 1978

In Plain Russian: Stories, trans. by Richard Lourie, Cape, London, 1980

Moscow 2042, trans. by Richard Lourie, Cape, London, 1988

Georgiy Vladimov

In addition to works in journals there are the following separate books:

Soviet

Bol'shaya ruda, Sovetskaya Rossiya, Moscow, 1962

Tri minuty molchaniya, Sovremennik, Moscow, 1976

Emigré

Vernyy Ruslan, Possev, Frankfurt, 1975

Tri minuty molchaniya, Possev, Frankfurt, 1982

Ne obrashchayte vnimanyya, maestro, Possev, Frankfurt, 1983

Criticism

There is to date no monograph on Vladimov.

English transmations of key works

'The Ore', in *Four Soviet Masterpieces*, trans. and with an Introduction by Andrew R. MacAndrew, Bantam, New York, London and Toronto, 1965

Faithful Ruslan: The Story of a Guard Dog, trans. by Michael Glenny, Cape, London, 1981

Three Minutes' Silence, trans. by Michael Glenny, Quartet, London, 1985

'Pay no Attention Maestro', trans. by Roger Keys, *The Literary Review* No. 59, May 1983, pp. 39–55

Index

Note: entries in **bold** indicate the main references to that subject

Index

Index